Islaamic Legal I

Dawah

Guidance from some of the Senior Scholars of our time, including -
'Abdul-'Azeez ibn 'Abdillaah ibn Baaz
Muhammad Naasiruddeen al-Albaanee
Muhammad ibn Saalih al-'Uthaymeen
The Permanent Committee for Islaamic Research & Verdicts

Compiled and Translated by
Abu'Abdul-Waahid Nadir Ahmad

Islaamic Legal Rulings Related to Da'wah
First Edition, Dhul-Hijjah 1433 / November 2012

فَمَن كَانَ يَرْجُواْ لِقَآءَ رَبِّهِ فَلْيَعْمَلْ عَمَلاً صَلِحًا وَلَا يُشْرِكْ بِعِبَادَةِ رَبِّهِ أَحَدَا

"So whoever hopes for the Meeting with his Lord, let him work righteousness and associate none as a partner in the worship of his Lord."
The Noble *Qur.aan* - Soorah al-Kahf, *Aayah* 110

British Library Cataloguing in Publication Data
A catalogue record for this book is available from the British Library.
ISBN 9781907589034

Every effort has been made to fulfil requirements with regard to reproducing copyright material. The Publisher will be glad to rectify any omissions at the earliest opportunity.

Compilation and Translation by - Abu'Abdul-Waahid Nadir Ahmad

Cover Design, Typesetting and Layout by - SumayyahScott.com

Published by - Fatwa-Online Publishing
al-Madeenah an-Nabawiyyah
Saudi Arabia
eMail: publishing@fatwa-online.com

Distributed by - Darussalam International
146 Park Road
London NW8 7RG
United Kingdom
Tel: +44.20.8539.4885
Fax: +44.20.8539.4889
eMail: info@darussalam.com

بسم الله الرحمن الرحيم

Contents

The Importance of Learning the Arabic Language[*]

Whilst every effort has been made to render this translation from it's original Arabic source to English, one must appreciate the rich nature of the Arabic language and how difficult it can be to accurately capture the <u>true</u> essence of the Arabic text in *any* language. Allaah (*Subhaanahu wa Ta'aala*) says:

إِنَّا أَنزَلْنَهُ قُرْءَانًا عَرَبِيَّا لَّعَلَّكُمْ تَعْقِلُونَ

Verily, We have sent it down as an Arabic Qur.aan in order that you may understand.[1]

This book and any other book translated from Arabic should never allow the reader to become complacent and hold back from learning the Arabic language, ever! Rather, it should only serve a <u>temporary</u> purpose in assisting the student of knowledge on his way until he has attained his goal in having learnt the Arabic language.

---

[*] Compiled by Abu 'Abdullaah Mohammed Akhtar Chaudhry
[1] The Noble Qur.aan - Soorah Yoosuf, Aayah 2.

9

When I began my Arabic language studies at the Islaamic University of Madeenah back in 1993, I remember being interviewed by Dr. V. Abdur-Raheem[2] to assess the level of my Arabic knowledge so as to ascertain exactly which class he should enrol me into; It was then that I sought his advice by asking him the question <u>every</u> Arabic language student[3] asks – *"O Shaykh! What is the best way to learn Arabic?"*, whereupon he advised: *"Arabic is not learnt by simply memorising the grammatical rules, rather, Arabic is learnt through necessity..."* – thereby guiding me to restrict my speech to the Arabic language as much as possible despite having <u>just</u> started my studies, *wAllaahul-Musta'aan*!

Poignantly, I recall a popular story our fellow Pakistani students at the University narrate about *Shaykh* Ihsaan Ilaahi Zaheer[4]. When the young

---

2 Author of the popular Duroos al-Lughatil-'Arabiyyah li-Ghayr an-Naatiqeen bihaa - Madeenah Arabic series of books, and at the time, Supervisor of the Institute of Arabic Language at the University. The Shaykh is currently the Supervisor of the Translation Department at the King Fahd Qur.aan Printing Complex in Madeenah.

3 My personal study notes prepared during my Arabic language studies at the Islaamic University of Madeenah and more study material – are all available for free download at http://www.fatwa-online.com

4 Born on 31 May 1945. He studied in Jaami'ah Islaamiyyah Gujranwala and Jaami'ah Salafiyyah Faisalabad. He then started teaching and giving weekly khutbahs up until he left for Saudi Arabia. He studied at the Islaamic University of Madeenah and graduated from the Faculty of Sharee'ah. During his final year at the Islaamic University of Madeenah, Shaykh 'Abdul-'Azeez Ibn Baaz asked him to deliver lectures on the Ahmadiyyah – this is a very rare achievement. His book on the subject was then printed in Madeenah, but the young Shaykh wished to include in the book "Graduate of the Islaamic University of Madeenah" – before he had actually graduated! So he asked Shaykh Ibn Baaz, who was the Chancellor at the time and he agreed to it. The young Shaykh then asked Shaykh 'Ibn Baaz: "What if I fail my degree?" Shaykh Ibn Baaz answered: "I will close the University!" Upon graduating, he returned to Pakistan and pursued further education and received degree classifications of M.A.s in Arabic, Islaamic Studies, Urdu and Farsi.

Shaykh arrived at the University as a student he was allocated a room in Building No.2 – which back then accommodated 6 students to a room. Upon discovering all his room mates were fellow Pakistanis he promptly made his way to the Dean of Student Accommodation and filed a complaint stressing that he had come to the University to learn the Arabic language and putting him in a room full of his fellow countrymen was detrimental to his efforts. He politely requested that he be placed in a room full of Arabs, whereupon his request was granted! *Subhaa-nAllaah*! Just listening to his Arabic audio lectures is testimony to his mastery of the language.

Imaam ash-Shaafi'ee said[5]: *'The language which Allaah favoured was the Arabic language as he revealed his Noble Book in this (Arabic) and he made this the language of the seal of the prophets Muhammad. And that is why we say that it is befitting for everyone who has the ability to learn Arabic – that they learn it, as it is the best language.'*

So, just imagine how much you have enjoyed reading a translated book; Now imagine how richer your experience would be if you were to read the original in Arabic!

He was taught by some of the major scholars of our time – namely: Shaykh Abdul Azeez Ibn Baaz, Shaykh Muhammad al-Ameen ash-Shanqeetee, Shaykh 'Abdul-Muhsin al-'Abbaad, Shaykh 'Atiyyah Muhammad Saalim, Shaykh Haafidh Muhammad Ghondalwee, Shaykh Abul-Barakaat Ahmad and Shaykh Muhammad Naasir-ud-Deen al-Albaanee.

He died on 30 March 1987, at the young age of 42; Shaykh 'Abdul-'Azeez Ibn Baaz led his funeral prayer in Riyadh, and the secondary prayer in al-Masjid an-Nabawee in Madeenah was attended by thousands. He was buried in the graveyard of al-Baqee' in Madeenah.

5 Iqtidaa Siraatil-Mustaqeem - Volume 1, Page 521.

Regarding the student of knowledge, *Shaykh* al-Albaanee was asked[6]: Is it obligatory upon a student of knowledge to learn and communicate in the Arabic language?

And the *Shaykh* responded: *Learning the Arabic language is an obligatory matter, as has been determined by the scholars, that:*

"If an obligatory act [A] requires you to undertake a secondary act [B] in order to fulfill the obligatory act [A], then that secondary act [B] becomes obligatory."

[That said], it is not possible for a student of knowledge to understand the Qur.aan and the Sunnah except by means of the Arabic language.

As for communicating in Arabic, then it is from the recommended acts, since there is no evidence to suggest its obligation.

Likewise, *Shaykh* 'Uthaymeen was asked[7]: It is apparent that many students of knowledge steer away from perfecting the rules of the Arabic language (grammar); Considering it's importance – what is your point of view?

And the *Shaykh* responded: *Yes, understanding the Arabic language is important, whether it be the rules of i'raab or the rules of balaaghah, all of these are important. However, based upon us being Arabs, and all Praise is for Allaah, then it is possible to learn without knowing the rules of the Arabic language. However, from that which is complete (and better) is for a person to learn the rules of the Arabic language. So, I encourage the learning of the Arabic language with all it's rules.*

---

6 Fataawa ash-Shaykh al-Albaanee fil-Madeenah wal-Imaaraat - Page 35.

7 Kitaabul-'Ilm - Page 145, Question No.42.

Likewise, Shaykhul-Islaam Ibn Taymiyyah (*rahima-hullaah*) said[8]: *"It is known that Arabic is Fard 'alal-Kifaayah and the Salaf would discipline their children for making grammatical mistakes. Due to this, we are ordered, whether it be an obligation or a recommendation, to preserve the Arabic (grammatical) rules, and to correct the tongues that have deviated from the correct speech. By doing so, we preserve the methodology of understanding the Qur.aan and the Sunnah. We also preserve the following of the Arabs in their manner of (correct) speech. If people were left with their grammatical mistakes, this would be considered a great deficiency and despicable mistake."*

Shaykh Ibn 'Uthaymeen was also asked[9]: *Baara-kAllaahu Feekum*, is the fact that the *Qur.aan* was revealed in the Arabic language a justification or an excuse for non-Arabs (for not acting upon it) due to it not being revealed in their language?

The *Shaykh* responded: *No, non-Arabs do not have an excuse or a justification in that the Qur.aan is not in their language; Rather it is upon them to learn the language of the Qur.aan, because if understanding the Book of Allaah or the Sunnah of the Messenger of Allaah (sal-Allaahu 'alayhi wa sallam) is dependant upon learning the Arabic language, then learning Arabic becomes waajib. This is because every action that has to be carried out, in order to be able to perform an obligation, acquires the ruling of being obligatory [or - All actions which if not performed first, an obligatory act cannot be performed, acquire the ruling of being obligatory (even if they are not an obligation within themselves, such as walking to the masjid for Salaatul Jamaa'ah (for*

---

8 Majmoo al-Fataawa - Volume 32, Page 252.

9 Fataawa Noor 'alad-Darb;
   Translated by Abu Abdul-Waahid Nadir Ahmad.

men), since one cannot perform jamaa'ah in the masjid unless he walks there, the act of walking in order to get to the masjid becomes waajib upon that individual, and so on...)].

Allaah (*Subhaanahu wa Ta'aala*) says:

وَمَاخَلَقْتُ الْجِنَّ وَالْإِنسَ إِلَّا لِيَعْبُدُونِ

And I created not the jinn and mankind except that they should worship Me (Alone). [10]

In this *aayah*, Allaah (*Subhaanahu wa Ta'aala*) has clearly defined the purpose of our creation – our purpose in this life, and outlined the means which shall assist us upon this path in the Noble *Qur.aan* and the authentic *Sunnah* – both of which originate in the Arabic language.

Considering this simple, yet essential fact, should provide us sufficient incentive to allocate time from our busy lives to learning Arabic which will subsequently open the doors to acquiring greater knowledge of this blessed religion of ours.

And what greater means to seeking knowledge can there be than to humble ourselves and sit at the feet of the inheritors[11] of the Prophets – the Scholars of *Ahlus-Sunnah* – and take directly fom them!

And as we take from them, we do so in order to worship our Lord upon

---

10 The Noble Qur.aan - Soorah adh-Dhaariyaat, Aayah 56.

11 Saheeh al-Bukhaaree, Sunan Abee Daawood/3641, Sunan at-Tirmidhee/2682, Sunan Ibn Maajah/223, Musnad Ibn Abee Shaybah/47, Musnad Ahmad/21715, Sunan ad-Daarimee/354, Saheeh Ibn Hibbaan/88: «*...and certainly, the Scholars are the inheritors of the Prophets...*».

sound knowledge, as Allaah (*Subhaanahu wa Ta'aala*) says:

قُلْ هَلْ يَسْتَوِى ٱلَّذِينَ يَعْلَمُونَ وَٱلَّذِينَ لَا يَعْلَمُونَ

Say: "Are those who know equal to those who know not?"[12]

'So he who worships Allaah upon sound knowledge will find great delight and immense pleasure in his worship, as opposed to he who worships Allaah without sound knowledge.'[13] Therefore, as we pursue this noble path, let us recall the words of the Messenger of Allaah (*sal-Allaahu 'alayhi wa sallam*) who said in this regard:

**«Whoever treads a path in search of knowledge,
Allaah will make easy for him the path to Paradise»**[14]

...the <u>ultimate</u> reward!

I close my sincere advice with the case of a sister who strived and struggled to learn the Arabic language, despite the odds; Despite maintaining a 24-hour routine with her husband, both caring for their two terminally ill children with Batten's disease, Zakkee - 12 and Zahraa - 10, she *still* found time to pursue her passion for learning the Arabic language.

Her care shift would finish daily at midnight when I would visit her to teach her for up to an hour, and after I left, she would revise what I had taught her until 2am when she would go to sleep. She would be up again

---

12 The Noble Qur.aan - Soorah az-Zumar, Aayah 9.

13 Shaykh Ibn 'Uthaymeen - Fat.h Dhil-Jalaali wal-Ikraam bi-Sharh Buloogh al-Maraam, Book of Purification - Pages 41-42.

14 Saheeh Muslim/38, Sunan at-Tirmidhee/2646, Sunan Ibn Maajah/223, Musannaf Ibn Abee Shaybah/26117, Musnad Ahmad/7427, Musnad al-Bazzaar/9128.

for the *Fajr* prayer and then resume her care shift at 8am.

My Sister, Umm Zakkee (*rahima-hAllaah*), died of breast cancer in the early hours of Saturday 16th *Ramadhaan* (1st December 2001) at the age of 35 years; Please remember her in your prayers.

May Allaah (*'Azza wa Jall*) permit her notes[15] to benefit all who seek to learn the Arabic language, and may He (*'Azza wa Jall*) cleanse my Sister of her sins and reward her with *al-Firdows al-A'laa*[16], *aameen*.

---

15 "Umm Zakkee's personal study notes to Dr. V. 'Abdur-Raheem's ((Lessons in Arabic Language)) – Book 2; [as taught at the Islaamic University of Madeenah]" – available for free download at http://www.fatwa-online.com

16 al-Muntakhab min Musnad 'Abd ibn Humayd/182, al-Ahaadeeth al-Mukhtaarah aw al-Mustakhraj min al-Ahaadeeth al-Mukhtaarah mimmaa lam Yukharrijhu al-Bukhaaree wa Muslim fee Saheehayhimaa/394, Mawaarid ath-Thamaan ilaa Zawaa.id Ibn Hibbaan/2434: *«...and if you ask Allaah, then ask Him for al-Firdows al-A'laa»*.

Biography of
Shaykh 'Abdul-'Azeez ibn 'Abdullaah ibn Baaz[*]
1909 - 1999

Abu 'Abdullaah Shaykh 'Abdul-'Azeez ibn 'Abdullaah ibn 'Abdur-Rahmaan Aal-Baaz was born in the city of Riyadh in *Dhul-Hijjah* 1330 A.H./1909 C.E.

He memorised the *Qur.aan* in his early age and then he acquired knowledge from many of the great scholars of the Kingdom. Some of his teachers were *Shaykh* Muhammad ibn 'Abdul-Lateef Aal-Shaykh, *Shaykh* Saalih ibn 'Abdul-'Azeez Aal-Shaykh and the eminent *Shaykh* Muhammad ibn Ibraaheem Aal-Shaykh who, in his time, was the *Mufti* of Saudi Arabia. *Shaykh* Ibn Baaz accompanied the eminent *Shaykh* and learned from him for about ten years. Thus he gained his religious education from the family of *Imaam* Muhammad ibn 'Abdul-Wahhaab.

Afterwards *Shaykh* Ibn Baaz was appointed as a Justice and he worked for fourteen years in the judiciary until he was deputed to the education faculty. He remained engaged in teaching for nine years at Riyadh Islaamic Law College, Riyadh Religious Institute. Then he was appointed

---

* Translated by Abu 'Abdullaah Mohammed Akhtar Chaudhry

Vice-Chancellor of the Islaamic University, al-Madeenah; but shortly afterwards, he was made the Chancellor with all the administrative powers. Later he was appointed President of the General Presidency of Islaamic Research, Ifta, Call and Propagation, Kingdom of Saudi Arabia.

He held the position of Grand *Mufti* of Saudi Arabia, the Presidency of many Islaamic Committees and Councils, the prominent among these being: Senior Scholars Committee of the Kingdom, Permanent Committee for Islaamic Research and Verdicts, the Founding Committee of Muslim World League, World Supreme Council for Mosques, Islaamic Jurisprudence Assembly Makkah; and the member of the Supreme Council of the Islaamic University at al-Madeenah, and the Supreme Committee for Islaamic Propagation, until he passed away on Thursday 27 *Muharram* 1420 A.H./May 13 1999 C.E. May Allaah (*Subhaanahu wa Ta'aala*) have Mercy upon his soul, aameen.

The *Shaykh*'s official website: http://www.binbaz.org.sa

Biography of
Shaykh Muhammad Naasiruddeen al-Albaanee[*]
1914 - 1999

He was born in the city of Ashkodera, then the capital of Albania in the year 1332 A.H./1914 C.E. into a poor family. His father al-Haaj Nooh Naj-jaatee al-Albaanee had completed *Sharee'ah* studies in Istanbul and returned a scholar to Albania. After Albania was taken over by atheism the family made *Hijrah* to Damascus. In Damascus *Shaykh* al-Albaanee completed his initial education and was then taught the *Qur.aan*, *Tajweed*, sciences of Arabic language, fiqh of the *Hanafee madh.hab* and further branches of the Deen by various *Shaykh*s and friends of his father.

He also learnt from his father the art of clock and watch repair - and became highly skilled in that and famous for it and derived his earnings through it. He began to specialise in the field of *hadeeth* and its related sciences by the age of 20 - being influenced by articles in 'al-Manaar' magazine.

He began to work in this field by transcribing *al-Haafiz* al-Iraaqee's monumental 'alMughnee 'an-hamlil-Asfaar fil-Asfaar fee takhreej maa fil-

---

lhyaa minal-Akhbaar' and adding notes to it.

He delved further into the field of *hadeeth* and its various sciences despite discouragement from his father. Furthermore, the books he needed were not to be found in his father's library which was composed mainly of various works of *Hanafee* Fiqh - and since he could not afford many of the books he required he would borrow them from the famous library of Damascus - 'al-Maktabah adth-Dthaahiriyyah' or sometimes from book sellers.

He became engrossed with the science of *hadeeth* to the extent that he would sometimes close up his shop and remain in the library for up to twelve hours - breaking off his work only for prayer - he would not even leave to eat, but would take two light snacks with him.

Eventually the library authorities granted him a special room to himself for his study and his own key for access to the library before normal opening time. Often he would remain at work from early morning until after 'Ishaa. During this time he produced many useful works - many of which are still waiting to be printed.

The *Shaykh* faced much opposition in his efforts to promote *tawheed* and the *Sunnah* but he bore this with patient perseverance. He was encouraged by some of the noble *Shaykh*s of Damascus who urged him to continue, amongst them *Shaykh* Bahjatul Bayjaar, *Shaykh* 'Abdul-Fattaah -the imam, and Towfeeq al-Barzah - *rahima-humullaah*.

After some time he started giving two weekly classes attended by students of knowledge and university teachers - in which he taught various books of *'aqeedah*, *fiqh*, *usool* and *hadeeth* sciences.

He also began organised monthly journeys for *da'wah* to the various cities of Syria and then Jordan.

After a number of his works appeared in print the *Shaykh* was chosen to teach *hadeeth* in the new University in Madeenah, Saudi Arabia, for three years from 1381 to 1383H where he was also a member of the University board.

After this he returned to his former studies and work in 'al-Maktabah adth-Dthaahiriyyah' leaving his shop in the hands of one of his brothers.

He visited various countries for *da'wah* and lectures - amongst them Qatar, Egypt, Kuwait, the Emirates, Spain and England. He was forced to emigrate a number of times moving from Syria to Jordan, then Syria again, then Beirut, then the Emirates, then again to 'Ammaan, Jordan. His works - mainly in the field of *hadeeth* and its sciences number over 100.

His students are many and include many Shaykhs of the present day amongst them:
Shaykh Hamdee 'Abdul-Majeed, *Shaykh* Muhammad 'Eed 'Abbaasee, Dr. 'Umar Sulaymaan al-Ashqar, *Shaykh* Muhammad Ibraheem Shaqrah, *Shaykh* Muqbil ibn Haadee al-Waadi'ee, *Shaykh* 'Alee Khushshaan, *Shaykh* Muhammad Jameel Zaynoo, *Shaykh* 'Abdur-Rahmaan Abdus-Samad, *Shaykh* 'Alee Hasan 'Abdul-Hameed al-Halabee, *Shaykh* Saleem al-Hilaalee.

The *Shaykh* passed away on Saturday 22 *Jumaadaa ath-Thaaniyah* 1420 A.H. / 2 October 1999 C.E. He was 87 years of age. May Allaah (*Subhaanahu wa Ta'aala*) have Mercy upon his soul, aameen.

The *Shaykh*'s official website: http://www.alalbany.net

Biography of
Shaykh Muhammad ibn Saalih al-'Uthaymeen[*]
1929 - 2001

Abu 'Abdullaah Muhammad ibn Saalih ibn Muhammad ibn 'Uthaymeen at-Tameemee an-Najdee was born in the city of Unayzah, Qaseem Region on 27th *Ramadhaan* 1347 A.H./1926 C.E. in a famous religious family.

He received his education from many prominent scholars like *Shaykh* 'Abdur-Rahmaan as-Sa'dee, *Shaykh* Muhammad Ameen ash-Shanqeetee and *Shaykh* 'Abdul-'Azeez ibn Baaz.

When he entered into teaching, a great number of students from inside and outside Saudi Arabia benefited from him. He had his own unique style of interpretation and explanation of religious points. He was from among those scholars who served Islaam without any type of religious prejudice and kept themselves away from the limitations of blind-following. He was distinguished in his great exertion of effort in religious matters and analogical deductions which clearly prove the religious understanding he possessed, and the correct usage of the principles of religion, he adopted.

---

* Translated by Abu 'Abdullaah Mohammed Akhtar Chaudhry

In giving religious verdicts, like *Shaykh* ibn Baaz, his *fataawa* were based on evidence from the *Qur.aan* and *Sunnah*. He had about fifty compilations to his credit. He taught Religious Fundamentals at the *Sharee'ah* Faculty of *Imaam* Muhammad ibn Sa'ood Islaamic University, Qaseem Branch. He was also a member of the Council of Senior Scholars of the Kingdom, and the *imaam* and *khateeb* of the big Mosque of Unayzah city.

The *Shaykh* passed away on Wednesday 15 *Shawwaal* 1421 A.H. / 10 January 2001 C.E. He was 74 years of age. May Allaah (*Subhaanahu wa Ta'aala*) have Mercy upon his soul, aameen.

The *Shaykh*'s official website: http://www.ibnothaimeen.com

Biography of
Shaykh Muqbil ibn Haadee al-Waadi'ee[*]
1933 - 2001

I come from Waadi'ah, which is a place to the east of the city of Sa'adah from the valley of Dammaaj. My name is Muqbil bin Haadee bin Muqbil bin Qaa'idah al-Hamdaanee al-Waadi'ee al-Khallaalee, from the tribe of Aali Raashid.[1]

All praise due to Allaah, most of the people of Waadi'ah, who neighbour Sa'adah defend me and the *Da'wah*. Some of them wish to defend the

---

[*] Translated by Abu Maryam Ismaa'eel Alercon
  Source: Tarjamah Abee 'Abdir-Rahmaan (pg. 16-29, with minor abridgement) [2nd Edition, 1999]

[1] Translator's Note: In her biographical account of her father, Umm 'Abdillaah Al-Waadi'iyyah said: "His father died while he was young and he didn't know him. So he grew up as an orphan and under the care of his mother for a period of time. She would ask him to work to make money and order him to look at the state of his community so that he could be like them. But he would turn away from this and say: 'I will go out to study.' So she would say: 'May Allaah guide you.' She would suppli cate for him to be guided, as several women who were around at that time informed me. Perhaps her supplication coincided with the time when supplications are ac cepted since he became one of the guided, guiding others." [Nubdhah Mukhtasarah: pg. 18]

24

Religion while others defend their tribal devotion. If it were not for Al-laah first, then them, the enemies of the (*Salafi*) *Da'wah*, particularly the *Shee'ah* of Sa'adah, would not have left behind any signs or traces of us.

I will mention some examples of them for which I ask Allaah to reward them, one of which was when I faced severe opposition in the Haadee Mosque because I turned people away from the (Shiite) *Da'wah* there. So some men from Waadi'ah and others stood by me to the point that Allaah saved me through their hands. The Shiites desired to rule against me. This was at the time of Ibraaheem al-Hamdee. And evil people amongst the Communists and Shiites raised their heads and imprisoned me for a period of eleven days during *Ramadhaan*. About fifty of the youth from Waad'iah would come to visit me in prison during some of the nights, while another hundred and fifty of their men would also go to the prison caretakers during these nights, so much so that the care-takers got fed up and released me from jail, all praise be to Allaah.

Another example is that the enemies of the *Da'wah* would sometimes come to Dammaaj with their weapons, so the people of Dammaaj would drive them away and they would be forced to leave in humiliation.

Another example is during our journeys. When I would say: "We wish to travel", they would compete with one other, may Allaah preserve them, to see who would accompany and guard me. So sometimes we would go out on some of our travels in about 15 cars!

During these days, the *Da'wah* was progressing in a superb manner be-cause, all praise be to Allaah, I had grown older. Perhaps at this point I have reached about 62 years of age. So it was the calamities and the advice from those who love the *Da'wah* that drove me to have kind-ness and to not keep up with the enemies, who don't have anything but insults and abuses.

Also, due to my teaching, writing and giving *Da'wah*, I was not able to find time to keep up with those enemies. So let them say what they want for my sins are many, and perhaps because of their slander, my sins will be lightened for me and instead fall upon their shoulders.

1. My Studies and Teachers

I studied at school until I completed the school's curriculum. Then a long time passed without me seeking knowledge since there was no one who would encourage me or assist me in seeking knowledge. And I used to love seeking knowledge. So I sought knowledge from the al-Haadee Mosque but I was not assisted in that.

After some time, I left my homeland (of Yemen) and went to the sacred lands (Makkah/Madeenah) and Najd. I would listen to the speakers and be fascinated by their sermons. So I sought the advice of some of the speakers on what beneficial books I should buy? They advised me to get Saheeh al-Bukhaaree, Buloogh al-Maraam, Riyaadh as-Saaliheen, and Fath-ul-Majeed, the explanation of Kitaab at-Tawheed. And they gave me copies of the textbooks from the *Tawheed* courses.

At that time, I used to work as a security guard in a building in Makkah, and so I would cling tightly to those books, and the material would stick to my head because what the people in our country did was the opposite of what was in these books, especially Fath-ul-Majeed. After some time had passed, I returned to my country and began to rebuke everything I saw that contradicted what was in those books, such as offering sacrifices to other than Allaah, building shrines over the graves, and calling unto the deceased. So news of this reached the Shiites and they began to censure what I was upon. One of them would say (the *hadeeth*): "Whoever changes his religion, then kill him." Another one sent a letter to my relatives saying: "If you don't prevent him, we will imprison him!" But after that, they agreed to let me enter the Haadee Mosque in order to study with them, so that they may (perhaps) remove the misconceptions that had clung to my heart.

So after that, I was admitted to study with them in the Haadee Mosque. The head of education there was the Judge Mutahhir Hanash. I studied the book al-'Aqd-uth-Thameen and ath-Thalaatheen Mas'alah, along with its explanation by Haabis. From the teachers that taught me there was Muhammad bin Hasan al-Mutamayyiz. One time we were discussing the subject of seeing Allaah in the Hereafter, so he began to mock and ridicule Ibn Khuzaimah and other *Imaams* of *Ahlus-Sunnah*, but I used to conceal my creed. Despite that, I was too weak to put my right hand over my left hand during prayer, and I would pray with my hands by my side. We studied the text of al-Azhaar up to the section on Marriage.

I also studied an explanation of the Laws of Inheritance from a large book that was above the standard level, but I did not benefit from it. So I saw that the assigned books were not beneficial, except for Grammar, since I studied the books al-Aajroomiyyah and Qatar an-Nadaa with them. Then I asked the Judge, Qaasim bin Yahyaa ash-Shuwayl, to teach me Buloogh al-Maraam. So we started it, but then we were disapproved of, so we left it.

So when I saw that the assigned study books were of a Shiite and Mu'tazlite nature, I agreed to only take from the books of Grammar. So I studied Qatar an-Nadaa several times under Isma'eel al-Hatbah, may Allaah have mercy on him, in the masjid that I would live in and he would pray in. And he would give us a lot of time and attention. One time, Muhammad bin Hooriyyah came to the masjid and I advised him to abandon astrology (tanjeem). So he advised the people there to kick me out of the study program, but they interceded on my behalf and he kept quiet.

Some of the Shiites would pass by me while I was studying Qatar an-Nadaa and say something with the meaning that education would not have any effect on me. But I would just remain silent and benefit from the books on Grammar. I did this until the revolution started in Yemen, when we left our country and settled in Najraan. There I studied with Abul-Husayn Majd-ud-Deen al-Mu'eed and benefited from him particularly in the Arabic Language. I stayed in Najraan for the length of two years. Then when I became sure that the war between the Republic party and the King's party (in Yemen) was all for the sake of worldly reasons, I resolved to travel to the sacred lands (Makkah/Madeenah) and to Najd. I lived in Najd for one and a half months in a school for *Qur.aan*ic memorisation, which was run by *Shaykh* Muhammad bin Sinaan al-Hadaa'ee. He was very hospitable to me because he saw that I benefited from the knowledge. And he advised me to stay for a while until he could send me to the Islamic University (of Madeenah). But the environment in Riyaadh changed for me and I decided to travel to Makkah.

I used to work whenever I found work, and I would seek knowledge at night, attending the lessons of *Shaykh* Yahyaa bin 'Uthmaan al-Paakistaanee on Tafseer Ibn Katheer, Saheeh al-Bukhaaree and Saheeh Muslim.

I would go over several books and there I met two noble *Shaykh*s from the scholars of Yemen:

First: The Judge, Yahyaa al-Ashwal. I would study Subul-us-Salaam of as-San'aanee with him and he would teach me any subject that I asked him about.

Second: *Shaykh* 'Abdur-Razzaaq ash-Shaahidhee al-Muhwaytee. He would also teach me whatever I asked him about.

Then the educational institute in Makkah opened and I took the entrance exam with a group of students, and I passed, all praise be to Allaah.

The most distinguished of our teachers there was *Shaykh* 'Abdul-'Azeez as-Subayyal. I, along with a group of students from the institute, would also study with *Shaykh* 'Abdullaah bin Muhammad bin Humayd, may Allaah have mercy on him, the book at-Tuhfah as-Saniyyah after *'Ishaa* at the Haram. He, may Allaah have mercy on him, would bring many points of benefit from Ibn 'Aqeel and other scholars' explanation. The lessons were above the level of my colleagues, so they began to slip away until he eventually stopped the class.

I also studied along with a group of students with *Shaykh* Muhammad as-Subayyal, may Allaah preserve him, the subject of the Laws of Inheritance.

After staying in the institute for some time, I left to go to my family in Najraan. Then I brought them to live with me in Makkah. We resided there together for the length of my studies in the institute and the Haram itself, which lasted six years.

The blessing of studying in the masaajid is well known. Do not ask about the friendly environment and relaxation we felt while in the *masaajid*. The Prophet (*sal-Allaahu 'alayhi wa sallam*) indeed spoke the truth when he said: "A group of people do not gather together in one of the Houses of Allaah, reciting the Book of Allaah and studying it amongst themselves, except that tranquility descends upon them, angels surround them, mercy engulfs them, and Allaah mentions them to those by Him."

So I would spend the day studying in the institute, and all of the lessons would assist my Creed and Religion. Then from after 'Asr till after the 'Ishaa prayer, I would go to the Haram and drink from the Zamzam water, about which the Prophet (*sallAllaahu 'alayhi wa sallam*) said:
    "Verily, it is a drink that satiates and a cure for diseases."

And we would listen to the speakers that came to Makkah from different lands to perform Hajj or 'Umrah.

From the teachers that we learned from at the Haram between *Maghrib* and *'Ishaa* was *Shaykh* 'Abdul-'Azeez bin Raashid an-Najdee, author of the book "Tayseer-ul-Wahyain fil-Iqtisaar 'alal-Qur'aani was-Saheehain", in which he has errors that we don't agree with him on. He, may Allaah have mercy on him, used to say: *"The authentic ahaadeeth that are not found in the two Saheeh Collections can be counted on one's fingers."* This statement of his stuck to my mind since I had objections to it. This was all the way until I decided to write "As-Saheeh-ul-Musnad mimmaa laysa fis-Saheehain" after which I became more certain about the falsehood of his statement, Allaah have mercy on him.

However, he was a man of *Tawheed*, who had strong knowledge of the Science of *Hadeeth* and was able to distinguish the authentic from the weak and the defective from the pure with regard to *hadeeth*. What amazed me about him was that he would call people away from taqleed (blind-following), to the point that he wrote a treatise called "At-Tawaagheet-ul-Muqanna'" [Masked Deities of Falsehood]. So the government, and likewise some of the senior scholars, thought that he intended them by it. So the committee of senior scholars gathered together to debate with him. They said: *"Did you intend us and the government with this book?"* So he replied: *"If you feel that you possess the characteristics that I mentioned in the book, then it includes you. And if you feel that you do not possess those characteristics that I mentioned in the book, then it doesn't include you."* Thereafter, the book was banned from entering into the Kingdom. I was informed about this.

One night, he was asked to give a class, but it was as if to only test him. So he began his class with Allaah's statement: *"Follow that which has been revealed to you from your Lord and do not follow false gods besides*

Him. Little do you remember." [Surah al-A'raaf: 3] He followed that with numerous ayaat that prove the prohibition of taqleed (blind-following). After this, he was restricted from teaching at the Haram, and we ask Al-laah's aid.

And from my teachers at the Grand Mosque (Haram) of Makkah who I benefited from was Shaykh Muhammad bin 'Abdillaah as-Sumaalee, for I attended his lessons for about seven or more months. And he was an ayah (manifest sign) in terms of knowledge of the narrators used by the two *Shaykh*s (Al-Bukhaaree and Muslim). I benefited immensely from him in the Science of *Hadeeth*. All praise to my Lord, since I started seeking knowledge, I didn't love anything except knowledge of the Book and the Sunnah.

After I completed the intermediate and secondary levels of the educational institute in Makkah, and after completing all of my religious lessons, I moved to Madeenah to go to the Islamic University there. Most of us transferred to the Faculty of *Da'wah* and Usool-ud-Deen. The most distinguished of those who taught us there were: *Shaykh* as-Sayyid Muhammad al-Hakeem and Shaykh Mahmood 'Abdul-Wahhaab Faa'id, both from Egypt. When vacation time came, I feared that time would go by wasted so I joined the Faculty of *Sharee'ah*, due to two reasons, the first of which was to acquire knowledge:

This was since some of the classes there were successive while others were combined. So it was a like a repetition of what we had studied in the Faculty of *Da'wah*. I completed both Faculty courses, all praise be to Allaah, and I was given two degrees. However, all praise be to Allaah, I give no regard to certificates; what merits recognition in my opinion is knowledge.

In the same year that I finished the two College courses, an advanced studies program opened in the Islamic University, which they called the Masters program. So I went for the interview exam and passed, all praise be to Allaah. The advanced studies course was on the Science of *Hadeeth*. All praise be to Allaah, I studied the subject that I loved the most. The most prominent of those who taught us there was *Shaykh* Muhammad al-Ameen al-Misree, may Allaah have mercy on him, *Shaykh* As-Sayyid Muhammad al-Hakeem al-Misree, and during the last part of my studies, *Shaykh* Hammaad bin Muhammad al-Ansaaree. On some nights, I would attend the classes of *Shaykh* 'Abdul-'Azeez bin Baaz in the Prophet's Mosque (in Madeenah) on the subject of Saheeh Muslim. I would also attend the gatherings of *Shaykh* al-Albaanee, which were specified to only the students of knowledge, in order to learn from him.

While I was in Makkah, I would teach some of the students of knowledge from the books Qatar-un-Nadaa and at-Tuhfah as-Saniyyah. And while I was in Madeenah, I would teach some of my brothers the book at-Tuhfah as-Saniyyah in the Prophet's Mosque. Then I promised my Muslim brothers that I would hold classes on the Jaami' (Sunan) of at-Tirmidhee, Qatar-un-Nadaa and al-Baa'ith-ul-Hatheeth for them in my house after 'Asr.

So a great wave of *Da'wah* spread from Madeenah, which filled the world in the time-span of six years. It was some righteous people who were ones who took on the task of financing it, while Muqbil bin Haadee and his Muslim brothers were the ones who took on the task of teaching their fellow brothers. As for traveling for the purpose of Calling to Allaah throughout all regions of the Kingdom, then this was shared between all of the brothers – the student of knowledge so that he can acquire knowledge and benefit others, and the common person so that he could learn. This was such that many of the common folk benefited and grew to love the (*Salafi*) *Da'wah*.

One of our Muslim brothers from amongst the students of knowledge was an *Imam* of a *masjid* in Riyadh. One time some people of knowledge rebuked him for using a *sutrah*. So he said: "We are unable to in front of you, but by Allaah, no one but a common person will get up to teach you the ahaadeeth of the *Sutrah*." So he called a brother from the general folk who loved the *Da'wah* and had memorised the ahaadeeth of the Sutrah from "Al-Lu'lu wal-Marjaan feemataffaqa 'alayhi ash-Shaykhaan." So he got up and narrated these *ahaadeeth*, after which the opposers felt ashamed and stayed quiet.

After this, the blind followers and the scholars of evil began to set in motion, and the reason for this stirring of the blind-followers, who were considered scholars in the eyes of the people, was because whenever they would find a young student of knowledge amongst our students and they would use a *hadeeth* as proof, the student would say to them: "Who reported the *hadeeth*?" And this was something they were not accustomed to. Then he would say to them: "What is the status (i.e. grading) of the hadeeth?" This was something that they also weren't accustomed to. So they would embarrass them in front of the people. And sometimes the student would say to them: "This is a weak *hadeeth*. There is so and so in its chain of narration and so and so declared him weak." So upon hearing this, it is as if the earth would become constricted beneath these blind-followers. And they would then go about spreading lies that these students were *Khawaarij*, when in fact the brothers were not from the *Khawaarij* who make it lawful to shed a Muslim's blood and who deem a Muslim a disbeliever on the count of sins.

However, there would occur some errors on the part of some of the new brothers, and this was because the beginner is almost always overwhelmed with excessive zeal. At that time, I was preparing my Master's dissertation, when all of a sudden one night, before I knew what was happening, they arrested me and arrested almost one hundred and fifty others. Some people were able to escape, but the earth trembled between those who opposed and those who agreed with out arrest. We remained in prison for a month or a month and a half. After that we were set free, all praise be to Allaah.

Shortly after this, the treatises from Juhaymaan were released and a group of us were again arrested.[2] During the interrogation, they asked me: *"Where you the one who wrote this?"* What, Juhaymaan can't write? So I denied this, and Allaah knows that I didn't write it nor did I assist in any part of it. But after staying in jail for three months, an order was made for foreigners to be deported.

When I arrived at Yemen, I went back to my village and stayed there for a while teaching the children *Qur.aan*. Before I knew it, it seemed like the whole world was in an all-out battle against me. It was as if I had come out to destroy the country, the Religion and the rulership. At that time, I didn't know any leader or tribal chief. So I would say: *"Allaah is sufficient for me and the best of Guardians."* When things would get tight, I would go to San'aa or to Haashid or to Dhimmaar, and also to Ta'iz, Ibb and Hudaydah to give Da'wah and to visit the Muslims brothers.

---

2 <u>Translator's Note</u>: This refers to Juhaymaan bin Muhammad al-'Utaybee, a deviant from Saudi Arabia who took over the Grand Mosque of Makkah with hundreds of followers in 1979, and held it for several days, after which the senior scholars allowed force to be used in the sacred site of the Ka'bah in order to regain it. The Saudi National Guard subdued them about two weeks later after much blood was shed and casualties were lost on the part of the rebels and the Saudi army. The remaining dissidents that were captured were later beheaded. Shaykh al-Albaanee mentioned this Juhaymaan in his book as-Saheehah (5/872), saying: "...And like the followers of the Saudi Juhaymaan, who caused the fitnah in the Grand Mosque in Makkah at the beginning of the 1400's (Hijree). He claimed that the awaited Mahdee was with him and sought from those present in the Mosque to give him bay'ah (allegiance). Some of the simple-minded, heedless and evil people followed him. Then Allaah put an end to their fitnah after they had shed much of the Muslims' blood."

After some days, some good-doers sent me my library from Madeenah. They sent the books to Sa'adah where the head of shipments there was malicious of the *Sunnah*. Some of our companions went to request the books from him, so he said: "Come back after *Zhuhr*, Allaah willing." But he didn't return after *Zhuhr*. Instead, some Shiites mobilized and requested the caretakers to confiscate the books because they were Wahaabbi books!

Do not ask about the monetary fees, hardships and injustice that occurred to me as a result of trying to get my books! Many of the brothers from the inhabitants of my country made great efforts to follow that up, including *Shaykh* 'Abdullaah bin Husayn al-Ahmar, *Shaykh* Hazaa' Dab'aan, the caretakers of the Guidance and Counseling Center, such as the Judge Yahyaa al-Fasayyal, may Allaah have mercy on him, and brother 'Aa'id bin 'Alee Mismaar. After a long difficulty, the people of Sa'adah sent a telegraph to the President 'Alee bin 'Abdillaah bin Saalih, so he assigned the case to the judge, 'Alee as-Samaan. The judge sent me a letter and promised that he would turn over the library to me. And he said: "The people of Sa'adah are very strict. They call the scholars of San'aa disbelievers." So I went to San'aa to get my books. Allaah decreed that my books arrive there while the judge 'Alee Samaan was out of the country on a mission. So when some of the brothers went to ask for it, the head of the Ministry of Endowments told them: "These books need to be inspected." So some of our Muslim brothers at the Center for Guidance and Counseling mobilised and went to request the books. So they said: *"These books are under our jurisdiction. We must examine them, so whatever is upright, we will hand over to al-Waadi'ee and whatever violates the Religion, we will keep it with us."* So by doing this, they discovered that the books were in fact purely religious and turned the them over to me without inspecting them, so may Allaah reward them.

I brought the books into my country, all praise be to Allaah. And my close ones, may Allaah reward them, built a small library and a small masjid. And they said: *"We will pray Jumu'ah here to avoid hardships and problems. Sometimes we would pray there with only six people present."*

One time the governor Haadee al-Hasheeshi asked for me, so I went to *Shaykh* Qaa'id Majlee, may Allaah have mercy on him, who then called him and said: *"What do you want from al-Waadi'ee?"* He said: *"Nothing, except to get to know him."* So he said: *"We will look for him in his institute."*

In another instance, some other leader asked for me and so Husayn bin Qaa'id Majlee went with me to see him. He (Majlee) began to talk against the *Shee'ah* and explain to him that we call to the *Qur.aan* and the *Sunnah* and that the *Shee'ah* hate us because of that because they fear that the truth will come out about them, so this leader said: "Indeed, the Shiites have tainted the history of Yemen, so as long as your *Da'wah* (call) is as you say it is, then call to it and we are with you."

After this I spent some time with my library. Only a few days had passed when some Egyptian brothers came and we started classes on some of the books of *Hadeeth* and the Arabic Language. After this, students continued to come from Egypt, Kuwait, the Sacred Lands (Makkah and Madeenah), Najd, 'Aden, Hadramaut, Algeria, Libya, Somalia, Belgium, and other Muslim and non-Muslim countries.

The number of students has now reached between six to seven hundred students, amongst which are a hundred and seventy families.[3] And Al-

---

3 Translator's Note: It must be re-emphasised here that this statement comes from the second edition of his autobiography, which was printed in 1999. Since then

laah is the One who provides them with sustenance. And all of this is not because of our might or power, nor due to the amount of knowledge we have or because of our courage or eloquence in speech. Rather, this is something that Allaah willed to be. So He was the One, all praise to Allaah, that granted us this blessing.

[End of Translation of Shaykh Muqbil's Autobiography]

2. His Death

Shaykh Muqbil bin Haadee al-Waadi'ee passed away on the 2nd of Jumaadal-Oolaa, 1422H (7/21/2001) due to a liver disease that he was suffering from for a long time, and due to which he traveled to America, Germany and Saudi Arabia during the last part of his life to seek treatment for. He was around seventy years of age when he died in Jeddah. His funeral prayer was held in Makkah and he was buried in the al-'Adl Cemetery near the graves of *Shaykh*s Ibn Baaz and Ibn al-'Uthaymeen, may Allaah have mercy on all of them.

3. The Scholars' Praise for him

Shaykh Muhammad bin Saalih al-'Uthaymeen said: *"Tell him that I consider him to be a mujaddid."*

Shaykh al-Albaanee said: *"So degrading and belittling these two Shaykhs (Rabee' and Muqbil), who call to the Qur.aan and the Sunnah and what the Salaf ss-Saalih were upon and who wage war against those who oppose this correct methodology. As is quite clear to everyone, it either comes from one of two types of people. Either it comes from someone who is ignorant or someone who follows his desires... If he is*

---

these numbers have continued to increase, such that in present times, the Shaykh's school, which is now taught and supervised by Shaykh Yahyaa al-Hajooree has around 1000 students and 500 families, all praise be to Allaah.

ignorant, then he can be taught. But if he is one who follows his desires, then we seek Allaah's refuge from the evil of this person. And we ask Allaah, Mighty and Sublime, to either guide him or break his back." [The Audio series Silsilah al-Hudaa wan-Noor: 1/851]

Shaykh Yahyaa al-Hajooree reported that *Shaykh* Rabee' al-Madkhalee said about him: *"He is the mujaddid in the lands of Yemen" and that he said: "there can't be found from the time of 'Abdur-Razaaq as-San'aanee to this present day someone who established the Da'wah and revived it as the likes of al-Waadi'ee."*[4]

---

4 Translator's Note: These quotes are from the book Nubdhah Mukhtasarah of Shaykh Muqbil's daughter Umm 'Abdillaah (pg. 46)

Biography of
Shaykh Ahmad ibn Yahyaa an-Najmee[*]
1928 - 2008

He is our noble *Shaykh*, the *'Allaamah*, the *Muhaddith*, the *Faqeeh*, the present *Mufti* of the district of Jaazaan and the carrier of the Flag of the Sunnah and *hadeeth* in it - Shaykh Ahmad Ibn Yahyaa Ibn Muhammad Ibn Shabeer an-Najmee Aali Shabeer from Banee Hummad, one of the well known tribes of the district of Jaazaan.

The *Shaykh*, may Allaah preserve him, was born in the village of Najaamiyyah on the 22nd of Shawaal of 1346H and was raised in the house of his two righteous parents - which have no equal in comparison.

Due to this, his parents both made a pledge to Allaah by him that they would not burden him with any type of worldly jobs, and Allaah made what they wished come true.

They would both constantly keep guard of their son to the point that they would not even let him play amongst the children. When he reached the age of puberty, they entered him into the schools of the village, where he learned to read and write. He learned to recite the *Qur'aan* in the na-

---

* Translated by Abu 'Maryam Ismaa'eel Alercon

tional school before the coming of the Shaykh 'Abdullaah al-Qar'aawee, *rahima-hullaah*, three times, the last of which occurred in 1358H when he remained there.

He first read the Qur'aan to *Shaykh* 'Abdu Ibn Muhammad 'Aqeel an-Najmee in 1355H. Then he read it to Shaykh Yahyaa Faqeeh 'Abasee, who was from Yemen and who had come to Najaamiyyah and stayed there. Our *Shaykh* studied under him in the year 1358H. But when Shaykh 'Abdullaah al-Qar'aawee arrived at Najaamiyyah, there occurred a debate between him and this teacher concerning the issue of Allaah's Rising - for he was *'asharee*. So *Shaykh* al-Qar'aawee defeated him and he fled from the town after that.

> **And so the roots of the people who did wrong were cut off - all praise be to Allaah, the Lord of the Worlds.** [2]

After their *'asharee* teacher left, the Shaykh, along with his two paternal uncles, Hasan Ibn Muhammad an-Najmee and Husayn Ibn Muhammad an-Najmee, began to frequently attend *Shaykh* al-Qar'aawee's classes for some days in the city of Saamitah, but this did not last. This was in the year 1359H. In 1360, in the month of Safar to be exact, our *Shaykh* joined the Madrasah *Salafiyyah* and recited the *Qur'aan*, this time under the order of *Shaykh* 'Abdullaah al-Qar'aawee (*rahima-hullaah*) to *Shaykh* 'Uthmaan Ibn 'Uthmaan Hamlee (*rahima-hullaah*). This was such that he recited the entire *Qur'aan* to him with tajweed and memorised the books "Tuhfatul-Atfaal", "Hidaayatul-Mustafeed", "Thalaathatul-Usool", "al-'Arba'een an-Nawawiyyah" and "al-Hisaab." And he perfected the discipline of handwriting.

---

2 The Noble *Qur.aan - Soorah* al-An'aam, *Aayah* 45

40

He would sit in the study circle, which *Shaykh* al-Qar'aawee had set up there, until the time when the younger students departed after the *Salaat az-Zhuhr*. Then he would attend the circle for the elder students, which *Shaykh* 'Abdullaah al-Qar'aawee was in charge of personally teaching. So he would sit in this class from after the *Salaat az-Zhuhr* till the time of the *Salaat al-'Ishaa*. Then after praying (*'Ishaa.*), he would return to his town of Najaamiyyah with his two uncles (Hasan and Husayn).

After four months, *Shaykh* 'Abdullaah al-Qar'aawee granted him permission to to be part of his study circle for elder students, which he taught himself. So he read to the *Shaykh* the following books: "ar-Raheebah" concerning Laws of Inheritance, "al-Aajroomiyyah" concening Arabic Grammar, "Kitaab at-Tawheed", "Buloogh al-Maraam", "al-Bayqooniyyah", "Nukhbat-ul-Fikr" with its explanation "Nuzhat-un-Nadhr", "Mukhtasaraat fee Seerah", "Tasreef al-Ghazee", "al-'Awaamil fee an-Nahw", "al-Waraqaat" concerning the Principles of *Fiqh*, and "al-'Aqeedah at-Tahaawiyyah" with its explanation from *Shaykh* 'Abdullaah al-Qar'aawee - this was before they had seen its explanation from Ibn Abil-'Izz al-Hanafee. He also studied parts of the book "al-Alfiyyah" of Ibn Maalik and "ad-Durar al-Bahiyyah" with its explanation "ad-Daraaree al-Madiyyah" concerning *Fiqh* - both of which are written by ash-Shawkaanee, rahimahullaah. This goes as well for other books - whether there was in them those which they studied as an assigned subject, like the previously mentioned books or what they studied for cultural education in some concise treatises and small pamphlets or those books, which they would reference when researching such as Naylul-Awtaar, Zaad al-Ma'aad, Noorul-Yaqeen, al-Muwatta and al-Ummuhaat.

In 1362H, *Shaykh* 'Abdullaah, *rahimahullaah*, distributed portions of the Ummahaat (*hadeeth* Books) he had present in his library to his students, which consisted of *Saheeh* al-Bukhaaree, *Sunan* Abee Daawood, *Sunan* an-Nasaa.ee, *Muwatta* of Imaam Maalik. So they (his elder stu-

41

dents) began to read these books to him, but they did not complete them because they had to depart due to a drought.

In 1364H, they returned and read them to him. so then *Shaykh* 'Abdullaah gave him the *ijaazah* (religious authorisation) to report from al-Ummahaat as-Sitt.

In 1369H, he studied under *Shaykh* Ibraheem Ibn Muhammad al-'Amoodee, *rahimahullaah*, the Judge of Saamitah at that time, two books - "Islaah al-Mujtami'a" and the book of *Shaykh* 'Abd-ur-Rahmaan Ibn Sa'adee, (*rahima-hullaah*) on *Fiqh*, which is organized in the form of question and answer, entitled: "al-Irshaad ilaa Ma'rifat-il-Ahkaam."

He also studied under *Shaykh* 'Alee Ibn ash-Shaykh Ziyaad as-Somalee at the order of *Shaykh* 'Abdullaah al-Qar'aawee, the subject of Grammar, studying the book "al-'Awaamil fin-Nahwi Mi.ah", as well as other books on Grammar and Morphology.

In 1384H, he attended the study circles of the *Shaykh*, the *Imaam*, the *'Allaamah*, the *Mufti* of the Saudi Lands, *Shaykh* Muhammad Ibn Ibraaheem Aal ash-Shaykh, *rahimahullaah*, for the length of close to two months. In these circles, he taught Tafseer Ibn Jareer at-Tabaree with the recitation of 'Abdul-'Azeez Ash-Shalhoob, with regard to the subject of *tafseer*. Likewise, in the same year, he attended the gatherings of our *Shaykh*, the *Imaam*, the *'Allaamah*, *Shaykh* 'Abdul-'Azeez Ibn Baaz, *rahimahullaah*, for the length of close to a month and a half. This class was on *Saheeh* al-Bukhaaree and occurred between the *Maghrib* and *'Ishaa*. prayers.

From what you have read it is clear that his teachers, in order, include:
1. *Shaykh* Ibraaheem Ibn Muhammad al-'Amoodee - the judge of Saamitah in his time

2. *Shaykh* Haafidh Ibn Ahmad al-Hakamee - (*rahima-hullaah*)

3. The *Shaykh*, the 'Allaamah, the Caller, the Reformer (*mujaddid*) of the southern part of the kingdom of Saudi Arabia, 'Abdullaah al-Qar'aawee - (*rahima-hullaah*)

4. *Shaykh* 'Abdu Ibn Muhammad 'Aqeel an-Najmee

5. *Shaykh* 'Uthmaan Ibn 'Uthmaan al-Hamlee

6. *Shaykh* 'Alee Ibn ash-Shaykh 'Uthmaan Ziyaad as-Somalee

7. The *Imaam*, the 'Allaamah, the former *Mufti* of the lands of Saudi Arabia, *Shaykh* Muhammad Ibn Ibraaheem Aal ash-Shaykh - (*rahima-hullaah*)

8. *Shaykh* Yahyaa Faqeeh 'Abasee al-Yemenee

Our *Shaykh*, may Allaah preserve him, has many many students. For whoever spent the amount of time that he spent in teaching, which is almost half a century, then you can just imagine how many his students will be. And if we were to list their number, then that would require a large book in itself. So I will only mention a short example of them, by which one can go by in determining his other students. So from among his students are:

1. Our *Shaykh*, the 'Allaamah, the *Muhaddith*, the Defender of the *Sunnah*, Rabee' Ibn Haadee al-Madkhalee

2. Our *Shaykh*, the 'Allaamah, the *Faqeeh*, Zayd Ibn Muhammad Haadee al-Madkhalee

3. Our *Shaykh*, the Noble Scholar, 'Alee Ibn Naasir al-Faqeehee

It is sufficient to just mention these three names here. And this is due to the widespread fame they have in the circles and gatherings of knowledge, so no one can blame us for doing so.

The *Shaykh* possesses a very high level of intelligence. The following is a story that indicates the intelligence and good memory he had since childhood:

The uncle, *Shaykh* 'Umar Ibn Ahmad Jardee al-Madkhalee said:
"When *Shaykh* Ahmad would attend classes at the Madrasah *Salafiyya-hin* Saamitah, along with his two uncles, Hasan an-Najmee and Husayn an-Najmee, during 1359 when he was 13, he would listen to the classes that *Shaykh* 'Abdullaah al-Qar'aawee gave to his elder students and he would memorise them." I say: This is what caused *Shaykh* 'Abdullaah al-Qar'aawee to let *Shaykh* Ahmad join his adult classes, which he would take charge of teaching himself. This was because of what the *Shaykh* (al-Qar'aawee) saw of his superiority, quickness in memorising and intelligence.

Our *Shaykh*, may Allaah preserve him, worked as a teacher in the schools of his *Shaykh*, 'Abdullaah al-Qar'aawee, as a volunteer. And when the pay positions began, he was assigned the duty of a teacher in his town of Najaamiyyah. This was in 1367H. Then in 1372H, he transferred to being Imaam and teacher in the town of Abu Subaylah in Baalhurrath.

On 1/1/1374H, when the educational institute in Saamitah was opened, he was assigned the position of a teacher in it until the year 1384H. He resigned from this position with the hopes of getting the opportunity to teach in the *Islaam*ic University of Madeenah, so he traveled there. However, certain circumstances took place which didn't allow that to occur, so he returned back to his district and Allaah decreed for him to be appointed the position of religious admonisher and guide for the Ministry of Justice of the District of Jaazaan. So he took the role of admonishing and advising in the best of manners.

On 1/7/1387H, he returned to being a teacher at the educational institute in the city of Jaazaan at his request. Then at the beginning of the school year of 1389H, he returned to teaching at the institute of Saamitah. He remained there as a teacher until he retired in 1/7/1410H.

Since that time up until the time that I am writing these lines, he has kept himself busy teaching in his home, in his local masjid and in other masaajid of the district, holding weekly classes as well as taking on the role of providing *fataawa* (for questions).

In doing all of this, he has acted in accordance with the final advice of his teacher, which was to remain constant in teaching and in taking care of the students, especially the foreign ones among them who left their families (to study). He had remarkable patience in accomplishing this, so we ask Allaah that He reward him on our behalf.

He also abided by his teacher, *Shaykh* al-Qar'aawee's final advice by continuing in his studies and in researching and learning from others. This is especially with regard to the sciences and principles of *hadeeth* and *fiqh*, for it was such that he surpassed his colleagues and had a powerful command in that matter. May Allaah bless his life and knowledge and benefit us with his efforts.

Our *Shaykh*, may Allaah preserve him, has written many books, some of which have been printed and some which have not. We ask Allaah that He facilitate the publishing of those books so that the benefit from them can be attained. From his books are:

1. Awdahul-Ishaarah fir-Radd 'alaa man abaaha al-Mamnoo' min az-Ziya-arah
2. Ta.seesul-Ahkaam Sharh 'Umdatul-Ahkaam - only a very, very small portion of it was printed.
3. Tanzeehush-Sharee'ah 'an Ibaahatil-Aghaanee al-Khalee'ah
4. Risaalatul-Irshaad ilaa Bayaanil-Haqq fee Hukmil-Jihaad

And there are other beneficial books, which he has presented for the Muslims, may Allaah reward him with the best of rewards and benefit Islaam and the Muslims through him. And may the peace and blessings of Allaah be on our prophet, Muhammad, his family and Companions, Ameen.

Biography of
Shaykh Dr. Saalih ibn Fowzaan al-Fowzaan[*]

He is the noble *Shaykh* Dr. Saalih ibn Fowzaan ibn 'Abdullaah from the family of Fowzaan from the people/tribe of ash-Shamaasiyyah.

He was born in 1354 A.H./1933 C.E. His father died when he was young so he was brought up by his family. He learnt the Noble *Qur.aan*, the basics of reading and writing with the imaam of the masjid of the town, who was a definitve reciter. He was the noble *Shaykh* Hamood Ibn Sulaymaan at-Talaal, who was later made a judge in the town of Dariyyah (not to be mistaken with the town of Dar'iyyah in Riyadh) in the region of Qaseem.

He later studied at the state school when it opened in ash-Shamaasiyyah in the year 1369 A.H./1948 C.E. He completed his studies at the Faysaliyyah school in Buraydah in the year 1371 A.H./1950 C.E. and was then appointed an infant school teacher. Then he joined the educational institute in Buraydah when it opened in the year 1373 A.H./1952 C.E., and graduated from there in the year 1377 A.H./1956 C.E. He then joined the

---

* Translated by Abu 'Abdullaah Mohammed Akhtar Chaudhry

Faculty of *Sharee'ah* (at the University of Imaam Muhammad) in Riyadh and graduated from there 1381 A.H./1960 C.E. Thereafter he gained his Masters degree in *fiqh*, and later a Doctorate. from the same faculty, also specialising in *fiqh*.

After his graduation from the Faculty of *Sharee'ah*, he was appointed a teacher within the educational institute in Riyaadh, then transferred to teaching in the Faculty of *Sharee'ah*. Later, he transferred to teaching at the Department for Higher Studies within the Faculty of the Principles of the Religion (*usool ad-deen*). Then he transferred to teaching at the Supreme Court of Justice, where he was appointed the head. He then returned to teaching there after his period of headship came to an end. He was then made a member of the Permanent Committee for Islaamic Research and Verdicts, where he continues to this day.

The noble *Shaykh* is a member of the Council of Senior Scholars, and member of the Fiqh Committee in Makkah (part of ar-Raabitah), and member of the Committee for Supervision of the Callers in Hajj, whilst also presiding over membership of the Permanent Committee for Islaamic Research and Verdicts. He is also the *imaam, khateeb* and teacher at the Prince Mut'ib Ibn 'Abdul-'Azeez *masjid* in al-Malzar.

He also takes part in responding to questions on the radio program 'Noorun 'alad-Darb', as he also takes part in contributing to a number of Islaamic research publications at the Council for (Islaamic) Research, Studies, Theses and Fataawa which are then collated and published. The noble *Shaykh* also takes part in supervising a number of theses at the Masters degree and Doctorate level.

He has a number of students of knowledge who frequent his regular gatherings and lessons .

He himself studied at the hands of a number prominent scholars and jurists, the most notable of whom were, the noble *Mashaayikh*:

'Abdul-'Azeez ibn Baaz (*rahima-hullaah*);

'Abdullaah ibn Humayd (*rahima-hullaah*);

Muhammad al-Ameen ash-Shanqeetee (*rahima-hullaah*);

'Abdur-Razzaaq 'Afeefee (*rahima-hullaah*);

Saalih Ibn 'Abdur-Rahmaan as-Sukaytee;

Saalih Ibn Ibraaheem al-Bulayhee;

Muhammad Ibn Subayyal;

'Abdullaah Ibn Saalih al-Khulayfee;

Ibraaheem Ibn 'Ubayd al-'Abd al-Muhsin;

Saalih al-'Alee an-Naasir;

He also studied at the hands of a number of scholars from al-Azhar University (Egypt) who specialised in *hadeeth*, *tafseer* and Arabic language.

He has played a major role in calling to Allaah and teaching, giving *fatwa*, *khutbah*s and knowledgeable refutations.

His books number many, however the following are just a handful which include Sharh al-'Aqeedatul Waasitiyyah, al-irshaad ilas-Saheehil-I'tiqaad, al-Mulakhkhas al-Fiqh.hee, Foods and the Rulings regarding Slaughtering and Hunting, which is part of his Doctorate. They also include at-Tahqeeqaat al-Mardiyyah in inheritance which is part of his Masters degree. Further titles include Rulings relating to the Believing Women, and a refutation of Yoosuf Qaradaawi's book al-Halaal wal-Haraam.

The *Shaykh*'s official website: http://www.alfawzan.ws

The Permanent Committee
for Islaamic Research and Verdicts[*]

A Royal Decree, number 137/1 and dated 08/07/1391 A.H. / (29/08/1971 C.E.) was issued for the establishment of the Council of Senior Scholars. Whereby, under section four it mentions:

'The Permanent Committee has been left the task of selecting its members from amongst the members of the Council [of Senior Scholars] in accordance with the Royal Decree. Its aim is to prepare research papers ready for discussion amongst the Council [of Senior Scholars], and issue *fataawa* on individual issues. This is by responding to the *fatwa*-seeking public in areas of *'aqeedah*, *'ibaadah* and social issues. It will be called: 'The Permanent Committee for Islaamic Research and Verdicts' (al-Lajnah ad-Daa.imah lil-Buhooth al-'Ilmiyyah wal-Iftaa.)'

Further, it is mentioned in section eight of the attachment to the Royal Decree:

'No *fatwa* will be issued by the Permanent Committee until the majority

---

* Translated by Abu 'Abdullaah Mohammed Akhtar Chaudhry

of its members have absolute agreement concerning it. Such, that the number [of scholars] studying each *fatwa* is no less then three members [of the Committee]. And if there exists an equal voice [differing in opinion], then the decision of the Head [of the Committee] will take precedence.'

The current members of the Permanent Committee include:
Head: *Shaykh* 'Abdul 'Azeez Aal ash-Shaykh;
Member: *Shaykh* 'Abdullaah Ibn Qu'ood;
Member: *Shaykh* 'Abdullaah Ibn Munee';
Member: *Shaykh* Saalih Ibn Fowzaan.

Amongst the members who have passed away include:
Shaykh Ibraaheem Ibn Muhammad Aal ash-Shaykh;
Shaykh 'Abdul 'Azeez Ibn Baaz;
Shaykh 'Abdur-Razzaaq Ibn 'Afeefee;
Shaykh Bakar 'Abdullaah Abu Zayd;
Shaykh 'Abdullaah Ibn Ghudayyaan.

From amongst the rules (applied) in forming the [Permanent] Committee was the importance attached to the majority view [of the Committee], and no doubt this gives each *fatwa* an element of knowledge-based strength, for certainly exchanging views simplifies [the task of] arriving at that which is correct. Noting therefore, the path which the Committee has taken is selecting the opinion(s) which are based upon *daleel* (proof) in addition to the *daleel* from the *Sunnah* being from authentic *ahaadeeth*. The Noble *Shaykh* 'Abdul 'Azeez Ibn Baaz has assisted in this issue from his (vast) knowledge of *hadeeth*. Likewise, as has *Shakyh* 'Abdur-Razzaaq Ibn 'Afeefee's [vast] knowledge of the various groups and differences in *'aqeedah* that we have today, added an element of knowledge-based strength to each *fatwa*.

Chapter 1
General Fataawa

1. Allaah Safeguards His Religion

Question: How does one respond to people who claim that since Allaah (*Subhaanahu wa Ta'aala*) has taken it upon Himself to safeguard His Religion, the efforts that the callers to Allaah put into it are useless?[1]

Response: The response is very simple, because this is the claim of those who reject 'cause'. There is no doubt that rejecting the causes of why things take place is misguidance as well as foolishness. Indeed Allaah safeguards this Religion, but He does so with causes, amongst them are the efforts that the callers to Allaah put into this religion by conveying it, explaining it and calling to it.

This is similar to one who says: 'Do not get married, if Allaah decrees for you to have a child then you shall have one.' Or one who says: 'Do not work for funds, if Allaah decrees wealth for you then you shall have it.'

---

1 Kitaab ad-Da'wah - Volume 2, Page 156

When Allaah (*Subhaanahu wa Ta'aala*) said:

إِنَّا نَحْنُ نَزَّلْنَا ٱلذِّكْرَ وَإِنَّا لَهُۥ لَحَٰفِظُونَ

"Indeed, it is We Who have sent down the Dhikr (i.e. the Qur.aan) and We will surely guard it (from corruption)."[2]

We know that Allaah said this knowing that He (*Subhaanahu wa Ta'aala*) is All-Wise and that there is nothing that takes place without a cause. So in order to safeguard this Religion, Allaah (*Subhaanahu wa Ta'aala*) decreed causes with which it will be safeguarded. It is for this reason that we find that the scholars of the *Salaf* wrote and warned against innovations and clarified the truth to the people, even though they knew that Allaah safeguards His Religion from innovations related to creed as well as actions. So, it is imperative that we carry out what Allaah has obligated upon us regarding defending, protecting and spreading the religion; safeguarding the religion is achieved by doing so.

Shaykh Muhammad ibn Saalih al-'Uthaymeen

2. Why Muslims are Lagging Behind

Question: Some of those who have weak *eemaan* claim that the reason *Muslims* are behind is because of their adherence to their religion. Their misconception, according to their claim, is that when the Western world abandoned and liberated themselves from all religions, they were able to achieve the level of sophistication that they now enjoy, and while adhering to our religion, we have become their followers as opposed to being their leaders. What is the response to these claims? They may also

---

2 The Noble *Qur.aan* - *Soorah* al-Hijr, *Aayah* 9

strengthen their argument by the abundance of rain, farms and vegetation present in the West, saying that this is proof that they are upon a correct path.[3]

Response: I say that this question can only be asked by someone who is either weak in *eemaan*, or doesn't have any *eemaan* altogether; one who is ignorant of history and oblivious of the causes of victory. When the *Muslims* held on to their religion in the beginning stages of *Islaam* they had honour, command, strength and dominance in all aspects of life.

On the contrary, some people say that the West only reached this level of knowledge due to what they learnt from the *Muslims* during the beginning stages of *Islaam*. However, the *Muslims* have neglected a great deal of their religion; they have also innovated in matters related to creed, sayings and actions, in the Religion of Allaah. This is why they fell far behind and are underdeveloped.

We know with certainty, and I call upon Allaah (*Subhaanahu wa Ta'aala*) as a witness to this, that if we returned to practicing this religion the same way our Righteous Predecessors practiced it, we would have honour, dignity and be victorious over all people. This is why when Heraclius, the king of Rome conferred with Abu Sufyaan – Rome at that time was considered to be a great empire – about what the Messenger (*sal-Allaahu 'alayhi wa sallam*) and his Companions were upon, he said:

> *"If what you say is true, he will soon occupy the lands beneath my very own feet."*

---

3 Alfaadh wa-Mafaaheem fee Meezaan ash-Sharee'ah - Page 914

When Abu Sufyaan and his companions left Heraclius's company, he said:

"The affair of Ibn Abi Kabshah (i.e. the Prophet) has certainly become grand, indeed the king of Asfar fears him."

As for industrial, technological and other developments that have taken place in atheist Western countries, our religion does not prohibit such developments, but if we only paid attention to such issues, we would sadly lose both the life of this world as well as our religion. However *Islaam* is not in opposition to such advancements, rather Allaah (*Subhaanahu wa Ta'aala*) said:

$$ وَأَعِدُّواْ لَهُم مَّا ٱسْتَطَعْتُم مِّن قُوَّةٍ وَمِن رِّبَاطِ ٱلْخَيْلِ تُرْهِبُونَ بِهِۦ عَدُوَّ ٱللَّهِ وَعَدُوَّكُمْ $$

"And prepare against them all you can of power, including steeds of war, to threaten thereby the enemy of Allaah and your enemy."[4]

Allaah (*Subhaanahu wa Ta'aala*) also says:

$$ هُوَ ٱلَّذِى جَعَلَ لَكُمُ ٱلْأَرْضَ ذَلُولًا فَٱمْشُواْ فِى مَنَاكِبِهَا وَكُلُواْ مِن رِّزْقِهِۦ $$

"It is He who has made the earth subservient to you (i.e. easy for you to walk on, live in and cultivate, etc.), so walk in the path thereof and eat of His provision."[5]

---

4 The Noble *Qur.aan* - *Soorah* al-Anfaal, *Aayah* 60

5 The Noble *Qur.aan* - *Soorah* al-Mulk, *Aayah* 15

He (*Subhaanahu wa Ta'aala*) says:

$$هُوَ ٱلَّذِى خَلَقَ لَكُم مَّا فِى ٱلْأَرْضِ جَمِيعًا$$

"It is He who created for you all that is on earth."[6]

Allaah (*Subhaanahu wa Ta'aala*) says:

$$وَفِى ٱلْأَرْضِ قِطَعٌ مُّتَجَٰوِرَٰتٌ$$

"And upon the earth are neighboring tracts..."[7]

There are other verses that clearly state that a person can work, attain and profit, but not on the account of the religion. These disbelieving nations are disbelievers from the foundation; the religions that they claimed to adhere to are false religions. Their religions and atheism are one and the same; there is no difference between them. Allaah (*Subhaanahu wa Ta'aala*) says:

$$وَمَن يَبْتَغِ غَيْرَ ٱلْإِسْلَٰمِ دِينًا فَلَن يُقْبَلَ مِنْهُ$$

"And whoever seeks a religion other than Islaam,
will never have it accepted..."[8]

Even though Jews and Christians have certain characteristics that differentiate them from others, in the Hereafter they are all the same. This is why the Prophet vowed that whoever from the Jews or Christians hears of him, and then chooses not to follow his religion would be amongst the dwellers of the Hellfire. So they are disbelievers in their foundation whether they affiliate themselves to Christianity, Judaism or not!

---

6   The Noble *Qur.aan* - *Soorah* al-Baqarah, *Aayah* 29

7   The Noble *Qur.aan* - *Soorah* ar-Ra'd, *Aayah* 4

8   The Noble *Qur.aan* - *Soorah* Aal-'Imraan, *Aayah* 85

As for the abundance of rain in their countries and so on, then this is a test and trial from Allaah (*Subhaanahu wa Ta'aala*). Furthermore they are rewarded for their good deeds during their life in this world, as the Prophet (*sal-Allaahu 'alayhi wa sallam*) informed 'Umar ibn al-Khattaab when 'Umar saw that a straw mat left marks on the Prophet's side. 'Umar cried at the sight and said; 'O Messenger of Allaah, the Persians and Romans live in luxury while you are in such a state?' So the Messenger of Allaah (*sal-Allaahu 'alayhi wa sallam*) said:

> **"O 'Umar, they are people who are hurriedly rewarded in their worldly life; does it not please you that they have the life of this world whereas we have the Hereafter?"**

Furthermore, there are disasters that take place in their countries such as droughts, earthquakes and hurricanes. This is well-known and is always being broadcasted in the news.

However, this questioner is blind, Allaah has blinded him of insight and so he is unable to perceive the reality of the situation. I advise him to repent to Allaah (*Subhaanahu wa Ta'aala*) from this behaviour before death takes him by surprise. He has to know that the only way we will have pride, honour, victory and leadership is by truthfully returning to our religion of *Islaam* in actions as well as speech. He must also know that the disbelievers are upon falsehood; they are not upon the truth, and their abode is the Fire as Allaah informed us in His Book and through His Messenger (*sal-Allaahu 'alayhi wa sallam*). These bounties that Allaah has given them in terms of luxuries are nothing but a test and trial for them, a rushed reward, so that when they pass away and depart from such luxuries only to enter the Hellfire, their regret, pain and sorrow will be even greater. It is from Allaah's (*Subhaanahu wa Ta'aala*) Wisdom to provide them these luxuries, even though they are not free from disasters such as earthquakes, droughts, hurricanes, floods and so on, as I have already explained.

I ask Allaah to grant this questioner guidance and success, to bring him back to the truth and grant us all understanding of our religion, indeed He is All-Generous, All-Bountiful, and all praise is due to Allaah, Lord of the worlds, and may the *salaah* and *salaam* be upon our Prophet Muhammad, his family and Companions.

Shaykh Muhammad ibn Saalih al-'Uthaymeen

3. Emerging from Being Behind

Question: Are *Muslims* behind, and how can we help them out of this state?[9]

Response: There is no doubt that no true believer is pleased with the state of the *Muslims* during present times. Indeed they have lagged behind due to inadequately fulfilling what Allaah has obligated upon them. They fell short in conveying the religion to the world and calling to Allaah (*Subhaanahu wa Ta'aala*) just as they fell short in preparing the strength that Allaah commanded them to prepare, as is in the saying of Allaah (*Subhaanahu wa Ta'aala*):

$$\text{وَأَعِدُّواْ لَهُم مَّا ٱسْتَطَعْتُم مِّن قُوَّةٍ وَمِن رِّبَاطِ ٱلْخَيْلِ تُرْهِبُونَ بِهِۦ عَدُوَّ ٱللَّهِ وَعَدُوَّكُمْ}$$

"And prepare against them all you can of power, including steeds of war to threaten thereby the enemy of Allaah and your enemy."[10]

They have also been neglectful concerning being cautious of their en-

---

9 Kitaab ad-Da'wah - Volume 2, Page 166

10 The Noble *Qur.aan* - *Soorah* al-Anfaal, *Aayah* 60

emy while Allaah (*Subhaanahu wa Ta'aala*) says:

$$خُذُواْ حِذْرَكُمْ$$

"Take every precaution for yourselves."[11]

He also says:

$$يَٰٓأَيُّهَا ٱلَّذِينَ
ءَامَنُواْ لَا تَتَّخِذُواْ بِطَانَةً مِّن دُونِكُمْ لَا يَأْلُونَكُمْ خَبَالًا$$

*"O you who believe! Take not as (your) Bitaanah
(advisors, consultants, protectors, helpers, friends)
those outside your religion since they will not fail
to do their best to corrupt you."*[12]

Just as He (*Subhaanahu wa Ta'aala*) says:

$$يَٰٓأَيُّهَا ٱلَّذِينَ ءَامَنُواْ لَا تَتَّخِذُواْ ٱلْيَهُودَ وَٱلنَّصَٰرَىٰٓ أَوْلِيَآءَ بَعْضُهُمْ
أَوْلِيَآءُ بَعْضٍ$$

*"O you who believe! Take not the Jews and the
Christians as Awliyaa' (friends, protectors, helpers), they are but Awliyaa of each other."*[13]

So these issues that *Muslim*s are lacking in have caused them to fall
behind. We hope that Allaah (*Subhaanahu wa Ta'aala*) alleviates them
by drawing the *Muslim*s back to the correct path that the Messenger of

---

11 The Noble *Qur.aan - Soorah* an-Nisaa, *Aayah* 102

12 The Noble *Qur.aan - Soorah* Aal-'Imraan, *Aayah* 118

13 The Noble *Qur.aan - Soorah* al-Maa.idah, *Aayah* 51

Allaah (*sal-Allaahu 'alayhi wa sallam*) directed them to by his saying:

"I left you upon clear guidance; its night is as clear as its day."

The Messenger of Allaah also said:

"I am leaving you with something that if you hold on to, you will never be lead astray: The Book of Allaah and my Sunnah."

So the cause of *Muslims* being behind is the fact that they did not act upon what Allaah and His Messenger (*sal-Allaahu 'alayhi wa sallam*) directed them to act upon; which is to hold fast to the Book of their Lord and the *Sunnah* of their Prophet. Likewise they were not cautious of their enemies, in order to secure themselves from their plots. However, this being the case, we do not say that there is no good at all or that the opportunity has passed away. There will continue to be goodness in this *ummah* no matter how weak it becomes. The Messenger (*sal-Allaahu 'alayhi wa sallam*) said:

"There shall always remain a group from my ummah upon the truth who are victorious; those who oppose them will not harm them, until the Command of Allaah is established."

So no matter how weak the *ummah* becomes, it will never be void of goodness. There will always be those who will establish the Religion of Allaah (*Subhaanahu wa Ta'aala*) amongst them, even if they are on a small island, and goodness will continue to be in this *ummah* as long as its sons and daughters return to it.

Shaykh Saalih ibn Fowzaan al-Fowzaan

<u>Question</u>: We say that we follow the Book and the *Sunnah* according to the understanding of the Righteous Predecessors, but Allaah only ordered us to worship Him with the Book and the *Sunnah*; so what is the use of this stipulation?[14]

<u>Response</u>: In the Name of Allaah, ar-Rahmaan, ar-Raheem. We use this stipulation because alot of the people of innovations, rather most likely all of them, claim that they follow the Book of Allaah and the *Sunnah* of the Messenger of Allaah (*sal-Allaahu 'alayhi wa sallam*). Even the *Ash'ariyyah* call themselves *Ahlus-Sunnah*.

When Ahmad ibn Naasir al-Iskandaraanee refuted al-Kashshaaf, who was *Ash'aree*, he claimed that he was supporting *Ahlus-Sunnah*. Likewise the *Maatureediyyah*, the followers of Abu Mansoor al-Maatureedee and others from the people of desires and innovations claim to be from *Ahlus-Sunnah*.

Furthermore the understanding of the *Salaf* is better for us than our own understanding; the Messenger (*sal-Allaahu 'alayhi wa sallam*) said:

> *"The best of people are my generation, then the subsequent generation, then the subsequent generation after them."*

So their understanding of the Book and the *Sunnah* is better for us than our understanding.

Shaykh Muqbil ibn Haadee al-Waadi'ee

---

14 Fataawa al-'Aqeedah - Page 135

<u>Question</u>: O noble *Shaykh*, the saying of the Prophet (*sal-Allaahu 'alayhi wa sallam*):

> ***"A time period will not come to pass except that the period that follows it will be worse."***

How can we reconcile between this saying and what we observe today concerning people's increasing interest in the Religion of Allaah? We are positive that this time period is better than periods before it because we notice that there are fewer evils and that people are turning to the Religion of Allaah. How do we reconcile between these two issues?[15]

<u>Response</u>: We must understand that the *Qur.aan* and the authentic *Sunnah* can never contradict reality. If something occurs that outwardly appears to be in contradiction to the apparent meanings of the *Qur.aan* and *Sunnah*, then know that you have misunderstood the texts of the *Qur.aan* and the *Sunnah* and they allude to something other than what you have understood, something that does not contradict reality.

As the brother mentioned; the reality during this time period is that youth, and all praise is due to Allaah, are turning to the Religion of Allaah in great numbers. We ask Allaah to grant them stability and guide them to the correct path. However, evil is widespread in relation to a lot of other people. Were these evils that are currently present amongst the *Muslims*, present in the past? In the past, we would never believe that a *Muslim* would drink alcohol; during present times alcohol is sold openly in stores: it is stacked into coolers just like other permissible drinks. We

---

15 Liqaa.aat al-Baab al-Maftooh - No.790

would never believe that someone would practice homosexuality; during present times a man has intercourse with another man as if the latter were his wife. These drugs that are destructive to whole nations; did we even used to know of them?

There is a lot of good in the *ummah* at present times but evil is present as well. If you compare the two you may say that the presence of good is greater than that of evil *inshaa.-Allaah*; but if evil is not deterred by good people then it will become greater than the good.

However, it is the rulers who are intended by this *hadeeth*, because Anas (*radhi-yAllaahu 'anhu*) mentioned this *hadeeth* due to some people approaching him; complaining about the treatment of al-Hajjaaj ibn Yoosuf ath-Thaqafee, so he said to them: 'Be patient for indeed the Messenger of Allaah (*sal-Allaahu 'alayhi wa sallam*) said:

> **"A time period will not come to pass except that the period that follows it will be worse."'**

So it is the rulers who are intended by this *hadeeth*, according to what is apparent to me. A time period will not come to pass except that the period after it will be worse.

The issue of the leadership of 'Umar ibn 'Abdil-'Azeez, may Allaah have mercy upon him, may arise. The rulers before him were worse than him, and he was without a doubt better than them, meaning he was better than those before him, especially those immediately before him. The response here is that there is no contradiction between this and the aforementioned *hadeeth*; the texts of the *Qur.aan* and *Sunnah* sometimes refer to something generally, as opposed to referring to every specific person or individual.

Shaykh Muhammad ibn Saalih al-'Uthaymeen

<u>Question</u>: Do you believe that people's present reception to *da'wah* is better than it was in the past; meaning that there is nothing today such as 'the collision between society and *da'wah*'?[16]

<u>Response</u>: People today are in dire need of *da'wah*. There is a great reception for it as a reaction to the increasing numbers of callers to false-hood, the outburst of the communist methodology and a great revival amongst *Muslim*s. So people today are turning to *Islaam*, embracing it and increasing their understanding of it according to the news that we hear from around the world.

I advise the scholars and all those who are involved in calling to Allaah to take advantage of this opportunity and exert all their efforts in calling to Allaah and teaching the people the reason for their creation; which is worshipping Allaah, obeying Him, reading His Book and so on. I advise them to engage in everything they possibly can, including delivering the *jumu'ah khutbah* along with other sermons during suitable occasions, authoring books and involving themselves with the different types of media outlets such as the radio, television and newspapers.

It is upon the scholars and the callers to Allaah (*Subhaanahu wa Ta'aala*) to take advantage of every opportunity and convey the *da'wah* using all possible legislated means, which are abundant, and all praise is due to Allaah. It is not befitting for them to refrain from calling to Allaah and teaching people. People these days accept whatever they are told, whether it is good or evil. So the people who possess knowledge of the Book of Allaah and the *Sunnah* of His Messenger (*Subhaanahu wa*

---

16 Majalatul-Buhooth al-Islaamiyyah - Volume 4, Page 143

Ta'aala) should take advantage of this opportunity and guide people to good upon a strong foundation built upon the Book of Allaah and the *Sunnah* of His Messenger (*sal-Allaahu 'alayhi wa sallam*). Every one of the callers must be keen upon knowing and understanding the issues they are calling to, relying on the Book of Allaah and the *Sunnah*, so that they do not call while being ignorant; rather it is imperative that they call with knowledge and insight. Allaah (*Subhaanahu wa Ta'aala*) says:

$$قُلْ هَٰذِهِۦ$$

$$سَبِيلِىٓ أَدْعُوٓاْ إِلَى ٱللَّهِ عَلَىٰ بَصِيرَةٍ أَنَا۠ وَمَنِ ٱتَّبَعَنِىٓ وَسُبْحَٰنَ$$

"Say (O Muhammad (sal-Allaahu 'alayhi wa sallam)): "This is my way; I call to Allaah (i.e. to the Oneness of Allaah – Islaamic Monotheism) with sure knowledge, I and whosoever follows me."[17]

This is from amongst the most important of conditions; that the scholar or caller to Allaah has knowledge and insight of what he is calling to and warning against. Beware of being lenient in this matter, because if a person is lenient in this issue he may call the people to falsehood or forbid them from the truth. So it is compulsory to be upon surety in these affairs, and that *da'wah* must be based upon knowledge, guidance and insight in all circumstances.

Shaykh 'Abdul-'Azeez ibn Baaz

7. Da'wah During Present Times

<u>Question</u>: How would you evaluate the reality of the *da'wah* during present times, and which issues need to be focused on, keeping the lat-

---

17 The Noble *Qur.aan - Soorah* Yoosuf, *Aayah* 108

est developments and current challenges in mind?[18]

Response: During present times Allaah (*Subhaanahu wa Ta'aala*) has facilitated the affair of calling to Allaah due to the availability of methods that were unavailable in the past. So the affairs of *da'wah* are alot easier because of the many different mediums that can be employed now. Establishing the proof upon people is now possible in a variety of methods, such as the radio, television, newspapers and so on; there are numerous methods. So it is essential for the people of knowledge and *eemaan*, and the followers of the messengers to carry out this task while co-operating with each other. It is upon them to convey Allaah's Message to His servants without fearing blame. They should not favour important personalities over simple folk, or the poor over the rich, rather they should convey the Religion of Allaah to His servants just as Allaah revealed and legislated it.

This may be an obligation upon you if you live in an area where no one else other than you can fulfil this task, similar to the ruling of enjoining good and forbidding evil, it is an obligation on every individual in certain circumstances and a collective obligation in others. So if you live in an area where no one is able to perform it or convey the Religion of Allaah except you, then it is compulsory upon you to do so. However, if there are others in your area conveying the Religion of Allaah and giving *da'wah*, then practicing it takes the ruling of being recommended in such a case. If you however, take the initiative and are keen upon practicing it then you would be considered to be a competitor upon practicing good and one who rushes to obey Allaah.

Amongst the evidences used to confirm that it is a collective obligation is the saying of Allaah (*Subhaanahu wa Ta'aala*):

---

18 Majmoo' Fataawa wa Maqaalaat Mutanawwi'ah - Volume 5, Page 256

وَلْتَكُن مِّنكُمْ أُمَّةٌ يَدْعُونَ إِلَى الْخَيْرِ

'Let there arise a group of people from amongst
you, inviting to all that is good.'[19]

al-Haafidh Ibn Katheer said in relation to this verse what means: a group
from amongst you must be appointed to carry out this great affair; calling to Allaah, spreading and conveying His Religion (*Subhaanahu wa
Ta'aala*).

It is also known that the Messenger (*sal-Allaahu 'alayhi wa sallam*)
called to Allaah and established His Religion in Makkah according to
his ability. His Companions (*radhi-yAllaahu 'anhum*) did likewise according to their abilities, and when they migrated, they called to Allaah
even more. When they (*radhi-yAllaahu 'anhum*) spread out in different
countries after the death of the Messenger (*sal-Allaahu 'alayhi wa sallam*) they also carried out this affair according to each one's individual
knowledge.

During times when callers to Allaah are few, evil is abundant and ignorance is rampant, like in our present state, calling to Allaah becomes an
obligation upon every one according to each person's individual ability.
If one lives in a town or city where there are others carrying out this task
and are conveying the affair of Allaah sufficiently, then calling to Allaah
takes the ruling of being 'recommended' in relation to everyone else in
that area. It takes this ruling because the proofs have been established
upon the creation and the affair of Allaah has been conveyed by others.
However, in regards to the rest of the world and the rest of mankind, it
is compulsory upon the scholars as well as the rulers to convey the affair

---

19 The Noble *Qur.aan - Soorah* Aal-'Imraan, *Aayah* 104

66

of Allaah according to their abilities by every available means. This is an obligation upon them according to their individual abilities.

Therefore it becomes clear that the ruling of calling to Allaah varies from being an obligation upon every individual to being a collective obligation upon everyone, depending on the circumstance. Calling to Allaah may be an obligation upon certain individuals, and also may be only 'recommended' upon others due to the fact that they live in an area where there are others who carry it out, and have therefore relieved them of this duty.

The obligation upon rulers and those who have extensive authority is even greater. It is upon them to convey the *da'wah* to whichever countries they are able to according to their abilities, using all available methods, as well as all live languages. It is imperative for them to convey the *da'wah* with these languages until the Religion of Allaah reaches everyone in their own languages, whether it is the Arabic language or other than it. Not only is this possible but it is also quite simple at present due to the availability of the previously mentioned mediums such as the radio, television, newspapers and other methods that were unavailable in the past. It is also imperative for those who deliver sermons to crowds during special occasions, to convey whatever they are able to in terms of the affair of Allaah (*Subhaanahu wa Ta'aala*). They must propagate it according to their abilities, while keeping the propagation of destructive methodologies and principles in mind, such as atheism; rejection of the Lord; rejection of religion; rejection of the afterlife; the spread of Christianity in alot of countries, as well as other misguided calls.

With this in mind, we say that calling to Allaah (*Subhaanahu wa Ta'aala*) at present times has indeed become a universal obligation upon all the scholars and all the *Muslim* rulers. It is obligatory for them to propagate the Religion of Allaah according to their abilities by writing, delivering sermons, the radio and every possible medium at their disposal. They must not hold back and depend on others. Indeed there is a great need for co-operation in this great affair during present times, alot greater than there was in the past, because the enemies of Allaah have united and are co-operating, using every possible means at their disposal to turn people away from the Religion of Allaah; sow suspicions concerning it and call the people to depart from it. So it is imperative upon the *Muslims* to confront these atheist activities with *Islaamic* activities and *da'wah* on all levels, with all possible mediums and methods. This is carrying out what Allaah has obligated upon His servants in relation to calling to His Path.

Shaykh 'Abdul-'Azeez ibn Baaz

8. Calling to Allaah is the Remedy

Question: What is the correct remedy which would save the *Islaamic* world from the storm that it is presently caught in?[20]

Response: Helping the *Islaamic* world emerge from the storm that it is currently caught in, a storm consisting of different methodologies, different creeds, politics, social as well as economical problems, can only be achieved by strictly adhering to *Islaam* and judging by the Legislation of Allaah in all affairs. Doing so will unify both the ranks and the hearts of the people. This is the correct remedy for the *Islaamic* world, rather it is a remedy for the whole world, with all the confusion, conflict, apprehension, and evil that is in it. Allaah (*Subhaanahu wa Ta'aala*) said:

---

20 Majmoo' Fataawa wa Maqaalaat Mutanawwi'ah - Volume 5, Page 261

يَـٰٓأَيُّهَا ٱلَّذِينَ
ءَامَنُوٓا۟ إِن تَنصُرُوا۟ ٱللَّهَ يَنصُرْكُمْ وَيُثَبِّتْ أَقْدَامَكُمْ

*"O you who believe! If you help (in the cause of) Allaah,
He will help you and make your foothold firm."*[21]

He (*Subhaanahu wa Ta'aala*) also said:

وَلَيَنصُرَنَّ ٱللَّهُ مَن يَنصُرُهُۥٓ ۗ إِنَّ ٱللَّهَ لَقَوِىٌّ
عَزِيزٌ ۝ ٱلَّذِينَ إِن مَّكَّنَّـٰهُمْ فِى ٱلْأَرْضِ أَقَامُوا۟ ٱلصَّلَوٰةَ
وَءَاتَوُا۟ ٱلزَّكَوٰةَ وَأَمَرُوا۟ بِٱلْمَعْرُوفِ وَنَهَوْا۟ عَنِ ٱلْمُنكَرِ ۗ
وَلِلَّهِ عَـٰقِبَةُ ٱلْأُمُورِ

*"Allaah will grant victory to those who help His
(Cause). Truly, Allaah is All-Strong, All-Mighty. (41)
Those (Muslim rulers) who, if We give them power
in the land, they establish the prayers, they pay the
zakaat (obligatory charity) and enjoin al-Ma'roof
(i.e. Islaamic Monotheism and all that Islaam orders one to do), and forbid al-Munkar (i.e. disbelief, polytheism and all that Islaam has forbidden)
[i.e. they make the Qur.aan as the law of their
country in all the spheres of life]. And with Allaah
rests the end of (all) matters (of creatures)."*[22]

Also His (*Subhaanahu wa Ta'aala*) saying:

---

21 The Noble *Qur.aan - Soorah* Muhammad, *Aayah* 7

22 The Noble *Qur.aan - Soorah* al-Hajj, *Aayahs* 40-41

وَعَدَ اللَّهُ الَّذِينَ ءَامَنُوا۟ مِنكُمْ وَعَمِلُوا۟

الصَّـٰلِحَـٰتِ لَيَسْتَخْلِفَنَّهُمْ فِى الْأَرْضِ كَمَا اسْتَخْلَفَ

الَّذِينَ مِن قَبْلِهِمْ وَلَيُمَكِّنَنَّ لَهُمْ دِينَهُمُ الَّذِى ارْتَضَىٰ لَهُمْ

وَلَيُبَدِّلَنَّهُم مِّنۢ بَعْدِ خَوْفِهِمْ أَمْنًا يَعْبُدُونَنِى لَا يُشْرِكُونَ بِى

شَيْـًٔا وَمَن كَفَرَ بَعْدَ ذَٰلِكَ فَأُو۟لَـٰٓئِكَ هُمُ الْفَـٰسِقُونَ

*"Allaah has promised those among you who be-
lieve and do righteous good deeds, that He will
certainly grant them succession to (the present
rulers) in the land, as He granted it to those before them, and that He will grant them the authority to practice their religion which He has chosen
for them (i.e. Islaam). And He will surely exchange
their fear with security (provided) they (believers) worship Me and do not associate anything (in
worship) with Me. But whoever disbelieved after
this, they are the Faasiqoon (rebellious, disobedi-
ent to Allaah)."*[23]

Furthermore Allaah (*Subhaanahu wa Ta'aala*) said:

وَاعْتَصِمُوا۟ بِحَبْلِ اللَّهِ جَمِيعًا وَلَا تَفَرَّقُوا۟

*"And hold fast, all of you together, to the Rope of Al-
laah (i.e. this Qur.aan), and be not divided among
yourselves..."*[24]

---

23 The Noble *Qur.aan* - *Soorah* an-Noor, *Aayah* 55

24 The Noble *Qur.aan* - *Soorah* Aal-'Imraan, *Aayah* 103

The verses of this meaning are plentiful. As long as rulers seek guidance and direction from other than the Book of Allaah and the *Sunnah* of His Messenger (*sal-Allaahu 'alayhi wa sallam*); as long as they judge by other than the legislation of *Islaam* and judge by laws that their enemies have placed for them; they will never emerge from the state they are in; a state of being behind and being hostile towards each other. Their enemies will continue to despise them as well as withhold their rights from them.

'Allaah wronged them not, but they wronged themselves.'

We ask Allaah to gather them upon guidance, rectify their hearts and deeds, grant them the blessing of steadfastly judging by the legislation of *Islaam* and abandoning anything that opposes it. Indeed He is the Guardian of this affair and able to carry it out, and may the *salaah* and *salaam* be upon our Prophet Muhammad, his family and Companions.

Shaykh 'Abdul-'Azeez ibn Baaz

9. Fortification Against Temptations

<u>Question</u>: What do you think youth should do in order to avoid paths that lead to temptation and follow the correct path, during present times?[25]

<u>Response</u>: The best path for the youth to follow in order to understand their religion and call to it is to adhere to the upright *manhaj* by studying and understanding it, as well as paying a great deal of attention to the Noble *Qur.aan* and the purified *Sunnah*.

---

25 Majmoo' Fataawa wa Maqaalaat Mutanawwi'ah - Volume 5, Page 262

I advise them to befriend the best people and surround themselves with righteous companions, including scholars who are known to be steadfast upon the truth, in order to benefit from them and their manners. I also advise them to get married to righteous women due to the saying of the Messenger (*sal-Allaahu 'alayhi wa sallam*):

> **"O youth, whoever amongst you has the means should get married."**

Shaykh 'Abdul-'Azeez ibn Baaz

10. The Islaamic Awakening

<u>Question</u>: Everyone is aware of the rapid spread of the 'Islaamic awakening' amongst *Muslims*, especially amongst the youth. Can you give some advice in directing this awakening?[26]

<u>Response</u>: The answer to this question has already preceded in previous questions relating to the activity of *Islaamic* movements that have been active since the beginning of this century or the end of the last century. We mentioned that they are upon goodness and that, praise be to Allaah, they are spread all over the world and continue to grow.

It is imperative for *Muslims* to support and co-operate with those responsible for them; it is imperative to support them financially and aid them. They should also beware of exceeding their limits or falling short because *Shaytaan* is involved in every *Islaamic da'wah* and all *Islaamic* works.

It is upon the people of knowledge and insight to support this call and advise those responsible to be upright and warn them from exceeding

---

26 Majmoo' Fataawa wa Maqaalaat Mutanawwi'ah - Volume 5, Page 158

their limits in order to avoid being detached or fall behind concerning Allaah's Rights. They must hold fast to the straight path which is being sincere to Allaah and following His Messenger (*sal-Allaahu 'alayhi wa sallam*) without being extreme or detached, henceforth they would be upright and would bear the fruits in the best manner.

More specifically it is upon the leaders of these movements to focus on this affair, and exert their efforts in it in order to avoid falling into extremity or being detached, and Allaah is the granter of success.

Shaykh 'Abdul-'Azeez ibn Baaz

11. Widespread Fataawa

<u>Question</u>: Issuing religious verdicts has become so prevalent that even small students of knowledge issue them; what do you have to say about this O, noble *Shaykh*?[27]

<u>Response</u>: The *Salaf*, may Allaah have mercy upon them, used to repel issuing religious verdicts from themselves because of its tremendous affair and great accountability, for fear that they would say something about Allaah which they have no knowledge of. One who issues religious verdicts is in actuality informing about Allaah and clarifying His Legislation. So if one says something about Allaah which he has no knowledge of, he has committed what is equal to *shirk*! Listen to the saying of Allaah (*Subhaanahu wa Ta'aala*):

$$\text{قُلْ إِنَّمَا حَرَّمَ رَبِّيَ ٱلْفَوَٰحِشَ مَا ظَهَرَ مِنْهَا وَمَا}$$
$$\text{بَطَنَ وَٱلْإِثْمَ وَٱلْبَغْىَ بِغَيْرِ ٱلْحَقِّ وَأَن تُشْرِكُوا۟ بِٱللَّهِ مَا لَمْ يُنَزِّلْ بِهِۦ}$$
$$\text{سُلْطَٰنًا وَأَن تَقُولُوا۟ عَلَى ٱللَّهِ مَا لَا تَعْلَمُونَ}$$

---

27 Kitaabul-'Ilm - Page 164

"Say (O Muhammad) The things that my lord has indeed forbidden are al-Fawaahish (great evil sins and every kind of unlawful sexual acts) whether committed openly or secretly, sins (of all kinds), unrighteous oppression, joining partners (in worship) with Allaah for which He has given no authority, and saying things about Allaah of which you have no knowledge of."[28]

So Allaah (*Subhaanahu wa Ta'aala*) equated *shirk* to saying about Him what one has no knowledge of. Allaah (*Subhaanahu wa Ta'aala*) said:

وَلَا تَقْفُ مَا لَيْسَ لَكَ بِهِ عِلْمٌ

إِنَّ ٱلسَّمْعَ وَٱلْبَصَرَ وَٱلْفُؤَادَ كُلُّ أُوْلَٰئِكَ كَانَ عَنْهُ مَسْئُولًا

"And follow not (O man i.e. say not, do not or witness not) that which you have no knowledge of. Verily the hearing, sight, and the heart, of each of these one will be questioned (by Allaah)."[29]

So one should not be hasty in issuing religious verdicts, rather one should wait, contemplate and review the issue. If there is little time, one should refer the issue to a more knowledgeable person in order to safeguard himself from speaking about Allaah without knowledge.

If a person is sincere and wants good, then Allaah will aid that person in reaching a correct religious verdict. Whoever has *taqwaa* of Allaah; He would grant him success and raise him in rank.

---

28 The Noble *Qur.aan* - *Soorah* al-A'raaf, *Aayah* 33

29 The Noble *Qur.aan* - *Soorah* al-Israa, *Aayah* 36

A person who issues religious verdicts without knowledge is more astray than an ignorant person; because an ignorant person says: "I do not know." He knows his capability in addition to being truthful. As for the one who compares himself to the most knowledgeable of scholars, rather he may even favour himself over them, and in doing so he would misguide himself as well as the people; he would make mistakes in issues that even the smallest students of knowledge wouldn't. So the evil of this person is tremendous and his danger is great.

Shaykh Muhammad ibn Saalih al-'Uthaymeen

12. Islaamic Unity

Question: How do we bring about *Islaam*ic unity to the *Muslim ummah* in our time? Everyday we see and hear about *Muslim*s killing fellow *Muslim*s and so on from our disunited Arab nations who have agreed to disagree in all affairs?[30]

Response: *Islaam*ic unity can only be achieved in the same way it was achieved during the time of the Prophet (*sal-Allaahu 'alayhi wa sallam*), which is by having the correct *'aqeedah*, true *eemaan*, and acting on the Book of Allaah (*Subhaanahu wa Ta'aala*) and the *Sunnah* of our Prophet Muhammad (*sal-Allaahu 'alayhi wa sallam*); calling to it and being patient upon the harms encountered while doing so.

Allaah is the granter of success and may the *salaah* and *salaam* be upon our Prophet Muhammad, his family and his Companions.

The Permanent Committee for Islaamic Research and Verdicts

---

30 Fataawa al-Lajnah ad-Daa.imah - Volume 2, Page 245

13. I 'created' Such and Such

Question: If I make something, a cup for instance, can I say that I created it, or is this considered to be delving into the affairs of the Names and Attributes of Allaah?[31]

Response: You mustn't say; 'I created it,' because creation is specific to Allaah (*Subhaanahu wa Ta'aala*) alone due to His saying:

اَللَّهُ خَٰلِقُ كُلِّ شَىْءٍ

"Allaah is the Creator of all things."[32]

One should say; 'I built it with the permission of Allaah,' or 'I made it.'

Allaah is the granter of success and may the *salaah* and *salaam* be upon our Prophet Muhammad, his family and his Companions.

The Permanent Committee for Islaamic Research and Verdicts

14. Performing one's Occupation Properly

Question: Some employees are lazy when it comes to their occupation. An individual from amongst them may let a whole year go by without enjoining good or forbidding evil; always arriving late to work saying: 'The manager has relieved me from my duty so there is no sin upon me.'

Is there a sin upon him in this case? Benefit us, may Allaah reward you.[33]

---

31 Fataawa al-Lajnah ad-Daa.imah - No.9406

32 The Noble *Qur.aan* - *Soorah* az-Zunar, *Aayah* 62

33 Majalatul-Buhooth al-Islaamiyyah - Volume 31, Page 115

Response: Firstly: It is legislated for every male and female *Muslim* to convey all the good that they have heard about Allaah (*Subhaanahu wa Ta'aala*) as has been indicated by the saying of the Messenger (*sal-Allaahu 'alayhi wa sallam*):

> **"May Allaah grant prosperity to one who hears a saying of mine, then memorises and reports it, just as he had heard it."**

He (*sal-Allaahu 'alayhi wa sallam*) also said:

> **"Convey my affair to the people, even if it were but a single verse."**

After addressing people, he (*sal-Allaahu 'alayhi wa sallam*) used to say:

> **"Those who are present must convey what they heard to those who are absent; for it may be that the message is conveyed to one who has a greater understanding than the one who initially heard it."**

Therefore, I advise everyone to convey all the good they have heard with insight and certainty. Whoever hears and memorises some knowledge, should then convey it to his family, his brothers and companions, so long as he believes that there is a benefit in this. He must pay close attention to the exact phrase that he hears and mustn't speak about something that he didn't memorise. By doing so he would become from amongst those who enjoin the truth and call to good.

As for employees who do not do their jobs, or do not perform them properly, it is as you have heard; it is from the signs of *eemaan* to act with trustworthiness and carefully preserve this as Allaah (*Subhaanahu wa Ta'aala*) said:

إِنَّ ٱللَّهَ يَأْمُرُكُمْ أَن تُؤَدُّواْ ٱلْأَمَٰنَٰتِ إِلَىٰٓ أَهْلِهَا

**"Verily, Allaah commands that you render back
the trusts to those whom they are due to..."**[34]

Trustworthiness is from the greatest traits of *eemaan*, and deception is
from the greatest traits of hypocrisy, as Allaah (*Subhaanahu wa Ta'aala*)
said when describing the believers:

وَٱلَّذِينَ هُمْ لِأَمَٰنَٰتِهِمْ وَعَهْدِهِمْ رَٰعُونَ

**Those who are faithfully true to their Amanaat (all
the duties which Allaah has ordained, honesty, moral
responsibility and trusts) and to their covenants.**[35]

He (*Subhaanahu wa Ta'aala*) also said:

يَٰٓأَيُّهَا ٱلَّذِينَ ءَامَنُواْ

لَا تَخُونُواْ ٱللَّهَ وَٱلرَّسُولَ وَتَخُونُوٓاْ أَمَٰنَٰتِكُمْ وَأَنتُمْ تَعْلَمُونَ

**"O you who believe! Betray not Allaah and His Mes-
senger, nor betray knowingly your Amanaat (the
things entrusted to you, and all the duties which
Allaah has ordained for you)."**[36]

So it is imperative for an employee to carry out the duties entrusted to
him with honesty and sincerity. He must carefully preserve them with-

---

34 The Noble *Qur.aan - Soorah* an-Nisaa, *Aayah* 58

35 The Noble *Qur.aan - Soorah* al-Mu.minoon, *Aayah* 8

36 The Noble *Qur.aan - Soorah* al-Anfaal, *Aayah* 27

out wasting any time in order to clear his conscious, feel good about his earnings and please his Lord. He should also be helpful, in regards to his occupation, his country and his employer. It is compulsory for the employee to fear Allaah and carry out what he/she is entrusted with as perfectly as possible, hoping to be rewarded by Allaah and fearing His punishment, acting upon the saying of Allaah (*Subhaanahu wa Ta'aala*):

إِنَّ ٱللَّهَ يَأْمُرُكُمْ أَن تُؤَدُّواْ ٱلْأَمَنَتِ إِلَىٰٓ أَهْلِهَا

"Verily, Allaah commands that you should render back the trusts to those whom they are due to..."[37]

Betrayal of trust is one of the characteristics of the hypocrites as the Prophet (*sal-Allaahu 'alayhi wa sallam*) informed us:

"A hypocrite has three signs: When he speaks he lies; when he makes a promise he breaks it; and when he is entrusted, he betrays his trust."

It is not permissible for a *Muslim* to resemble hypocrites; rather it is compulsory for the *Muslim* to distance himself from their attributes and safeguard his trust. He must pay a great deal of attention to carrying out his job without wasting any time, even if his manager is lenient and doesn't ask him to do anything. He should not sit around and do nothing at work or be laid-back in that matter. Rather it is upon him to work hard until he becomes better than his supervisor in carrying out his duties; being true to his trust as well as being a good role model for others.

Shaykh 'Abdul-'Azeez ibn Baaz

---

37 The Noble *Qur.aan* - *Soorah* an-Nisaa, *Aayah* 58

Chapter 2
The Ruling of Calling to Allaah

1. The Ruling of Calling to Allaah

<u>Question</u>: We would like you to explain the ruling of calling to Allaah (*Subhaanahu wa Ta'aala*) as well as its numerous virtues.[1]

<u>Response</u>: t it is compulsory to call to Allaah (*Subhaanahu wa Ta'aala*); it is an obligation. There is alot of evidence to support this; amongst it is the saying of Allaah (*Subhaanahu wa Ta'aala*):

وَلْتَكُن مِّنكُمْ أُمَّةٌ يَدْعُونَ إِلَى ٱلْخَيْرِ وَيَأْمُرُونَ بِٱلْمَعْرُوفِ
وَيَنْهَوْنَ عَنِ ٱلْمُنكَرِ وَأُوْلَٰئِكَ هُمُ ٱلْمُفْلِحُونَ

"Let there arise from amongst you a group of people inviting to all that is good (Islaam), enjoining al-Ma'roof (i.e. Islaamic Monotheism and all that Islaam orders one to do) and forbidding al-Munkar (polytheism and disbelief and all that Islaam has forbidden). And it is they who are the successful."[2]

---

1 Majmoo' Fataawa wa Maqaalaat Mutanawwi'ah - Volume 5, Page 255

2 The Noble *Qur.aan* - *Soorah* Aal-'Imraan, *Aayah* 104

His (*Subhaanahu wa Ta'aala*) saying as well:

ٱدۡعُ إِلَىٰ سَبِيلِ رَبِّكَ بِٱلۡحِكۡمَةِ
وَٱلۡمَوۡعِظَةِ ٱلۡحَسَنَةِ وَجَٰدِلۡهُم بِٱلَّتِى هِىَ أَحۡسَنُ

"Call (mankind, O Muhammad to the way of your Lord (i.e. Islaam) with wisdom (i.e. with the Divine Revelation and the Qur.aan), fair preaching, and debate with them in a manner that is best."[3]

His (*Subhaanahu wa Ta'aala*) saying as well:

وَٱدۡعُ إِلَىٰ رَبِّكَ وَلَا تَكُونَنَّ مِنَ ٱلۡمُشۡرِكِينَ

"Call to your Lord and be not from amongst the al-Mushrikoon (those who associate partners with Allaah)."[4]

His Saying:

قُلۡ هَٰذِهِۦ
سَبِيلِىٓ أَدۡعُوٓاْ إِلَى ٱللَّهِ عَلَىٰ بَصِيرَةٍ أَنَا۠ وَمَنِ ٱتَّبَعَنِى

'Say (O Muhammad): "This is my way; I call to Allaah (i.e. to the Oneness of Allaah – Islaamic Monotheism) with sure knowledge, I and whosoever follows me".'[5]

Allaah clarified that the *du'aat* are the followers of the Messenger (*sal-Allaahu 'alayhi wa sallam*) and they are the people of knowledge and insight. It is well-known that it is compulsory to follow him (*sal-Allaahu*

---

3 The Noble *Qur.aan* - *Soorah* an-Nahl, *Aayah* 125

4 The Noble *Qur.aan* - *Soorah* al-Qasas, *Aayah* 87

5 The Noble *Qur.aan* - *Soorah* Yoosuf, *Aayah* 108

'alayhi wa sallam) and tread upon his *manhaj* as Allaah (*Subhaanahu wa Ta'aala*) said:

لَّقَدۡ كَانَ لَكُمۡ فِى رَسُولِ ٱللَّهِ أُسۡوَةٌ
حَسَنَةٌ لِّمَن كَانَ يَرۡجُواْ ٱللَّهَ وَٱلۡيَوۡمَ ٱلۡأٓخِرَ وَذَكَرَ ٱللَّهَ كَثِيرًا

'Indeed in the Messenger of Allaah (Muhammad) you have a good example to follow for he who hopes for (the Meeting with) Allaah and the Last Day, and remembers Allaah much.'[6]

The scholars have stated that calling to Allaah (*Subhaanahu wa Ta'aala*) is a collective obligation depending on the areas where it is carried out. Every area or region is in need of *da'wah* activities; it is a collective obligation. If a sufficient group of people carry it out, the obligation is absolved from the rest of the people in that area. The ruling of *da'wah* in relation to them now becomes 'recommended' as well as a pious honourable deed.

If people in a certain region do not call to Allaah in a sufficient manner, there is a sin upon all those living in that region. It then becomes compulsory upon everyone in that region to call to Allaah according to each person's ability. As for countries in general, it is obligatory to appoint a group charged with carrying out the *da'wah* to Allaah (*Subhaanahu wa Ta'aala*), explaining and conveying His Message to all corners of the world with all possible means. Indeed the Messenger of Allaah (*sal-Allaahu 'alayhi wa sallam*) used to send callers and letters to the people in general, and to kings and rulers specifically, and call them to Allaah (*Subhaanahu wa Ta'aala*).

Shaykh 'Abdul-'Azeez ibn Baaz

---

6 The Noble *Qur.aan - Soorah* al-Ahzaab, *Aayah* 21

2. Is Calling to Allaah an Obligation upon Every Muslim?

Question: Is calling to Allaah obligatory upon every male and female *Muslim*, or is it specific to the scholars and students of knowledge?[7]

Response: There is no difference between a great or famous scholar, a serious student of knowledge or a common *Muslim* if a person has knowledge and insight of what he is calling to. As long as that person has certain knowledge of the issue he is calling to, in this case the Messenger (*sal-Allaahu 'alayhi wa sallam*) said:

> *"Convey my affair to others, even if it were but a single verse."*

It is not a condition for a caller to attain a great level of knowledge, but it is a condition to be knowledgeable of what he is calling to. It is impermissible to call upon ignorance and depend on emotions.

This is why we find that brothers, who call to Allaah while only having a small amount of knowledge, prohibit things that Allaah has not prohibited, and obligate things that Allaah has not obligated upon His servants, due to having strong emotions. This is a very dangerous affair. Prohibiting what Allaah has permitted is the same as permitting what Allaah has prohibited. So if they, for example, rebuke others for permitting a certain issue, others will consequently rebuke them for prohibiting that same issue. Allaah (*Subhaanahu wa Ta'aala*) has made both affairs equivalent in saying:

---

7 Kitaab ad-Da'wah - Volume 2, Page 158

وَلَا تَقُولُوا لِمَا تَصِفُ أَلْسِنَتُكُمُ

الْكَذِبَ هَٰذَا حَلَٰلٌ وَهَٰذَا حَرَامٌ لِّتَفْتَرُوا عَلَى اللَّهِ الْكَذِبَ

إِنَّ الَّذِينَ يَفْتَرُونَ عَلَى اللَّهِ الْكَذِبَ لَا يُفْلِحُونَ ۝

مَتَٰعٌ قَلِيلٌ وَلَهُمْ عَذَابٌ أَلِيمٌ

"And say not concerning that which your tongues put forth falsely: "This is lawful and this is unlawful," so as to invent lies against Allaah. Verily, those who invent lies against Allaah will never prosper. A passing brief enjoyment (will be theirs), but they will have a painful torment."[8]

Shaykh Muhammad ibn Saalih al-'Uthaymeen

---

8 The Noble *Qur.aan - Soorah* an-Nahl, *Aayah*s 116-117

Chapter 3
The Priorities of Calling to Allaah

1. What are the Priorities of Da'wah

Question: Is the main priority of *da'wah* performing good works such as building *masaajid* and helping the needy, or is it calling governments to apply the *Islaam*ic legislation and fight corruption in all its forms?[1]

Response: It is compulsory for the scholars to start with what the messengers - may the *salaah* and *salaam* be upon all of them - started with, regarding non-*Muslim* societies and countries. And it is calling them to singling out Allaah in worship and abandoning worshipping other than Him. It is calling them to believe in His Names and Attributes and confirming them in a way that is befitting to Him (*Subhaanahu wa Ta'aala*) while believing, loving and following His Messenger (*sal-Allaahu 'alayhi wa sallam*).

It is also upon them to call the *Muslim*s everywhere, to hold fast to the Legislation of Allaah and be steadfast upon it. It is upon them to advise

---

1 Majmoo' Fataawa wa Maqaalaat Mutanawwi'ah - Volume 5, Page 85

the rulers and help the needy, just as it is upon them to continue to call to Allaah; be keen upon performing good works; visit the rulers and encourage them to perform good works, as well as encourage them to judge by the *Islaam*ic legislation and compel people to abide by it due to the saying of Allaah (*Subhaanahu wa Ta'aala*):

فَلَا وَرَبِّكَ لَا يُؤْمِنُونَ حَتَّىٰ يُحَكِّمُوكَ فِيمَا شَجَرَ بَيْنَهُمْ ثُمَّ لَا يَجِدُواْ فِىٓ أَنفُسِهِمْ حَرَجًا مِّمَّا قَضَيْتَ وَيُسَلِّمُواْ تَسْلِيمًا

"But no, by your Lord, they can have no Faith, until they make you (O Muhammad) judge between them in all disputes, and find no resistance in themselves against your decisions, and accept (them) with full submission."[2]

Also His (*Subhaanahu wa Ta'aala*) saying:

أَفَحُكْمَ ٱلْجَٰهِلِيَّةِ يَبْغُونَ وَمَنْ أَحْسَنُ مِنَ ٱللَّهِ حُكْمًا لِّقَوْمٍ يُوقِنُونَ

"Do they then seek the judgment of (the days of) Ignorance? And who is better in judgment than Allaah for a people who have firm Faith."[3]

The verses of this meaning are plentiful.

Shaykh 'Abdul-'Azeez ibn Baaz

---

2 The Noble *Qur.aan - Soorah* an-Nisaa, *Aayah* 65

3 The Noble *Qur.aan - Soorah* al-Maa.idah, *Aayah* 50

2. Do the Priorities of Da'wah Change?

Question: Do the priorities of *da'wah* change depending on changing times or different societies? Is it required to begin with the same method that the Messenger of Allaah (*sal-Allaahu 'alayhi wa sallam*) began with in every time period, in terms of calling people to *'aqeedah* firstly?[4]

Response: There is no doubt that the fundamentals and priorities of *da'wah* do not change due to changing time periods. They have remained the same since the Messenger (*sal-Allaahu 'alayhi wa sallam*) was sent and will continue to be the same until the Hour is established. There may be certain principles however, that have been properly understood by a certain community while having nothing present amongst them to negate or contradict these particular principles. In this case the caller should concentrate on other affairs that these people lack or are weak in.

The foundations of calling to *Islaam* never change. The Messenger (*sal-Allaahu 'alayhi wa sallam*) said to Mu'aadh ibn Jabal (*radhi-yAllaahu 'anhu*) when he sent him to the people of Yemen:

> *"Call them firstly to testify that none have the right to be worshipped except Allaah and that Muhammad is the Messenger of Allaah. If they accept this from you, inform them that Allaah has enjoined five prayers upon them to be performed daily. If they accept this from you, inform them that Allaah has enjoined Sadaaqh (zakaat) upon them which is to be taken from the rich amongst them and to be given to the poor amongst them."*

---

4 Kitaab ad-Da'wah - Volume 2, Page 154

These are the foundations of *da'wah*; it is obligatory to organise them in this manner when calling non-*Muslims*. If we are calling *Muslims* who know the first foundation of *tawheed* however, while not lacking in its understanding or having any issues that invalidate it, then we call them to what is next in order as is clear in this *hadeeth*.

Shaykh Muhammad ibn Saalih al-'Uthaymeen

Chapter 4
The Methodoloy of Calling to Allaah

1. How Do I Start Calling to Allaah?

Question: If a person wants to call to Allaah; how should he start and what should he begin with?[1]

Response: It seems that the questioner would like to call to Allaah. Calling to Allaah must be carried out with wisdom, fair preaching and lenience towards people; not with harshness, reprehension or admonishment.

The caller must start with the most important issues first, and then follow them with issues that are next in importance, just as the Messenger of Allaah (*sal-Allaahu 'alayhi wa sallam*) used to do when sending messengers to different areas. He used to order them to start with the most important issues and then follow them with what is next in importance. He said to Mu'aadh (*radhi-yAllaahu 'anhu*) when he sent him to Yemen:

---

1 Kitaab ad-Da'wah - Volume 2, Page 155

"Call them firstly to testify that none have the right to be worshipped except Allaah and that Muhammad is the Messenger of Allaah. If they accept this from you, inform them that Allaah has enjoined five prayers upon them that are to be performed daily. If they accept this from you then inform them that Allaah has enjoined (zakaat) upon them, to be taken from the rich amongst them and given to the poor amongst them."

Therefore the caller must start with the most important issues and must carefully select the appropriate opportunity, time and place for his call. It may be appropriate to invite a person he wishes to call to Allaah to his house and speak to him there; it may be more appropriate to visit that person himself and call him to Allaah there. It may also be appropriate to call him at certain times and not at others. In any case, the intelligent, insightful *Muslim* knows how to conduct himself when calling the people to the truth.

Shaykh Muhammad ibn Saalih al-'Uthaymeen

2. The Best Manner in Calling to Allaah

Question: Due to your extensive experience in the field of *da'wah*, we would like to ask; what is the best way to call to Allaah?[2]

Response: The way to call to Allaah - as Allaah (*Subhaanahu wa Ta'aala*) clarified - is clear in the Book of Allaah and *Sunnah* of His Prophet (*sal-Allaahu 'alayhi wa sallam*); Allaah (*Subhaanahu wa Ta'aala*) says:

---

2 Majalatul-Buhooth al-Islaamiyyah - Volume 40, Page 145

ٱدۡعُ إِلَىٰ سَبِيلِ رَبِّكَ بِٱلۡحِكۡمَةِ
وَٱلۡمَوۡعِظَةِ ٱلۡحَسَنَةِ وَجَٰدِلۡهُم بِٱلَّتِى هِىَ أَحۡسَنُ

*"Invite (mankind, O Muhammad) to the Way of
your Lord with wisdom (i.e. with the Divine Inspiration and the Qur.aan), fair preaching and debate with them in a manner that is best."*[3]

Allaah (*Subhaanahu wa Ta'aala*) also says:

فِيمَا رَحۡمَةٍ مِّنَ
ٱللَّهِ لِنتَ لَهُمۡ وَلَوۡ كُنتَ فَظًّا غَلِيظَ ٱلۡقَلۡبِ لَٱنفَضُّوا۟ مِنۡ حَوۡلِكَ

*"And by the Mercy of Allaah, you dealt with them
gently. And had you been severe and harsh hearted,
they would have dispersed from around you..."*[4]

Allaah (*Subhaanahu wa Ta'aala*) said, in the account of Moosaa and
Haaroon, when He sent them to Pharaoh:

فَقُولَا لَهُ قَوۡلًا لَّيِّنًا لَّعَلَّهُ يَتَذَكَّرُ أَوۡ يَخۡشَىٰ

*"And speak to him mildly, perhaps he may accept
admonition or fear Allaah."*[5]

So the caller must carefully select a good method and use wisdom when
calling to Allaah. Wisdom is knowledge of the sayings of Allaah as well as
the noble Prophetic narrations; fine sermon and kind words that have

---

3 The Noble *Qur.aan - Soorah* an-Nahl, *Aayah* 125

4 The Noble *Qur.aan - Soorah* Aal-'Imraan, *Aayah* 159

5 The Noble *Qur.aan - Soorah* Taha, *Aayah* 44

an effect upon people's hearts; words that remind them of the afterlife, death, Heaven and the Hellfire. This method is implemented in order for people's hearts to accept the *da'wah*, gain interest in it and listen attentively to what the caller is saying.

Similarly, if the one being called has a misconception, the caller must heal and remove it using the best manner, not with harshness and force, but with the best manner. He should speak about the misconception and then remove it with evidences.

The caller to Allaah shouldn't tire, weaken or get upset and therefore chase those being called away. Rather he must carefully select and employ the appropriate manner, explanation and evidence. He must endure the issues that upset him and deliver his sermon with calmness and gentleness; Allaah may facilitate its acceptance by those listening.

Shaykh 'Abdul-'Azeez ibn Baaz

3. The Best Manner in Enjoining Good and Forbidding Evil

Question: There are two books written about the best manner in calling to Allaah and the best manner in enjoining good and forbidding evil. The authors of these books notice alot of faults that the *Muslim*s fall into and are hurt by what they witness; they (the *Muslim* readers) would like to know if there is anything that they can do to change the evil that is present?[6]

Response: Indeed Allaah (*Subhaanahu wa Ta'aala*) has clarified the method of calling to Allaah and the obligations upon the caller; for He

---

6 Majmoo' Fataawa wa Maqaalaat Mutanawwi'ah - Volume 4, Page 240

(*Subhaanahu wa Ta'aala*) said:

$$\text{قُلۡ هَٰذِهِۦ}$$

$$\text{سَبِيلِيٓ أَدۡعُوٓاْ إِلَى ٱللَّهِۚ عَلَىٰ بَصِيرَةٍ أَنَا۠ وَمَنِ ٱتَّبَعَنِيۖ}$$

'Say (O Muhammad): "This is my way; I call to Allaah
(i.e. to the Oneness of Allaah – Islaamic Monotheism)
with sure knowledge, I and whosoever follows me". [7]

So the caller to Allaah must have knowledge as well as insight of what he enjoins and prohibits; thus refraining from speaking about Allaah without knowledge. He must be sincere to Allaah in this issue, as opposed to a *madh.hab* or people's opinions. Rather he must call to Allaah, seeking His reward, His Forgiveness as well as seeking the rectification of the people's condition. It is essential that he is sincere and has knowledge; Allaah (*Subhaanahu wa Ta'aala*) says:

$$\text{ٱدۡعُ إِلَىٰ سَبِيلِ رَبِّكَ بِٱلۡحِكۡمَةِ}$$

$$\text{وَٱلۡمَوۡعِظَةِ ٱلۡحَسَنَةِۖ وَجَٰدِلۡهُم بِٱلَّتِي هِيَ أَحۡسَنُۚ}$$

"Call (mankind, O Muhammad) to the way of your
Lord (i.e. Islaam) with wisdom (i.e. with the Divine
Revelation and the Qur.aan), fair preaching and
debate with them in a manner that is best." [8]

This verse explains how to call to Allaah, and that it must be carried out with wisdom, which is knowledge, using evidences from the Book of Allaah and the *Sunnah*. Knowledge in this verse was named wisdom be-

---

7 The Noble *Qur.aan - Soorah* Yoosuf, *Aayah* 108

8 The Noble *Qur.aan - Soorah* an-Nahl, *Aayah* 125

cause it deters falsehood and assists in following the truth. Knowledge may be accompanied by debating and arguing in a manner that is best when needed. It may be sufficient to clarify the truth with its evidences to some people because they seek the truth; whenever the truth becomes clear to them, they follow it. These types of people are not in need of preaching. Other people may be hesitant or unconcerned; so they are in need of preaching in a manner that is best. So the caller to Allaah preaches and reminds the ignorant; those who are oblivious or carefree, he reminds them of Allaah whenever needed until they are convinced of the truth and adhere to it.

Some people may have some misconceptions and therefore argue about them; they need these misconceptions to be cleared. So the caller to Allaah should clarify the truth with its evidences and debate with him in a manner that is best; in order to remove these misconceptions with evidences from the legislation. However he must use kind words, a fine manner and gentleness; not harshness and force, so that he does not end up chasing them away from the truth and cause them to persist upon falsehood. Allaah (*Subhaanahu wa Ta'aala*) said:

$$ فَبِمَا رَحْمَةٍ مِّنَ اللَّهِ لِنتَ لَهُمْ وَلَوْ كُنتَ فَظًّا غَلِيظَ ٱلْقَلْبِ لَٱنفَضُّواْ مِنْ حَوْلِكَ $$

"And by the Mercy of Allaah, you (Muhammad) dealt with them gently. And had you been severe and harsh-hearted, they would have dispersed from around you..."[9]

He also said when he sent Moosaa and Haaroon to Pharoah:

---

9 The Noble *Qur.aan* - *Soorah* Aal-'Imraan, *Aayah* 159

فَقُولَا لَهُ قَوْلًا لَّيِّنًا لَّعَلَّهُ يَتَذَكَّرُ أَوْ يَخْشَىٰ

"And speak to him mildly, perhaps he may accept admonition or fear Allaah."[10]

The Messenger of Allaah (*sal-Allaahu 'alayhi wa sallam*) said in an authentic *hadeeth*:

> *"Indeed gentleness is not practiced in any affair except that it beautifies it, and it is not removed from any affair except that it spoils it."*

He (*sal-Allaahu 'alayhi wa sallam*) also says:

> *"Whoever is deprived of gentleness is deprived of everything that is good."*

So the caller to Allaah (*Subhaanahu wa Ta'aala*) should seek and act upon the truth; he must be gentle with those he is calling, and strive to be sincere. He should rectify affairs using the method that was drawn out by Allaah, which is calling to His Religion with wisdom, fine sermon and debating in the best manner. In addition to this he must have insight and knowledge in order to convince those who are seeking the truth, remove misconceptions from those who are affected by them and soften the hearts of those who are unconcerned, stern or avert to the truth. Hearts are indeed softened by the call to Allaah, fine sermon and pointing out the blessings that Allaah has in store for those who accept the truth, and the danger that they will face by rejecting the call to the truth, and other methods of preaching.

---

10 The Noble *Qur.aan* - *Soorah* Taha, *Aayah* 44

It is upon the callers who are appointed by rulers and authorised to enjoin good and forbid evil, to act with legislated manners and be sincere to Allaah with regards to their occupation. They are to act with the same etiquette as the callers to Allaah with regards to lenience and avoid use of force, except when needed as is the case with aggressors, the arrogant and those who oppose the truth. In these cases authoritative deterrents should be used, acting on the saying of Allaah (*Subhaanahu wa Ta'aala*):

وَلَا تُجَـٰدِلُوٓاْ أَهۡلَ ٱلۡكِتَـٰبِ إِلَّا بِٱلَّتِى هِىَ أَحۡسَنُ إِلَّا ٱلَّذِينَ ظَلَمُواْ مِنۡهُمۡ

"And do not debate with the people of the book except in a manner that is best except with those of them who do wrong..."[11]

Acting also, on the saying of the Messenger of Allaah (*sal-Allaahu 'alayhi wa sallam*):

"Whoever amongst you who sees something evil must change it with his hands; if he is unable to do so, he must change it with his tongue; if he is unable to do that, he is to hate it with his heart and that is the weakest of faith."

In relation to those who are not aggressors, they should be treated in the same manner as the caller to Allaah would treat them while forbidding them from evil and calling them to good. They should be forbidden from evil with wisdom and gentleness and the evidences should be

---

11 The Noble *Qur.aan - Soorah* al-'Ankaboot, *Aayah* 46

pointed out for them until they refrain from evil, adhere to the truth and abandon the falsehood they were upon. This of course is according to each individuals ability, as Allaah (*Subhaanahu wa Ta'aala*) says:

فَٱتَّقُوا۟ ٱللَّهَ مَا ٱسْتَطَعْتُمْ

"So keep your duty to Allaah and fear Him as much as you can..."[12]

As the Messenger (*sal-Allaahu 'alayhi wa sallam*) also said in the afore-mentioned *hadeeth*:

"Whoever from amongst you who sees something evil."

Amongst the general verses that confirm this, is the saying of Allaah (*Subhaanahu wa Ta'aala*):

وَٱلْمُؤْمِنُونَ وَٱلْمُؤْمِنَٰتُ بَعْضُهُمْ
أَوْلِيَآءُ بَعْضٍ يَأْمُرُونَ بِٱلْمَعْرُوفِ وَيَنْهَوْنَ عَنِ ٱلْمُنكَرِ

"The believers, men and women, are Awliyaa' (helpers, supporters, friends, protectors) of one another; they enjoin al-Ma'roof (i.e. Islaamic Monotheism and all that Islaam orders one to do), and forbid (people) from al-Munkar (i.e. polytheism and disbelief of all kinds, and all that Islaam has forbidden)."[13]

His (*Subhaanahu wa Ta'aala*) saying as well:

---

12 The Noble *Qur.aan* - *Soorah* at-Taghaabun, *Aayah* 16

13 The Noble *Qur.aan* - *Soorah* at-Towbah, *Aayah* 71

كُنتُمْ خَيْرَ أُمَّةٍ أُخْرِجَتْ لِلنَّاسِ تَأْمُرُونَ بِالْمَعْرُوفِ
وَتَنْهَوْنَ عَنِ الْمُنكَرِ وَتُؤْمِنُونَ بِاللَّهِ

"You (true believers in Islaamic Monotheism, and real followers of Prophet Muhammad and his Sunnah) are the best of people ever raised up from mankind; you enjoin al-Ma'roof (i.e. Islaamic Monotheism and all that Islaam has ordained) and forbid al-Munkar (polytheism, disbelief and all that Islaam has forbidden), and you believe in Allaah."[14]

Allaah (*Subhaanahu wa Ta'aala*) has warned those who abandon this way and cursed them through the tongue of Daawood and 'Eesaa, son of Maryam; He said in His Noble Book in *Soorah* al-Maa.idah:

لُعِنَ الَّذِينَ
كَفَرُوا مِنْ بَنِي إِسْرَائِيلَ عَلَىٰ لِسَانِ دَاوُدَ وَعِيسَى
ابْنِ مَرْيَمَ ذَٰلِكَ بِمَا عَصَوا وَّكَانُوا يَعْتَدُونَ ۝
كَانُوا لَا يَتَنَاهَوْنَ عَن مُّنكَرٍ فَعَلُوهُ لَبِئْسَ
مَا كَانُوا يَفْعَلُونَ

"Those amongst the Children of Israeel who disbelieved were cursed by the tongue of Daawood and 'Eesaa, son of Maryam. That was because they disobeyed (Allaah and the Messengers) and were ever transgressing beyond bounds.) They used not to forbid one another from al-Munkar (wrong, evil-

---

14 The Noble *Qur.aan* - *Soorah* Aal-'Imraan, *Aayah* 110

***doing, sins, polytheism, disbelief) which they com-
mitted. Vile indeed was what they used to do.*"[15]**

Thus the affair is grand and the responsibility great. This is an obligation upon the people of faith, those with the ability, such as rulers, scholars, as well as individual *Muslim*s who possess the ability and enough knowledge to forbid evil and enjoin good. It is not just for a specific group; even though a specified group would have its own obligations and a greater burden. However this does not necessitate that the obligation is absolved from others, rather it is compulsory for others to assist and co-operate with them in forbidding evil and enjoining good, until goodness is abundant and evil is minimal. Especially if the specific group appointed to carry out this task is not fulfilling its duty or achieving the intended goal, rather the affair is getting worse and evil is on the rise; consequently it becomes compulsory upon those with the ability to assist them in all circumstances.

If the intended goal is achieved by an appointed group who are doing a satisfactory job however, the obligation is then absolved from others in that particular area or country. This is because enjoining good and forbidding evil is a collective obligation; if the intended goal is achieved by a specified group or volunteers, such that evil is being eliminated and good is being enjoined, its ruling becomes 'recommended' in relation to everyone else. In the case of a specific form of evil that no one else other than you is able to remove, or there is no one else present to enjoin good and forbid evil, it becomes compulsory upon you to carry out the task as long as you know of its presence and have the ability to forbid it. It is indeed binding upon you to do so in such a case, and whenever there are others present with you, it becomes a collective obligation

---

15 The Noble *Qur.aan - Soorah* al-Maa.idah, *Aayah*s 78-79

upon all of you; whoever from amongst you who sufficiently carries out the obligation would achieve the objective; but if all of you abandon it then all of you would fall into sin.

In summary, this is an obligation upon everyone, a collective obligation. So whenever it is being carried out by a group of individuals from a society or tribe who are achieving the intended objective, the obligation is then absolved from everybody else.

Likewise is the case of calling to Allaah; if everybody abandons this duty, they all fall into sin, and whenever a sufficient group of individuals call to Allaah, direct the people to good and forbid evil, it then becomes a great 'recommended act' upon everybody else, due to co-operating in good and assisting one another upon piety and good.

Shaykh 'Abdul-'Azeez ibn Baaz

4. Lenience When Calling to Allaah

Question: Some of those whom we consider to be steadfastly practicing the religion, treat people harshly, cold-heartedly and some of them are always frowning. What advice do you have for them, and what are the obligations upon a *Muslim* towards his brother in *Islaam*, especially if he is deficient in practicing the religion?[16]

Response: The purified *Sunnah*, the *Sunnah* of the Prophet (*sal-Allaahu 'alayhi wa sallam*), confirms that it is obligatory for the *Muslim* to call to Allaah with wisdom, lenience and kindness. Allaah (*Subhaanahu wa Ta'aala*) said to His Messenger Muhammad (*sal-Allaahu 'alayhi wa sallam*):

---

16 Kitaab ad-Da'wah - No.1291

100

$$\text{ٱدْعُ إِلَىٰ سَبِيلِ رَبِّكَ بِٱلْحِكْمَةِ}$$

$$\text{وَٱلْمَوْعِظَةِ ٱلْحَسَنَةِ وَجَٰدِلْهُم بِٱلَّتِي هِيَ أَحْسَنُ}$$

"Invite (mankind, O Muhammad) to the Way of your Lord (i.e. Islaam) with wisdom (i.e. with the Divine Inspiration and the Qur.aan), fair preaching, and debate with them in a manner that is best."[17]

He (*Subhaanahu wa Ta'aala*) also said to him:

$$\text{فَبِمَا رَحْمَةٍ مِّنَ}$$

$$\text{ٱللَّهِ لِنتَ لَهُمْ وَلَوْ كُنتَ فَظًّا غَلِيظَ ٱلْقَلْبِ لَٱنفَضُّوا مِنْ حَوْلِكَ}$$

"And by the Mercy of Allaah, you (Muhammad (sal-Allaahu 'alayhi wa sallam) dealt with them gently. And had you been severe and harsh-hearted, they would have dispersed from around you..."[18]

Allaah (*Subhaanahu wa Ta'aala*) said when He sent Moosaa and Haaroon to Pharaoh:

$$\text{فَقُولَا لَهُ قَوْلًا لَّيِّنًا لَّعَلَّهُ يَتَذَكَّرُ أَوْ يَخْشَىٰ}$$

"And speak to him mildly, perhaps he may accept admonition or fear Allaah."[19]

The Messenger of Allaah stated:

"Indeed Allaah gives through gentleness that which He does not give through harshness."

---

17 The Noble *Qur.aan - Soorah* an-Nahl, *Aayah* 125

18 The Noble *Qur.aan - Soorah* Aal-'Imraan, *Aayah* 159

19 The Noble *Qur.aan - Soorah* Taha, *Aayah* 44

He (*sal-Allaahu 'alayhi wa sallam*) used to say to his messengers when sending them out to call to Allaah:

> *"Make things easy and do not make things difficult; give glad tidings and do not drive people away from you."*

He also said:

> *"Indeed you (Muslims) were only sent to make things easy, and you were not sent to make things difficult."*

This is what the caller must be like; gentle, always smiling and open-hearted, in order for his call to be more readily accepted by those he is calling to Allaah.

It is also imperative that his call is solely to Allaah (*Subhaanahu wa Ta'aala*) and not to himself. One should not try to be victorious over others or take revenge of those who have opposed the path, because if he calls to Allaah alone, by doing so he would be sincere. Allaah would make his affair easy for him and guide whomsoever He pleases from amongst His slaves through him.

On the other hand, if he is calling to himself, wishing to be victorious, feeling that others are his enemies and wishes to take revenge, indeed the call would be deficient and its blessing may be removed.

Therefore my advice to my brothers from amongst the callers to Allaah is to feel these feelings; meaning to call the creation as a mercy to the creation, while glorifying the Religion of Allaah (*Subhaanahu wa Ta'aala*) and supporting it.

Shaykh Muhammad ibn Saalih al-'Uthaymeen

5. Behaving with Hikmah

Question: What is *hikmah* and how does a *Muslim* act upon it?[20]

Response: *Hikmah* is being in harmony with proper manners and rulings. Faults in one's behaviour are contradictory to *hikmah*.

Some callers to Allaah call in a manner that lacks *hikmah*; if one of them sees a person practicing something that he believes is incorrect, he harshly rebukes him, raising his voice in the process. For example, if someone enters the *masjid* and sits without praying *tahiyyatul-masjid* first, some people would raise their voices at him in reprimand. Hikmah however, is to explain the ruling to him and cite the *hadeeth* as evidence.

Likewise this methodology must be implemented with all obligations, prohibitions and personal dealings between people, such as financial affairs. *Hikmah* must be implemented in them, for how many people waste their money and then borrow from someone else for the most trivial of reasons.

Shaykh Muhammad ibn Saalih al-'Uthaymeen

6. Calling the Ignorant

Question: O, noble *Shaykh*, we notice that common *Muslim*s, within the country as well as out of the country, are turning away from the Religion of Allaah (*Subhaanahu wa Ta'aala*); they are not interested in knowing or learning it. They are ignorant of even the simplest of matters, matters that a *Muslim* is not permitted to be ignorant of.

---

20 Majmoo' Duroos wa Fataawa al-Haram al-Makkee - Volume 3, Page 362

How do we deal with them? Are they legislatively pardoned, and where does the responsibility fall with regards to them?[21]

Response: It is compulsory for them to learn issues that they are in need of from the Religion of Allaah. They must learn what they need from the rulings of purification, prayers, *zakaat*, fasting, *hajj* and so on. Knowledge of these issues is an obligation upon every *Muslim* as the scholars have stated, thus it is obligatory upon them to ask about it.

The mediums that assist in gaining knowledge have been facilitated at present, and all praise is due to Allaah. Transportation has been facilitated; the distances that used to take two days for a person to travel across now only take a couple of hours. Communication has also been facilitated; telephones are now available, so people are able to call the scholars and ask them. Therefore they are not pardoned in reality.

Having said this, we also say that it is an obligation upon the scholars to travel to countries where ignorance is predominant, in order to teach people the affairs of their religion. Indeed the Messenger of Allaah (*sal-Allaahu 'alayhi wa sallam*) used to send callers to different countries to teach people their religion and guide them.

Shaykh Muhammad ibn Saalih al-'Uthaymeen

7. Calling the Culturally Influenced

Question: What is the best way to call those who are influenced by certain cultures or societies?[22]

---

21 Liqaa.aat al-Baab al-Maftooh - No.830

22 Majmoo' Fataawa wa Maqaalaat Mutanawwi'ah - Volume 4, Page 240

<u>Response</u>: The caller to Allaah (*Subhaanahu wa Ta'aala*) should clarify the mistakes, innovations and other such issues present within the methodologies that these people are influenced by; the ways that they affiliate themselves to and the communities that they live in. Likewise the caller should clarify any issues in opposition to the legislation of *Islaam* that are present in their societies and communities. He is to call them to compare everything that they are uncertain of to the upright scale, which is the Book of Allaah and the *Sunnah* of His Messenger (*sal-Allaahu 'alayhi wa sallam*). Whatever is in agreement to either one or both of them is acknowledged by the legislation, and whatever is in disagreement to them is rejected; no matter whose opinion it is.

In the past, the people of knowledge used to compare issues which were differed upon to the proofs of the legislation. Whatever is in accordance to the legislation stays, and whatever is in opposition to the legislation must be discarded, even if it were the opinion of a great personality. This is because the truth is above all. Likewise this method must be implemented with regards to all habits and manners that are in opposition to the legislation of *Islaam*. Such habits must be discarded even if they were from the manners of their parents, elders, predecessors or others. Everyone must adhere to all the orders of Allaah and His Messenger because this is the way to salvation as Allaah (*Subhaanahu wa Ta'aala*) said:

$$وَأَنَّ هَٰذَا صِرَاطِي مُسْتَقِيمًا فَاتَّبِعُوهُ وَلَا تَتَّبِعُوا السُّبُلَ فَتَفَرَّقَ بِكُمْ عَن سَبِيلِهِ ذَٰلِكُمْ وَصَّاكُم بِهِ لَعَلَّكُمْ تَتَّقُونَ$$

And verily, this is my straight path, so follow it, and follow not (other) paths, for they will separate you from His path. This He has ordained for you

that you may become Muttaqoon (pious)[23]

Allaah is the granter of success.

Shaykh 'Abdul-'Azeez ibn Baaz

8. Giving Out Cassettes/CDs/DVDs

Question: I love calling to Allaah and am very keen about it. However, I lack a good method. Is it sufficient for me to choose a suitable cassette by one of the scholars or callers to Allaah, and give it to a relative or to *Muslims* in general as a gift?[24]

Response: Yes, if the cassette is by a scholar who is known to have the correct *'aqeedah* and a great deal of knowledge. If you gift it to your brothers then you have done well and will obtain an equal amount of reward as the scholar due to the saying of the Messenger (*sal-Allaahu 'alayhi wa sallam*):

> **"Whoever directs someone to good will obtain an
> equal reward as the one who practices it."**

There is no problem for you yourself to speak in a fine manner about affairs that you have knowledge of, such as encouraging people to pray in congregation, to give *zakaat*, warn them from backbiting and *nameemah*, disobeying their parents, cutting off their relations and everything evil that Allaah has forbidden. These affairs and their likes are known to all *Muslims* whether they are scholars or not.

Shaykh 'Abdul-'Azeez ibn Baaz

---

23 The Noble *Qur.aan* - *Soorah* al-An'aam, *Aayah* 153

24 Majalatul-Buhooth al-Islaamiyyah - Volume 36, Page 126

9. Giving Out Beneficial Cassettes and Books

Question: I am a young man who would like to become a caller to Al-laah; however I lack a suitable method. Is it sufficient for me to give out beneficial cassettes or books? Benefit me; may Allaah reward you with good![25]

Response: Yes, there is no doubt that a person may not be able to call to Allaah himself, but may be able to give out beneficial books and cassettes.

However, based upon the fact that he doesn't have the ability to call to Allaah himself, he must not distribute books or tapes until he presents them to students of knowledge first, in order to let the students examine the mistakes these books or cassettes may contain. He should do so, so that he does not inadvertently give out material that contains errors. He can also make an agreement with a student of knowledge in which the student writes something in calling to good that this individual can distribute.

Shaykh Muhammad ibn Saalih al-'Uthaymeen

10. Different Methods in Giving Da'wah

Question: Amongst the callers to Allaah, are those who apply the method of upbringing and teaching; others apply the method of delivering sermons and reminders in places where women gather. What is your opinion and which of the two is more successful?[26]

---

25 Kitaab ad-Da'wah - Volume 2, Page 171

26 Kitaab ad-Da'wah - Volume 2, Page 170

Response: I believe this to be from the blessings of Allaah (*Subhaanahu wa Ta'aala*) upon His servants, that He made them have different approaches with regards to the mediums or methods that they use in calling to Allaah.

One person delivers sermons; Allaah (*Subhaanahu wa Ta'aala*) has blessed him with eloquence, the ability to speak proficiently and have an effect on people. In his case, giving sermons is considered to be the best method for him. Allaah (*Subhaanahu wa Ta'aala*) blesses another person with softness, lenience and kindness, with which he affects the hearts of the people. This type of caller has a better method than the previously mentioned one, especially if he is proficient at speaking. Other callers may have knowledge but lack communication skills. The blessings of Allaah (*Subhaanahu wa Ta'aala*) are spread out between His servants, and He has raised some over others in levels.

My opinion is that each person should use the method that he believes is the most beneficial and useful, as well as one that is most suited to him. One should not delve into affairs that he is unable to handle. Rather he should be sure of himself, seeking aid from Allaah (*Subhaanahu wa Ta'aala*), so that if certain issues were raised he would be able to handle them properly.

Shaykh Muhammad ibn Saalih al-'Uthaymeen

11. Da'wah in Evil Places

Question: Some people go to immoral places claiming that they only go there to call to Allaah. Is it permissible for a person to go to such places, the homes of *Shaytaan*, in order to promote *Islaam* to those who do not want it; their actions proving this?[27]

Response: All praise is due to Allaah alone and may the *salaah* and *salaam* be upon His Messenger, his family and Companions.

If he has hope that they may accept, he may sit with them in order to direct them to the truth, advise them and carry out the obligation of conveying the message and establishing the proofs upon them. Just as the Messenger of Allaah (*sal-Allaahu 'alayhi wa sallam*) used to do when passing by the gatherings of the polytheists in order to call them to the truth. If they accept, then all praise is due to Allaah, otherwise he is to leave them in order to protect himself from their evil and distance himself from it.

The Permanent Committee for Islaamic Research and Verdicts

12. Serving Islaam

Question: Which is better; serving *Islaam* using political methods or by calling people to return to the path of the Messenger (*sal-Allaahu 'alayhi wa sallam*)?[28]

Response: It is compulsory to serve *Islaam* by calling the people to the Book of Allaah and the *Sunnah* of His Messenger (*sal-Allaahu 'alayhi wa sallam*); with the methodology that Allaah directed and ordered His Messenger (*sal-Allaahu 'alayhi wa sallam*) to follow in His saying:

$$ \text{ٱدْعُ إِلَىٰ سَبِيلِ رَبِّكَ بِٱلْحِكْمَةِ وَٱلْمَوْعِظَةِ ٱلْحَسَنَةِ ۖ وَجَٰدِلْهُم بِٱلَّتِي هِىَ أَحْسَنُ} $$

---

27 Fataawa al-Lajnah ad-Daa.imah - No.9406

28 Fataawa al-Lajnah ad-Daa.imah - No.7674

*"Call (mankind, O Muhammad) to the Way of your
Lord with wisdom (i.e. with the Divine Inspiration
and the Qur.aan), fair preaching and debate with
them in a manner that is best."*[29]

His saying as well:

قُلْ هَـٰذِهِۦ

سَبِيلِىٓ أَدْعُوٓاْ إِلَى ٱللَّهِ عَلَىٰ بَصِيرَةٍ أَنَا۠ وَمَنِ ٱتَّبَعَنِى

*"Say (O Muhammad): "This is my way; I call to Al-
laah (i.e. to the Oneness of Allaah – Islaamic Monotheism) with sure knowledge, I and those who
follow me."*[30]

The Messenger of Allaah (*sal-Allaahu 'alayhi wa sallam*) clarified the
method of calling to Allaah with his sayings, writings and actions; he
said:

*"Whoever amongst you sees something evil must
change it with his hands; if he is unable to do so,
he must change it with his tongue; if he is unable
to do that, he is to hate it with his heart and that is
the weakest of faith."*

He said to Mu'aadh when he sent him to Yemen:

*"You are travelling to a People of the Book, so call
them firstly to testify that none have the right to be
worshipped except Allaah and that Muhammad is*

---

29 The Noble *Qur.aan - Soorah* an-Nahl, *Aayah* 125

30 The Noble *Qur.aan - Soorah* Yoosuf, *Aayah* 108

the Messenger of Allaah. If they accept this from you, inform them that Allaah has enjoined five prayers upon them that are to be performed daily. If they accept this from you, inform them that Allaah has enjoined Sadaqah (zakaat) upon them, which is to be taken from the rich amongst them and given to the poor amongst them."

In the *hadeeth* of Sahl ibn Sa'd (*radhi-yAllaahu 'anhu*), the Messenger of Allaah (*sal-Allaahu 'alayhi wa sallam*) said to 'Alee (*radhi-yAllaahu 'anhu*) when he gave him the banner on the day of the battle of Khaybar:

"Proceed with calmness and tranquility until you enter their land; then call them to Islaam and inform them of what has been obligated upon them in relation to the rights of Allaah in Islaam. For by Allaah, if Allaah guides a single person through you, it is better for you than the best of camels."

The Messenger of Allaah (*sal-Allaahu 'alayhi wa sallam*) also wrote to kings of different nations; calling them to *Islaam* and ordering them to worship Allaah alone. He mentioned in his letters to the People of the Book:

قُلْ يَٰٓأَهْلَ ٱلْكِتَٰبِ تَعَالَوْا۟ إِلَىٰ كَلِمَةٍ سَوَآءٍ بَيْنَنَا وَبَيْنَكُمْ أَلَّا نَعْبُدَ إِلَّا ٱللَّهَ وَلَا نُشْرِكَ بِهِۦ شَيْـًٔا وَلَا يَتَّخِذَ بَعْضُنَا بَعْضًا أَرْبَابًا مِّن دُونِ ٱللَّهِ

"Say (O Muhammad): "O people of the Scripture (Jews and Christians): Come to a word that is just between you and us, that we worship none but Allaah, that we associate no partners with Him and that

111

none of us take others as lords besides Allaah.""[31]

He promised them double the reward if they accept and warned them of bearing the punishment of their sins as well as the sins of their people if they rejected.

He called to *Islaam* with his actions as well, for he was a complete example in implementing *tawheed* and worshipping Allaah. He behaved with the highest standard of manners when dealing with people and in his whole life in general. He was never angered for personal reasons nor did he ever take revenge for himself; he was only angered when the sacredness of Allaah was violated. He was just as Allaah described him in His Noble Book, saying:

$$وَإِنَّكَ لَعَلَىٰ خُلُقٍ عَظِيمٍ$$

"...to the believers (he is) full of pity, kind, and merciful."[32]

His saying as well:

$$بِالْمُؤْمِنِينَ رَءُوفٌ رَّحِيمٌ$$

"Indeed, you (O Muhammad) have an exalted standard of character."[33]

This is the policy of the prophetic call to Allaah; full of wisdom and fine judgement. It was drawn out for us by the Messenger of Allaah (*sal-Allaahu 'alayhi wa sallam*). So it is upon the callers of *Islaam*ic groups

---

31 The Noble *Qur.aan - Soorah* Aal-'Imraan, *Aayah* 64

32 The Noble *Qur.aan - Soorah* at-Towbah, *Aayah* 128

33 The Noble *Qur.aan - Soorah* al-Qalam, *Aayah* 4

to call with this method; the method of wisdom, fine sermon and debating in the best manner. They must assess everyone they call according to their respected levels and speak to each individual on a level that he/she understands. Allaah may support His religion through them and direct their attention towards their enemies, not their brothers. Indeed He is All-Able to answer supplications.

The Permanent Committee for Islaamic Research and Verdicts

13. How to Forbid Evil

Question: We notice that alot of the youth who are keen on forbidding evil do not know how to go about doing so. What advice do you have for them and what is the best way to forbid evil?[34]

Response: I advise them to verify all issues to ascertain that they are in fact accurate. They must gain knowledge first, in order to be certain concerning what is good and what is evil based upon legislated evidences, so that their rebuttal is based upon insight due to the saying of Allaah (*Subhaanahu wa Ta'aala*):

قُلْ هَٰذِهِۦ

سَبِيلِىٓ أَدْعُوٓاْ إِلَى ٱللَّهِ عَلَىٰ بَصِيرَةٍ أَنَا۠ وَمَنِ ٱتَّبَعَنِى

'Say (O Muhammad): "This is my way; I call to Allaah (i.e. to the Oneness of Allaah – Islaamic Monotheism) with sure knowledge, I and those who follow me".'[35]

---

34 Majmoo' Fataawa wa Maqaalaat Mutanawwi'ah - Volume 5, Page 57

35 The Noble *Qur.aan* - *Soorah* Yoosuf, *Aayah* 108

I also advise that rebuttal should be carried out with gentleness, consisting of kind speech and good manners in order for it to be accepted, and in order for them to rectify affairs more than they ruin them due to the saying of Allaah (*Subhaanahu wa Ta'aala*):

$$\text{ٱدْعُ إِلَىٰ سَبِيلِ رَبِّكَ بِٱلْحِكْمَةِ}$$
$$\text{وَٱلْمَوْعِظَةِ ٱلْحَسَنَةِ ۖ وَجَٰدِلْهُم بِٱلَّتِى هِىَ أَحْسَنُ}$$

"Call (mankind, O Muhammad) to the Way of your Lord with wisdom (i.e. with the Divine Inspiration and the Qur.aan), fair preaching and debate with them in a way that is best."[36]

As well as His saying:

$$\text{فَبِمَا رَحْمَةٍ مِّنَ}$$
$$\text{ٱللَّهِ لِنتَ لَهُمْ ۖ وَلَوْ كُنتَ فَظًّا غَلِيظَ ٱلْقَلْبِ لَٱنفَضُّوا۟ مِنْ حَوْلِكَ}$$

"And by the Mercy of Allaah, you (Muhammad) dealt with them gently. And had you been severe and harsh-hearted, they would have dispersed from around you..."[37]

The saying of the Messenger (*sal-Allaahu 'alayhi wa sallam*):

"Whoever is deprived of gentleness is deprived of everything that is good."

His (*sal-Allaahu 'alayhi wa sallam*) saying as well:

---

36 The Noble *Qur.aan - Soorah* an-Nahl, *Aayah* 125

37 The Noble *Qur.aan - Soorah* Aal-'Imraan, *Aayah* 159

"Indeed gentleness is not implemented in any af-
fair except that it beautifies it, and it is not re-
moved from any affair except that it ruins it."

The *ahaadeeth* of this like are plentiful.

The callers to Allaah, those who direct the people to good and forbid
them from evil should be the first to practice what they call to and the
last to fall into what they forbid from, so as to avoid resembling those
whom Allaah (*Subhaanahu wa Ta'aala*) has admonished in His saying:

$$\text{أَتَأْمُرُونَ ٱلنَّاسَ بِٱلْبِرِّ}$$

$$\text{وَتَنسَوْنَ أَنفُسَكُمْ وَأَنتُمْ تَتْلُونَ ٱلْكِتَٰبَ أَفَلَا تَعْقِلُونَ}$$

"Do you enjoin al-Birr (piety and righteousness
and each and every act of obedience to Allaah)
on the people and you forget (to practice it) your-
selves while you recite the Scripture [the Torah)]!
Have you then no sense?"[38]

His saying as well:

$$\text{يَٰٓأَيُّهَا ٱلَّذِينَ ءَامَنُوا لِمَ تَقُولُونَ مَا لَا تَفْعَلُونَ ۝}$$

$$\text{كَبُرَ مَقْتًا عِندَ ٱللَّهِ أَن تَقُولُوا مَا لَا تَفْعَلُونَ}$$

"O you who believe! Why do you say that which you
do not do? Most hateful it is with Allaah that you
say that which you do not do."[39]

---

38 The Noble *Qur.aan* - *Soorah* al-Baqarah, *Aayah* 44

39 The Noble *Qur.aan* - *Soorah* as-Saff, *Aayah*s 2-3

Also, in order for people to take them as examples and benefit from their speech as well as their actions, and Allaah is the granter of success.

Shaykh 'Abdul-'Azeez ibn Baaz

14. Is Da'wah 'Towqeefiyyah' or 'Towfeeqiyyah'?

Question: Is *da'wah* '*towqeefiyyah*' or '*towfeeqiyyah*'?[40]

Response: Calling to Allaah is '*towqeefiyyah*' in the sense that the caller must follow the methodology that Allaah directed the callers to follow, which is with wisdom, fine sermon, and debating in the issues related to *ijtihaad*. Debates must be carried out in the finest manner with the intention of arriving at the truth and not to merely overcome or defeat the opponent, or to blindly follow or obstinately cling to one's own opinion. Allaah (*Subhaanahu wa Ta'aala*) said:

$$ادْعُ إِلَىٰ سَبِيلِ رَبِّكَ بِالْحِكْمَةِ وَالْمَوْعِظَةِ الْحَسَنَةِ وَجَادِلْهُم بِالَّتِي هِيَ أَحْسَنُ$$

"Call (mankind, O Muhammad) to the way of your Lord (i.e. Islaam) with wisdom (i.e. with the Divine Revelation and the Qur.aan), fair preaching, and debate with them in a manner that is best."[41]

The caller to Allaah should forbid evil acts physically, providing he has the ability and is qualified to do so. If he is unable to do so however, he should forbid evil with his tongue. If he is not able to that, he should

---

40 Fataawa al-Lajnah ad-Daa.imah - Volume 3, Page 379

41 The Noble *Qur.aan* - *Soorah* an-Nahl, *Aayah* 125

at least hate that evil act with his heart, and that is the weakest level of *eemaan*.

Calling to Allaah is a collective obligation; if a sufficient group carries it out, the obligation is absolved from everybody else. Its obligation falls specifically upon those whom *da'wah* cannot be established without.

As for it happening, then this is *'towfeeqiyyah'*: meaning that whomsoever Allaah wishes success for in carrying out the obligation of calling to Allaah, Allaah would make him love *da'wah* and make the means of performing it easy upon him; a blessing and mercy from Allaah (*Subhaanahu wa Ta'aala*).

Allaah is the granter of success and may He send His *salaah* upon our Prophet Muhammad and upon his family and Companions.

The Permanent Committee for Islaamic Research and Verdicts

15. Methodology of Criticism between the Callers of Ahlus-Sunnah

All praise is due to Allaah, Lord of the worlds and may the peace and blessings be upon our faithful Prophet Muhammad, his family, Companions and whoever acts upon his *Sunnah* to the Day of Judgement.[42]

To proceed:

Indeed Allaah (*Subhaanahu wa Ta'aala*) orders people to act with justice and perform good deeds, and He prohibits injustice, oppression and

---

42 Majmoo' Fataawa wa Maqaalaat Mutanawwi'ah - Volume 7, Page 311

enmity. Allaah has sent His Prophet Muhammad (*sal-Allaahu 'alayhi wa sallam*) with the same religion that He had sent all His Messengers with; consisting of the call to *tawheed* and being sincere to Allaah alone. He ordered him to establish justice and forbade him from everything that is in contradiction to it, such as worshipping other than Allaah, splitting, dispersing, enmity and aggression with regards to the rights of His servants.

At present alot of those who affiliate themselves with knowledge and calling to good, speak ill of alot of their brothers. They speak about the students of knowledge, callers and lecturers. They do so either secretly in private gatherings; they may sometimes record such gatherings and circulate the recordings, or they may do so in public, in general lectures in the *masaajid*. This approach is in contradiction to the order of Allaah and His Messenger (*sal-Allaahu 'alayhi wa sallam*) from a number of angles.

Firstly: This is a form of aggression over *Muslim*'s rights, rather over an exclusive group of people who include students of knowledge and callers to *Islaam*; those who exert their efforts to enlighten people, direct them, and rectify their *'aqeedah* and *manhaj*, as well as try hard to organise lessons, lectures and write beneficial books.

Secondly: This splits the unity of the *Muslims* and tears apart their ranks; while they are in utter need of unity and being distant from dispersal, splitting and excessive gossip. Especially if the callers that are being spoken about are from *Ahlus-Sunnah wal-Jamaa'ah*, who are known for battling innovations and superstitions; standing up against those who call to them and exposing their plots and faults. We do not see any benefit in this kind of conduct, except for the lurking enemies from amongst the non-*Muslims*, hypocrites or the people of innovations.

Thirdly: This type of conduct assists and supports biased people amongst the Masons, Orientalists and atheists; people who are notorious for speaking about callers to *Islaam*, lying about them and inciting people against them. It is not from the rights of brotherhood to help these hasty enemies against our brothers such as the students of knowledge, the callers or others.

Fourthly: This behaviour corrupts the hearts of the general public as well as those specifically involved. It also propagates lies and false rumours and is a cause for excessive backbiting and tale-carrying. It opens the doors of evil upon weak souls who struggle against this kind of behaviour, those who have become accustomed to spreading misconceptions, instigating *fitnah* and are keen on harming the believers with what they have not earned.

Fifthly: A lot of this gossip that is being spread has no reality and is mere conjecture, which the *Shaytaan* has beautified for those who engage in such activities and deceived them with. Allaah (*Subhaanahu wa Ta'aala*) said in the *Qur.aan*:

يَٰٓأَيُّهَا ٱلَّذِينَ ءَامَنُوا۟ ٱجۡتَنِبُوا۟ كَثِيرًا مِّنَ ٱلظَّنِّ إِنَّ بَعۡضَ ٱلظَّنِّ إِثۡمٌ وَلَا تَجَسَّسُوا۟ وَلَا يَغۡتَب بَّعۡضُكُم بَعۡضًا

O you who believe! Avoid a lot of suspicion; indeed some suspicions are sins. And spy not, and do not backbite one another.[43]

The believer should interpret his brother's speech in the best way. It has been narrated that some of the *Salaf* said:

---

43 The Noble *Qur.aan - Soorah* al-Hujuraat, *Aayah* 12

"Do not think ill of a word that your brother has said while you are able to find a good interpretation for it."

Sixthly: Concerning issues where we find some opinions of the scholars or students of knowledge in matters where it is permissible to hold opinions. One who holds a particular opinion should not be blamed or rebuked if he is from amongst those who are qualified to derive opinions. If someone else disagrees with him in that particular issue, then it is more befitting that he debates with him in a manner that is best while being keen on reaching the truth through the quickest path, and while repelling the whispers and provocations of the *Shaytaan*. If this is not possible and one sees that he is obligated to explain the contradicting view, then this should be done with the best of speech and the most pleasant of indications; without attacking, dispraising or transgressing in speech, which in turn may lead others to reject and turn away from the truth. This should also be carried out without speaking about a specific person, accusing people's intentions or speaking excessively without justification. The Messenger of Allaah (*sal-Allaahu 'alayhi wa sallam*) used to say in situations like this:

> ***"What is the matter with people who say such and such things?"***

Therefore I advise the brothers who spoke ill of the callers to repent to Allaah (*Subhaanahu wa Ta'aala*) from what their tongues have uttered and what their hands have written, which in turn corrupted the hearts of some youth and filled them with hatred and malice, as well as occupied them from gaining beneficial knowledge. They should also repent from promoting gossip, searching for what they perceive to be mistakes in others, and taking this task upon themselves.

I also advise them to make amends for what they have caused, whether

120

it is in writing or other than that; this would free them from this conduct. I advise them to remove what they have attached to the minds of their listeners and focus on fruitful deeds which are beneficial to Allaah's servants and bring people closer to Him. They should beware of hastily uttering rulings of *takfeer*, *tabdee'* or *tafseeq* over others without evidence. The Messenger of Allaah (*sal-Allaahu 'alayhi wa sallam*) said:

> **"Whoever says; 'You disbeliever' to his brother, then this ruling shall return to either one of them."**

If something from the sayings of the people of knowledge is problematic, it is legislated for the callers to the truth and the students of knowledge to return to the recognised scholars in those issues. They must ask them so they can clarify and give a detailed explanation of the issue in order to remove any uncertainty or misconception, acting upon the saying of Allaah (*Subhaanahu wa Ta'aala*) in *Soorah* an-Nisaa:

وَإِذَاجَاءَهُمْ أَمْرٌمِّنَ ٱلْأَمْنِ

أَوِٱلْخَوْفِ أَذَاعُواْبِهِۦ وَلَوْرَدُّوهُ إِلَى ٱلرَّسُولِ وَإِلَىٰٓ أُوْلِى

ٱلْأَمْرِ مِنْهُمْ لَعَلِمَهُ ٱلَّذِينَ يَسْتَنۢبِطُونَهُۥ مِنْهُمْ وَلَوْلَافَضْلُ

ٱللَّهِ عَلَيْكُمْ وَرَحْمَتُهُۥ لَٱتَّبَعْتُمُ ٱلشَّيْطَـٰنَ إِلَّا قَلِيلًا

When a matter concerning (public) safety or fear comes to them, they publicise it (among the people); if only they had referred it to the Messenger or to those charged with authority among them, the proper investigators would have understood it from them (directly). Had it not been for the Grace and Mercy of Allaah upon you, you would have followed Shaytaan, except a few of you.[44]

---

44 The Noble *Qur.aan* - *Soorah* an-Nisaa, *Aayah* 83

We ask Allaah to rectify the state of all the *Muslim*s and gather their hearts and deeds upon piety; to enable all the *Muslim* scholars and callers to the truth to do what Allaah is pleased with and what benefits His servants. I ask Allaah to guard them from the causes of splitting and differing; to support the truth and disgrace falsehood through them; indeed He is the Custodian of this affair and is All-Able to carry it out, and may the *salaah* and *salaam* be upon our Prophet Muhammad, his family, Companions and whoever follows his guidance to the Day of Judgement.

Shaykh 'Abdul-'Azeez ibn Baaz

16. An Explanation of the Previous Article

Question: Noble *Shaykh*, you issued a statement a few weeks ago about the methodology of criticism between the callers. Different people have interpreted it in different ways; what is your opinion of this?[45]

Response: All praise is due to Allaah and may the *salaah* and *salaam* be upon the Messenger of Allaah and whoever acts upon his guidance.

To Proceed:

Concerning the statement which the questioner is alluding to, I intended to advise my brothers through it, the scholars and the callers to *Islaam*, that when they criticise their brothers due to their statements, lectures or seminars, that this should be done in a manner that is far from admonishing or specifying them, because this may cause hostility and enmity between all those involved.

---

45 Majmoo' Fataawa wa Maqaalaat Mutanawwi'ah - Volume 7, Page 315

It was the way of the Prophet that if he heard that some of his companions said things that do not coincide with the *Islaam*ic legislation, he would notify them by saying:

"What is the matter with people who say such things?"

He would then clarify the issue. An example of this is when he heard that someone said: "I will stay up all night in prayer without sleep."

And another said: "As for me, I will not stop fasting."

A third said: "As for me, then I will not marry."

The Messenger addressed the people, praised his Lord and said:

"What is the matter with people who say such things?"

So my intention is the same as the Prophet's, meaning that the indication should be in a manner that is like this: 'Some people are saying such and such but the correct opinion is this.' So criticism should be void of admonishing anyone in particular, but with the intention of explaining the legislated issue so that the love between brothers, callers and the scholars remains. I did not intend specific people with it; I intended all of the scholars and callers in general, whether they are within the country or out of it.

So my advice to everyone is that the method of advising and criticising others should be anonymous, not specific, because the intention is to clarify mistakes or errors and clarify the truth without having to admonish any particular person. May Allaah grant everyone success.

Shaykh 'Abdul-'Azeez ibn Baaz

<u>Question</u>: The enemies of Allaah are keen on propagating rancour in *Muslim* lands in a variety of ways; what methods do you think we should apply to confront these tidal waves that threaten *Muslim* communities?[46]

<u>Response</u>: This activity is not surprising from the callers of Christianity, Judaism and other disbelievers and methodologies of destruction, because Allaah (*Subhaanahu wa Ta'aala*) has informed us of this in His Book saying:

وَلَن تَرْضَىٰ عَنكَ ٱلْيَهُودُ وَلَا ٱلنَّصَارَىٰ حَتَّىٰ تَتَّبِعَ مِلَّتَهُمْ قُلْ إِنَّ هُدَى ٱللَّهِ هُوَ ٱلْهُدَىٰ وَلَئِنِ ٱتَّبَعْتَ أَهْوَاءَهُم بَعْدَ ٱلَّذِى جَاءَكَ مِنَ ٱلْعِلْمِ مَا لَكَ مِنَ ٱللَّهِ مِن وَلِيٍّ وَلَا نَصِيرٍ

Never will the Jews nor the Christians be pleased with you (O Muhammad) untill you follow their religion. Say: "Verily, the Guidance of Allaah (i.e. Islaamic Monotheism) is the (only) Guidance. And if you (O Muhammad) were to follow their (Jews and Christians) desires after what you have received of Knowledge (i.e. the Qur.aan), then you would neither have a Walee (protector or guardian) or a Helper to protect you from Allaah."[47]

Allaah says as well:

وَلَا يَزَالُونَ يُقَـٰتِلُونَكُمْ حَتَّىٰ يَرُدُّوكُمْ عَن دِينِكُمْ إِنِ ٱسْتَطَـٰعُواْ

46 Majmoo' Fataawa wa Maqaalaat Mutanawwi'ah - Volume 5, Page 204

47 The Noble *Qur.aan* - *Soorah* al-Baqarah, *Aayah* 120

"And they will never cease fighting you until they turn you back from your religion if they can."[48]

Due to this they exert all their efforts in trying to influence *Islaam*ic countries, using different methods to accomplish this, such as spreading doubts and confusion. They persevere upon this way without tiring. The church; jealousy and hatred motivate and direct them to carry this out. So it is compulsory for *Muslim* rulers and the people of knowledge to confront the efforts of the enemies of *Islaam* with opposing efforts and direct and educate the children of the *Muslims*. The *ummah* of *Islaam* has taken the trust of this religion upon itself as well as the trust of conveying it, so if we are keen on equipping the sons and daughters of the *Muslims* in *Muslim* communities with knowledge and understanding of the religion, and get them accustomed to practicing it while they are young, then we have nothing to fear for them with the Permission of Allaah. As long as they are holding on to the Religion of Allaah, glorifying it, practicing its legislation and battling what is in opposition to it, the opposite of that will take place; the enemies are the ones who will fear them because Allaah (*Subhaanahu wa Ta'aala*) says:

يَـٰٓأَيُّهَا ٱلَّذِينَ

ءَامَنُوٓاْ إِن تَنصُرُواْ ٱللَّهَ يَنصُرْكُمْ وَيُثَبِّتْ أَقْدَامَكُمْ

"O you who believe! If you help (in the cause of) Allaah, He will help you and make your foothold firm."[49]

He also says:

قُل لِّلَّذِينَ كَفَرُواْ سَتُغْلَبُونَ

وَتُحْشَرُونَ إِلَىٰ جَهَنَّمَ وَبِئْسَ ٱلْمِهَادُ

---

48 The Noble *Qur.aan* - *Soorah* al-Baqarah, *Aayah* 217

49 The Noble *Qur.aan* - *Soorah* Muhammad, *Aayah* 7

'Say (O Muhammad) to those who disbelieve: "You will be defeated and gathered together in Hell, and worst indeed is that place of rest".'[50]

The verses of this like are plentiful.

So the most important factor in confronting this surge is to prepare a generation of people that have knowledge of the reality of *Islaam*, and this is accomplished by directing and bringing them up within the home, the family, through educational curriculums, the media and society.

In addition to this is the role of the rulers and instructions from *Islaam*ic leaders, to be keen on performing beneficial deeds, to constantly re-mind the people with what benefits them and cultivate the *'aqeedah* within them.

الَّذِينَ ءَامَنُوا۟ وَتَطْمَئِنُّ
قُلُوبُهُم بِذِكْرِ اللَّهِ أَلَا بِذِكْرِ اللَّهِ تَطْمَئِنُّ الْقُلُوبُ

"Indeed, with the remembrance of Allaah do hearts find peace."[51]

There is no doubt that being heedless is from the causes that allow the enemies of *Islaam* to influence *Muslim* lands with their culture and knowledge, which gradually distances the *Muslims* from their religion. Immorality will therefore increase amongst them and they would be affected by the ideologies of their enemies. Allaah (*Subhaanahu wa Ta'aala*) orders the believing party to practice patience and enjoin it

---

50 The Noble *Qur.aan - Soorah* Aal-;Imraan, *Aayah* 12

51 The Noble *Qur.aan - Soorah* ar-Ra'd, *Aayah* 28

upon others, and to strive in His Cause by any means:

يَـٰٓأَيُّهَا ٱلَّذِينَ ءَامَنُوا۟ ٱصْبِرُوا۟
وَصَابِرُوا۟ وَرَابِطُوا۟ وَٱتَّقُوا۟ ٱللَّهَ لَعَلَّكُمْ تُفْلِحُونَ

"O you who believe! Practice patience and perse-
vere upon it, and guard your territory by station-
ing army units permanently at the places from
where the enemy can attack you, and fear Allaah,
so that you may be successful."[52]

His saying as well:

وَٱلَّذِينَ
جَـٰهَدُوا۟ فِينَا لَنَهْدِيَنَّهُمْ سُبُلَنَا ۚ وَإِنَّ ٱللَّهَ لَمَعَ ٱلْمُحْسِنِينَ

"As for those who strive hard in Our Cause, We will
surely guide them to Our paths (i.e. Allaah's reli-
gion – Islaamic Monotheism). And verily, Allaah is
with the Muhsinoon (good-doers)."[53]

I ask Allaah with His Most Beautiful Names and Lofty Attributes to rectify
the state of the *Muslim*s; to grant them understanding in their religion;
to unify their leaders upon the truth and to rectify their inner state; indeed He is *Jawaad*, *Kareem*, and may the peace and blessings be upon
our Prophet Muhammad, his family and Companions.

Shaykh 'Abdul-'Azeez ibn Baaz

---

52 The Noble *Qur.aan* - *Soorah* Aal-'Imraan, *Aayah* 200

53 The Noble *Qur.aan* - *Soorah* al-'Ankaboot, *Aayah* 69

Question: What is the best way to confront the rivals of *Islaam*ic movements?[54]

Response: There is no doubt that the *Islaam*ic movement everywhere has opposition and enemies that join together against it. There are organised movements; some that are evident and others secretive that assist and support them in a variety of ways and draw up plans for them. In this circumstance my opinion is that it is binding upon *Muslim* countries as well as the masses of *Muslims* to support these *Islaam*ic movements in every place, with sincere *du'aat* who are known to possess knowledge, are passionate about *Islaam*, truthful, patient and have the correct *'aqeedah*. They must also be supported financially, which would help them carry out the task of calling to the Religion of Allaah, propagating it and refuting the opposition. They must also support them with books, articles and beneficial editorials, written in a variety of languages according to the areas in which these movements are located.

Supervisors should be appointed for these movements; who visit them every now and then in order to find out how active and truthful they are, and find out what their needs are as well as direct them to a befitting path to traverse upon. These supervisors should also help in solving the problems that may confront these movements, and find out about the individuals and the organisations that help and support the enemies whether secretly or publicly, in order for the movements to be cautious of them and deal with them in a suitable manner.

No doubt what I have mentioned requires truthful efforts by faithful

---

54 Majmoo' Fataawa wa Maqaalaat Mutanawwi'ah - Volume 5, Page 253

souls who seek [the pleasure of] Allaah and the afterlife.

We ask Allaah to grant the *Islaam*ic movement and the *Muslim*s everywhere with what will aid them with establishing and practicing the truth and grant them understanding and stability upon it; indeed He is the best of those who are asked.

Shaykh 'Abdul-'Azeez ibn Baaz

19. Advice on Extremism

Question: What advice can you give some youth who become overzealous and incline towards extremeness?[55]

Response: It is compulsory for youth as well as everyone else to beware of using force, being extreme and excessive due to the saying of Allaah (*Subhaanahu wa Ta'aala*):

$$\text{يَٰٓأَهۡلَ ٱلۡكِتَٰبِ لَا تَغۡلُوا۟ فِى دِينِكُمۡ}$$

"O people of the Scripture! Do not exceed the limits in your religion."[56]

Allaah (*Subhaanahu wa Ta'aala*) said as well:

$$\text{فَبِمَا رَحۡمَةٍ مِّنَ}$$
$$\text{ٱللَّهِ لِنتَ لَهُمۡۖ وَلَوۡ كُنتَ فَظًّا غَلِيظَ ٱلۡقَلۡبِ لَٱنفَضُّوا۟ مِنۡ حَوۡلِكَ}$$

"And by the Mercy of Allaah you dealt with them gen-

---

55 Majmoo' Fataawa wa Maqaalaat Mutanawwi'ah - Volume 5, Page 273

56 The Noble *Qur.aan* - *Soorah* an-Nisaa, *Aayah* 171

tly. And had you been severe and harsh hearted,
they would have dispersed from around you..."[57]

This is also due to the saying of Allaah (*Subhaanahu wa Ta'aala*) to
Moosaa and Haaroon when He sent them to Pharaoh:

فَقُولَا لَهُ قَوْلًا لَّيِّنَا لَّعَلَّهُ يَتَذَكَّرُ أَوْ يَخْشَىٰ

"And speak to him mildly, perhaps he may accept
admonition or fear Allaah."[58]

The Prophet (*sal-Allaahu 'alayhi wa sallam*) said:

"Beware of extremism in the religion, for indeed it
is only extremism that destroyed those before you."

Due to this, I advise all the *du'aat* to avoid extremism; it is upon them
to be balanced, which is traversing upon the way of Allaah, upon the
judgement of His Book and the *Sunnah* of His Prophet (*sal-Allaahu
'alayhi wa sallam*).

Shaykh 'Abdul-'Azeez ibn Baaz

20. When to Translate the Friday Sermon

Question: What is the ruling concerning translating the *jumu'ah khutbah* into a language other than Arabic after it has finished, but before the
Friday prayer is established? If this is not permissible, when should the
translation take place?[59]

---

57 The Noble *Qur.aan - Soorah* Aal-'Imraan, *Aayah* 159

58 The Noble *Qur.aan - Soorah* Taha, *Aayah* 44

59 ar-Rihlah al-Akheerah li-Imaam al-Jazeerah - Page 153

Response: We advise the *imaam* to read the verses of the *Qur.aan* and the *ahaadeeth* in Arabic. If they are in need of explaining such as if an Arab does not understand them, then he should explain them firstly in Arabic and then translate their meanings. Meaning that after the *imaam* reads a *Qur.aan*ic verse or *hadeeth* in Arabic, he should then translate their meanings immediately; he shouldn't delay the translation. The translation shouldn't be delayed until after the prayer. I have already received some questions concerning this issue; if he does so, some people may leave without hearing the sermon. What I have mentioned is what should be done.

Shaykh Muqbil ibn Haadee al-Waadi'ee

21. Translating the Friday Sermon

Question: Is it permissible to deliver the *jumu'ah khutbah* in other than the Arabic language if most of those attending are non-Arabs; is it permissible to deliver it in English for example? We ask this because the *Imaam* starts by praising Allaah and sending the *salaah* and *salaam* upon the Messenger of Allaah. He then reads out *khutbatul-haajah* in the Arabic language and then continues in the English language even if he comes across a verse from the *Qur.aan* or a *hadeeth*; he reads them in English.[60]

Response: No, he should read the *Qur.aan* or *hadeeth* in Arabic and then translate them, as has already preceded. If the Arabs themselves do not understand the meaning of the verses he is reciting, he should explain them firstly and then translate for non-Arabs in order for them to understand, and from Allaah alone do we seek assistance.

Shaykh Muqbil ibn Haadee al-Waadi'ee

---

60 ar-Rihlah al-Akheerah li-Imaam al-Jazeerah - Page 154

Chapter 5
The Mediums of Da'wah

1. Are the Mediums of Da'wah Towqeefiyyah?

Question: O, noble *Shaykh*, during the summer vacation some schools open up summer camps in order to keep the youth occupied with beneficial activities such as lectures, seminars, competitions and other such activities. They also keep the students occupied by playing soccer and acting in plays. Some of the youth however, object by saying that this is neither befitting nor permissible and that this is not the way of the Messenger (*sal-Allaahu 'alayhi wa sallam*). They say that it is compulsory that these classes take place in the *masaajid* and that the mediums of calling to Allaah are *towqeefiyyah* (i.e. to be carried out exactly like how the Messenger of Allaah (*sal-Allaahu 'alayhi wa sallam*) carried them out and that different or new mediums cannot be employed).

Due to this alot of youth are confused and so we would like you to explain this matter in detail; explaining the difference between 'methods' and 'objectives' in order for the issue to become clear, may Allaah reward you with good![1]

---

1 Liqaa.aat al-Baab al-Maftooh - No.767

<u>Response</u>: In the Name of Allaah, *ar-Rahmaan, ar-Raheem*. All praise is due to Allaah, Lord of the worlds and may the *salaah* and *salaam* be upon our Prophet Muhammad, his family, his Companions and all those who follow him to the Day of Judgement.

To Proceed:

There is no doubt that the government, may Allaah grant it success, is to be thanked for initiating these summer centres, because great evils and tribulations are prevented through them. What if this great number of youth started touring the markets, parks and mountains; what kind of evil do you think would take place due to this?

I believe that every intelligent person who is in touch with reality will assume that alot of deviation would occur amongst the youth, and alot of bad manners and immoral thoughts would be picked up by them as well. These camps, and to Allaah belongs all praise, are started to safeguard alot of these youth, and I do not say that it safeguards most of the youth or all the youth, as this is not the case. Alot of good takes place in these centres; including invitations sent out to the people of knowledge to deliver lectures there, which leads to teaching alot of knowledge, delivering beneficial sermons and causing unity between the youth and the scholars; there is no doubt that there are great benefits in this.

Activities within these centres such as entertaining oneself by playing soccer, permissible forms of plays and the like, this is from wisdom; if the soul is always indulged in serious activities it would bore and tire. The Companions of the Messenger of Allaah (*radhi-yAllaahu 'anhum*) said:

"O, Messenger of Allaah, while we are in your company and you mention Heaven and the Hellfire to us, it is as if we can actually see them with our

133

own eyes, but when we return to our families and children we forget."

So the Messenger of Allaah (*sal-Allaahu 'alayhi wa sallam*) said:

"Hour by hour."

Meaning that the person feels like the first case at times and like the second at others.

He (*sal-Allaahu 'alayhi wa sallam*) also said to 'Abdullaah ibn 'Amr ibn al-'Aas (*radhi-yAllaahu 'anhum*) when he said: "I will stay up all night in prayer and will not stop fasting for as long as I live."

He said:

"Did you say this?"

He replied: "Yes, O Messenger of Allaah."

He (*sal-Allaahu 'alayhi wa sallam*) said:

"Indeed your Lord has a right upon you; you have a right upon yourself; your family has a right upon you and your guests have rights upon you; so give every one of them their due rights."

Listen to the story of the people who asked about the deeds that the Messenger of Allaah (*sal-Allaahu 'alayhi wa sallam*) used to perform in private, while at home. They were told of his deeds and it was as if they belittled them, so they said:

"The Messenger (*sal-Allaahu 'alayhi wa sallam*) has been forgiven all his past and future sins. This is not the case with us."

One of them then said: "I will not sleep at night."

What he meant by this is that he would stay up all night in prayers.

Another said: "I will fast continuously and will never stop."

The third said: "I will not eat meat."

The fourth said: "I will not get married."

So when the Prophet (*sal-Allaahu 'alayhi wa sallam*) heard of this he said:

> **"What is the matter with people who say such things? As for me, I fast at times and I don't at others; I pray at night and I sleep as well; I also marry. So whoever does not act upon my Sunnah is not from me."**

Therefore, providing the soul with a due portion of a permissible form of entertainment is without a doubt from the wisest of affairs. Furthermore, soccer, including having the ability to remove boredom, also has physical benefits; it is an activity that strengthens the body. However, it must be regulated with the following conditions:

Firstly: The players must not wear high shorts like the foolish do; indeed this is impermissible. It is not permissible for *Muslim* youth to wear such shorts. If we were to say that thighs are *'awrah* then the ruling is clear, because it is not permissible to expose or to look at the *'awrah*.

If we were to say that the thighs are not *'awrah* then for youth to expose their thighs is a *fitnah* for them as well as an immoral act that must be prevented.

<u>Secondly</u>: It mustn't lead to vulgar language consisting of insults and the likes of such behaviour, for indeed anything that leads to vulgar language, which is far from having good manners, is impermissible.

<u>Thirdly</u>: Procedures that are considered to be bad manners must not be practiced, as some players do if one team wins the other. Players run around hugging each other, climbing over each other's shoulders and the likes of such actions that are contradictory to good mannerisms. Were it not for the fact that these actions came to us from countries that neither have manners nor religion, we would have been the first to denounce them (had they started by us). Even if young immature children, that have not reached the age of ten yet, were to engage in such actions, they should be directed to abandon them.

As for the objection that it is compulsory for lessons to be in the *masaajid*, then this is incorrect. Lessons can be given in the *masaajid*, in schools, colleges, homes and in other places.

I say to the brother who has come with this objection: a person must have a wide ranging sense of perception and awareness, and must place things in their perspective places. One should not be superficial, watching from above the rooftops. Rather he should be perceptive and think deeply about issues, examining the benefits and harms that are resultant of such issues. The broad, comprehensive, great principle of the *Islaam*-ic legislation is to 'achieve the benefits and repel the harms'. Indeed it (Islaam) brought the benefits and repelled the harms. No one doubts that if we ordered these summer camps to carry out all their activities in the *masaajid*, people would not be able to bear this; not even the common folk.

Therefore we say: these camps have been establishments of knowledge for a long period of time without any objections from the part of the

Muslims; they study in them as well as publish books there. All of this was unknown at the time of the Messenger of Allaah (*sal-Allaahu 'alayhi wa sallam*). The only evidence they can use as a proof for a connection between the two is the issue of the people of as-Safah. But did the Messenger (*sal-Allaahu 'alayhi wa sallam*) prohibit this? No he did not. Schools are now places for knowledge. The Book of Allaah, the *Sunnah* of the Messenger (*sal-Allaahu 'alayhi wa sallam*), the sayings of the scholars and the disciplines that are a means of gaining knowledge such as grammar and so on, are taught there.

So we say to the brother who has objected to this affair; know that the religion is broader than what you think. It attains the benefits wherever they may be, so long as they don't include harms that are equal to or greater than the benefits themselves; in this case they are prohibited.

As for his claim that the mediums of calling to Allaah are '*towqeefiyyah*'; the word 'medium' in itself indicates that they are not '*towqeefiyyah*', as long as they remain mediums. We are to employ them as long as they are not prohibited within themselves, because mediums take on the same ruling as the objectives. Do we not use microphones to call the people to Allaah? Was this medium present at the time of the Messenger (*sal-Allaahu 'alayhi wa sallam*)? Do we not read books and wear glasses in order to clarify text or enlarge it? These are mediums that are used to read books and gain knowledge. Were they present at the time of the Messenger (*sal-Allaahu 'alayhi wa sallam*)? Do we not place a miniature speaker in the ears of the hearing-impaired in order for them to hear the good that is being said? The answer is; of course we do. Were these things present at the time of the Messenger (*sal-Allaahu 'alayhi wa sallam*)?

As long as we acknowledge that they are mediums (they are permissible). Yes, if it is a prohibited medium within itself, it is prohibited to use it. If one was to say for example; these people will not even come close to you unless you play musical instruments that they can dance to; we say that we cannot use this medium in calling to Allaah because it is prohibited within itself. Therefore mediums are permissible depending on what they are mediums to, as long as they are not *Islaami*cally prohibited within themselves. If so, then indeed they are to be banned.

I myself approve of these summer camps; I consider them to be amongst the good works of the government and I encourage everyone responsible for children to enrol them in these centres.

However, there is an issue that we must be wary of; it is that young children should not intermingle with youth or adults because of what this consists of in terms of *fitnah*, which is to be avoided. It is also imperative for those responsible for these centres to be trustworthy people who possess knowledge, piety and are well-mannered, according to each individuals' ability, for indeed perfection is for Allaah alone.

It is due to this foundation that when the scholars spoke about the issue of appointing judges, saying that it is obligatory for a judge to be trustworthy; they mentioned that if there is no one trustworthy enough to be appointed as a judge, then the best of the sinners and the closest of them to trustworthiness is to be appointed, because Allaah (*Subhaanahu wa Ta'aala*) says:

$$\text{فَٱتَّقُوا۟ ٱللَّهَ مَا ٱسْتَطَعْتُمْ}$$

So keep your duty to Allaah and fear Him as much as possibly you can.[2]

---

2 The Noble *Qur.aan* - *Soorah* at-Taghaabun, *Aayah* 16

Furthermore, it is upon those responsible, such as parents, brothers and so on, to gather information regarding a camp before enrolling their children in it. They should look, for example, at the appearance of its students in relation to piety, and at the individuals who take the students out for trips and so on, in order to safeguard their children.

We ask Allaah to grant everyone success, and I repeat, especially for the students of knowledge, their intellect must be extensive and their assessment deep. They shouldn't judge affairs according to their outward appearance, and should think about the objectives of the *Islaam*ic legislation and what it aims to accomplish in terms of benefiting the creation. They should not ban something that is beneficial or something that repels a greater evil, except if there is a prohibition in the legislation in regards to it. Whenever there is such a prohibition, then we know that there is no benefit in what has been prohibited and that its harms are greater than its benefits.

Shaykh Muhammad ibn Saalih al-'Uthaymeen

2. Differing in the Mediums of Da'wah

Question: From amongst the issues that the callers to Allaah (*Subhaanahu wa Ta'aala*) have differed in, is the issue of the mediums of calling to Allaah. Some of them say that they are forms of worship that are *towqeefiyyah* (to be carried out exactly like the Messenger of Allaah (*sal-Allaahu 'alayhi wa sallam*) carried them out and that one cannot introduce new methods), and they therefore rebuke those who carry out different types of educational and physical activities or plays that are used as mediums to attract youth and call them to Allaah. Others hold the opinion that mediums are renewed by changing times, and that it is permissible for callers to use every permissible medium to call people to Allaah (*Subhaanahu wa Ta'aala*). We would like you to clarify the correct opinion in this matter.[3]

<u>Response</u>: All praise is due to Allaah, Lord of the worlds. There is no doubt that calling to Allaah is a form of worship as Allaah ordered in His saying:

$$ادْعُ إِلَىٰ سَبِيلِ رَبِّكَ بِالْحِكْمَةِ وَالْمَوْعِظَةِ الْحَسَنَةِ وَجَٰدِلْهُم بِالَّتِي هِيَ أَحْسَنُ$$

Call (mankind, O Muhammad) to the way of your Lord (i.e. Islaam) with wisdom (i.e. with the Divine Revelation and the Qur.aan), fair preaching and debate with them in a manner that is best.[4]

The person who is calling to Allaah should keep in mind that he is acting upon the Order of Allaah (*Subhaanahu wa Ta'aala*) and that he is drawing closer to Allaah by doing so. There is no doubt that the best method to call with, is with the Book of Allaah and the *Sunnah* of His Messenger (*sal-Allaahu 'alayhi wa sallam*). For indeed the Book of Allaah (*Subhaanahu wa Ta'aala*) is the greatest way of preaching to people:

$$يَٰٓأَيُّهَا النَّاسُ قَدْ جَآءَتْكُم مَّوْعِظَةٌ مِّن رَّبِّكُمْ وَشِفَآءٌ لِّمَا فِي الصُّدُورِ وَهُدًى وَرَحْمَةٌ لِّلْمُؤْمِنِينَ$$

O mankind! There has come to you good advice from your Lord (i.e. the Qur.aan, enjoining all that is good and forbidding all that is evil), and a healing for that (disease of ignorance, doubt, hy-

---

3 Kitaab ad-Da'wah - Volume 2, Page 167

4 The Noble *Qur.aan* - *Soorah* an-Nahl, *Aayah* 125

pocrisy and differences) which is in your breasts, – a guidance and a mercy (explaining lawful and unlawful things) for the believers.[5]

Likewise the Messenger of Allaah (*sal-Allaahu 'alayhi wa sallam*) spoke with the most eloquent of speech when preaching. He sometimes delivered sermons to his companions in a manner which they described as being one that: 'Filled the eyes with tears and the hearts with fear.'

Therefore this is the best medium for those who are able to employ it in their sermons; meaning the Book of Allaah and the *Sunnah* of His Messenger (*sal-Allaahu 'alayhi wa sallam*). There is nothing wrong in adding other permissible mediums if one sees the need to do so, with the condition that they do not consist of anything impermissible, such as lying, acting out the roles of non-*Muslims*, the Companions (*radhiyAllaahu 'anhum*) or honourable *Imaams* in plays.

Amongst the conditions, is that the play should not include males imitating females or vice versa, because this will institute the curse of the Messenger of Allaah (*sal-Allaahu 'alayhi wa sallam*) upon the performer; for indeed he cursed men who imitate women and women who imitate men.

The point is that if one uses these mediums occasionally, in order to bring people together, then I do not see anything wrong with it as long as they do not consist of something forbidden.

However using these mediums excessively and rendering them as the official method in calling to Allaah while refraining from using the Book

---

5 The Noble *Qur.aan - Soorah* Yunus, *Aayah* 58

of Allaah and the *Sunnah* of His Messenger (*sal-Allaahu 'alayhi wa sal-lam*), in a manner that would lead people to being impassive to everything except such mediums; then I do not approve of this. Rather I believe this to be prohibited, because advising and directing people to other than the Book and the *Sunnah* when calling to Allaah is an abominable act.

However I do not see a problem with using them occasionally as long as they do not contain something impermissible.

Shaykh Muhammad ibn Saalih al-'Uthaymeen

3. The Minbar and the Masjid

Question: The *minbar* and the *masjid* are two issues in *Islaam* that alot of people have written about. Some say that people have drifted away from using the *minbar* as a means to call to Allaah. Others say that they have been prohibited from the most precious and purest places on earth; the Houses of Allaah, because they are unable to sit in them to study or be taught. Others say that the *minbar* is being used for purposes other than calling to Allaah; it is used to call to certain dates or groups and so on.[6]

Response: There is no doubt that the *masjid* and the *minbar* are two historical tools that have been used for providing guidance to the *Muslims* in specific and to all people in general; teaching them beneficial matters and conveying the Message of their Lord (*Subhaanahu wa Ta'aala*) to them. Indeed Allaah sent the messengers, may peace be upon all of them, in order to convey the Message of their Lord to the

---

6 Majmoo' Fataawa wa Maqaalaat Mutanawwi'ah - Volume 5, Page 80

people and teach them the Legislation of Allaah. This is what Allaah sent all the messengers to do, beginning with Aadam to Nooh, and those who came after him. All of them were sent to convey the Message of Allaah through the *masjid* and *minbar*, whether the *minbar* was inside the *masjid* or other places, and whether the *minbar* was built or not. A camel can be used as a *minbar*, as well as a horse or other mountable animals. A *minbar* may be an elevated place in which the message can be conveyed from.

The point is that Allaah (*Subhaanahu wa Ta'aala*) legislated for His slaves to convey the Message of their Lord and teach the people the religion He sent His Messengers with by any possible means. However the *masjid* and the *minbar* are the most important tools in conveying this message and spreading the *da'wah*. A great deal of attention must be paid by the scholars as well as teachers to this great message, and it must be restored to its original state. It is compulsory upon them to teach the people the affairs of their religion using the *masjid*, because it is a gathering place for the *Muslims* during *jumu'ah* and other occasions. It is also compulsory upon them to convey the issues that Allaah obligated upon the people in both their worldly and religious affairs, using other methods as well; such as the radio, television, newspapers, giving sermons in gatherings and suitable occasions, authoring books and using every possible method in which the Legislation and Message of Allaah (*Subhaanahu wa Ta'aala*) can be conveyed.

This is what the people of knowledge and *eemaan*, the followers and successors of the messengers must carry out. They must convey the Message of Allaah and teach the people His Legislation in order for the elderly as well as the young, male, as well as female, those in agreement, as well as those in opposition, gain understanding of their religion, so that the evidences are established and all excuses are cut off.

It is not permissible for the leaders or anyone else to stand between the people and the *minbar* except if they have knowledge that a particular individual is using it to call to falsehood or is not qualified to call to Allaah. These are to be barred wherever they may be.

As for those who call to the truth and guidance while being qualified to do so, it is imperative to encourage and aid them upon this task of theirs. The methods which they use to convey the Legislation of Allaah should also be facilitated for them as Allaah (*Subhaanahu wa Ta'aala*) said:

وَتَعَاوَنُوا۟ عَلَى ٱلْبِرِّ وَٱلتَّقْوَىٰ وَلَا تَعَاوَنُوا۟ عَلَى ٱلْإِثْمِ وَٱلْعُدْوَٰنِ

Help one another upon al-Birr and at-Taqwaa (virtue, righteousness and piety); but do not help one another in sin and transgression.[7]

He (*Subhaanahu wa Ta'aala*) also said:

وَٱلْعَصْرِ ۝ إِنَّ ٱلْإِنسَٰنَ لَفِى خُسْرٍ ۝ إِلَّا ٱلَّذِينَ ءَامَنُوا۟ وَعَمِلُوا۟ ٱلصَّٰلِحَٰتِ وَتَوَاصَوْا۟ بِٱلْحَقِّ وَتَوَاصَوْا۟ بِٱلصَّبْرِ ۝

By al-'Asr (the time). Indeed, man is in loss, except those who believe (in Islaamic Monotheism), do righteous good deeds and recommend one another to the truth.[8]

The Messenger of Allaah (*sal-Allaahu 'alayhi wa sallam*) said:

"The religion is Naseehah (sincere advice)."

---

7 The Noble *Qur.aan* - *Soorah* al-Maa.idah, *Aayah* 2

8 The Noble *Qur.aan* - *Soorah* al-'Asr

144

It was said: "To whom O, Messenger of Allaah?"

He said:

> **"To Allaah, His Book, His Messenger and the rulers**
> **of the Muslims as well as the common folk."**

There are many verses in the Book of Allaah and *ahaadeeth* in the *Sunnah* of His Messenger indicating this meaning.

It is upon all the people of knowledge everywhere, those who uphold the Book of Allaah and the *Sunnah* to carry out the task of calling to Allaah; teaching, enjoining good and forbidding evil according to their individual abilities due to the saying of Allaah (*Subhaanahu wa Ta'aala*):

$$\text{فَٱتَّقُواْ ٱللَّهَ مَا ٱسْتَطَعْتُمْ}$$

> **So keep your duty to Allaah and fear Him as much**
> **as you possibly can.**[9]

It is upon them to convey the Message of Allaah wherever they are; at home, in the *masjid*, along pathways, in a car, plane, train, and in every place. There is no specified place for conveying the *da'wah*, rather it is required to be carried out everywhere according to each individual's ability due to the saying of Allaah (*Subhaanahu wa Ta'aala*):

$$\text{فَهَلْ عَلَى ٱلرُّسُلِ إِلَّا ٱلْبَلَٰغُ ٱلْمُبِينُ}$$

> **Are the Messengers then charged with anything**
> **but to clearly convey the Message?**[10]

---

9 The Noble *Qur.aan - Soorah* at-Taghaabun, *Aayah* 16

10 The Noble *Qur.aan - Soorah* an-Nahl, *Aayah* 35

His (*Subhaanahu wa Ta'aala*) saying as well:

$$يَٰٓأَيُّهَا ٱلرَّسُولُ بَلِّغۡ مَآ أُنزِلَ إِلَيۡكَ مِن رَّبِّكَ$$

*O Messenger (Muhammad)! Convey (the Message)
which has been sent down to you from your Lord.*[11]

The saying of the Messenger of Allaah (*sal-Allaahu 'alayhi wa sallam*):

*"Convey my affair to the people, even if it were but
a single verse."*

His (*sal-Allaahu 'alayhi wa sallam*) saying as well:

*"May Allaah grant prosperity to one who hears a
saying of mine, memorises it and then reports it
just as he heard. It may be that the one whom it is
reported to has a greater understanding than the
one who initially heard it."*

When he (*sal-Allaahu 'alayhi wa sallam*) gave sermons he used to
say:

*"Those of you who are present are to convey to
those who are absent."*

When he delivered the *khutbah* in 'Arafaat during *hajjatul wadaa'* to the
greatest of gatherings, he said to them at the end, while on his camel:

*"Those who are present are to convey to those who
are absent, for it may be that the one whom the*

---

11 The Noble *Qur.aan* - *Soorah* al-Maa.idah, *Aayah* 67

message is conveyed to has a greater understanding than the one who initially hears it."

He also said:

"You will be questioned about me, so what will you say?"

They said:

"We bear witness that you conveyed [the message], carried out [your duty] and sincerely advised [us]."

So he raised his finger to the sky and then pointed towards the people saying:

"O, Allaah! Bear witness, O, Allaah! Bear witness."

When he sent 'Alee (*radhi-yAllaahu 'anhu*) to Khaybar to call the Jews to *Islaam* and battle them if they did not accept the *da'wah*; he (*sal-Allaahu 'alayhi wa sallam*) said to him:

"Call them to Islaam and inform them of what has been obligated upon them in relation to the Rights of Allaah. For by Allaah, if Allaah guides a single person through you, this is better for you than the best of camels."

There is a *hadeeth* narrated by Sahl ibn Sa'd al-Ansaaree (*radhi-yAllaahu 'anhu*) that was authentically reported by both al-Bukhaaree and *Muslim*. Also, in Saheeh Muslim, a *hadeeth* narrated by Abu Mas'ood al-Ansaaree (*radhi-yAllaahu 'anhu*) that the Messenger of Allaah (*sal-Allaahu 'alayhi wa sallam*) said:

"Whoever directs someone to a good deed is rewarded with an equal reward to the one who practices it."

There are alot of verses in the *Qur.aan* as well as alot of *ahaadeeth* concerning calling to Allaah, directing and enjoining the people with good and forbidding them from evil.

So it is upon all the people of knowledge and *eemaan*, amongst the rulers as well as others, in *Muslim* as well as non-*Muslim* countries, to convey the Message of Allaah and teach the people their religion. They are to practice wisdom and gentleness while doing so, as well as use the appropriate methods which encourage people to accept the truth and do not chase them away from it, as Allaah (*Subhaanahu wa Ta'aala*) said:

ٱدۡعُ إِلَىٰ سَبِيلِ رَبِّكَ بِٱلۡحِكۡمَةِ
وَٱلۡمَوۡعِظَةِ ٱلۡحَسَنَةِ وَجَٰدِلۡهُم بِٱلَّتِي هِيَ أَحۡسَنُ

Invite (mankind, O Muhammad to the way of your Lord (i.e. Islaam) with wisdom (i.e. with the Divine Revelation and the Qur.aan), fair preaching and debate with them in a manner that is best. [12]

He (*Subhaanahu wa Ta'aala*) also said:

وَلَا تُجَٰدِلُوٓاْ أَهۡلَ ٱلۡكِتَٰبِ إِلَّا بِٱلَّتِي هِيَ أَحۡسَنُ إِلَّا
ٱلَّذِينَ ظَلَمُواْ مِنۡهُمۡ

And do not debate with the people of the book except in a manner that is best except with those of them who do wrong... [13]

---

12 The Noble *Qur.aan* - *Soorah* an-Nahl, *Aayah* 125

13 The Noble *Qur.aan* - *Soorah* al-'Ankaboot, *Aayah* 46

He (*Subhaanahu wa Ta'aala*) said as well:

وَمَنْ أَحْسَنُ قَوْلًا مِّمَّن دَعَا إِلَى ٱللَّهِ وَعَمِلَ صَلِحًا وَقَالَ
إِنَّنِى مِنَ ٱلْمُسْلِمِينَ

And who is better in speech than one who [says:
"My Lord is Allaah (believes in His Oneness)," and
then stands firm (acts upon His Order), calls to
Allaah's (Islaamic Monotheism), does righteous
deeds and says: "I am one of the Muslims."[14]

He (*Subhaanahu wa Ta'aala*) said while commanding His Messenger
(*sal-Allaahu 'alayhi wa sallam*):

فَبِمَا رَحْمَةٍ مِّنَ
ٱللَّهِ لِنتَ لَهُمْ وَلَوْ كُنتَ فَظًّا غَلِيظَ ٱلْقَلْبِ لَٱنفَضُّوا مِنْ حَوْلِكَ

And by the Mercy of Allaah, you (Muhammad) dealt
with them gently. And had you been severe and
harsh-hearted, they would have dispersed from
around you, so pardon them, and ask (Allaah's)
forgiveness for them...[15]

Allaah (*Subhaanahu wa Ta'aala*) said when He sent Moosaa and Haaroon to Pharoah:

فَقُولَا لَهُ قَوْلًا لَّيِّنًا لَّعَلَّهُ يَتَذَكَّرُ أَوْ يَخْشَىٰ

And speak to him mildly, perhaps he may accept
admonition or fear Allaah.[16]

---

14 The Noble *Qur.aan* - *Soorah* Fussilat, *Aayah* 33

15 The Noble *Qur.aan* - *Soorah* Aal-'Imraan, *Aayah* 159

16 The Noble *Qur.aan* - *Soorah* Taha, *Aayah* 44

In an authentic *hadeeth*, the Messenger of Allaah (*sal-Allaahu 'alayhi wa sallam*) said:

> *"Indeed gentleness is not practiced in any affair except that it beautifies it, and it is not removed from any affair except that it spoils it."*

He (*sal-Allaahu 'alayhi wa sallam*) also said:

> *"Whoever is deprived of gentleness is deprived of everything that is good."*

There are plenty of verses in the *Qur.aan* and *ahaadeeth* of this like.

So it is obligatory upon all *Muslim*s to understand their religion and ask the people of knowledge about issues that are confusing to them due to the saying of the Messenger of Allaah (*sal-Allaahu 'alayhi wa sallam*):

> *"Allaah grants understanding in the religion to those whom He wishes good for."*

It is upon the people of knowledge to teach and make people understand their religion, as well as convey the knowledge that Allaah has granted them. They should compete in carrying this affair out with honesty, trustworthiness and patience until they convey the Religion of Allaah to His servants and until they teach the people what Allaah obligated upon them and what He forbade them from.

This should be done through the *masaajid*, circles of knowledge within the *masaajid* or elsewhere, and during the *jumu'ah* or *'Eed khutbah* as well as other occasions.

Not everyone has the ability to study in schools, universities and colleges, and not everyone is able to find a school that would teach him the Religion of Allaah; His Purified Legislation, the Noble *Qur.aan* as it was sent down and the purified *Sunnah* as it was transmitted by the Messenger (*sal-Allaahu 'alayhi wa sallam*).

It is also compulsory upon the people of knowledge and *eemaan* to convey the *da'wah* to the people by using the *minbar*s of the radio, television, newspapers, the *jumu'ah* and the *'Eed*. It is upon them to do so in everyplace, with lessons in circles of knowledge, whether in the *masaajid* or elsewhere.

It is upon every student of knowledge whom Allaah blessed with the understanding of the religion, and every scholar whom Allaah blessed with insight, to take advantage of the knowledge that Allaah has given them. They must take advantage of every opportunity to call to Allaah; in order to convey the Message of Allaah, teach the people the *Islaam*ic Legislation, order them to do good and forbid them from evil. They must explain to the people issues that may be hidden from them concerning what Allaah has obligated upon them or forbidden them from.

This is obligatory upon all the people of knowledge, who are the successors of the messengers and the inheritors of the prophets. It is upon them to convey the Message of Allaah and teach His Legislation to His servants. It is upon them to sincerely advise to Allaah, His Book, His Messenger, the rulers of the people and the common folk, and practice patience while carrying this out. It is upon all the rulers to assist, encourage and provide them with everything that would facilitate this task because Allaah (*Subhaanahu wa Ta'aala*) says:

وَتَعَاوَنُواْ عَلَى ٱلْبِرِّ وَٱلتَّقْوَىٰ وَلَا تَعَاوَنُواْ عَلَى ٱلْإِثْمِ وَٱلْعُدْوَٰنِ

Help one another upon al-Birr and at-Taqwaa

(virtue, righteousness and piety)...[17]

The Messenger of Allaah (*sal-Allaahu 'alayhi wa sallam*) said:

"Allaah is in the aid of whoever aids his brother."

He (*sal-Allaahu 'alayhi wa sallam*) also says:

"Allaah is in the aid of a servant as long as the servant aids his brother."

I ask Allaah (*Subhaanahu wa Ta'aala*) to grant us, all our *Muslims* brothers, the scholars in specific and the students of knowledge in general, success, guidance and assist us upon conveying the truth. Indeed He is All-Generous, All-Bountiful, and may the *salaah* and *salaam* be upon our Prophet Muhammad, his family and his Companions.

Shaykh 'Abdul-'Azeez ibn Baaz

4. The Role of Islaamic Record Companies

Question: You are aware of the great efforts that *Islaamic* record companies exert in directing and advising people. Some evil people have tarnished their reputations accusing them of being materialistic amongst other things; we would like your eminence to clarify this issue so that the reality is not misunderstood by those who have no insight.[18]

Response: There is no doubt that recording beneficial lectures and ser-

---

17 The Noble *Qur.aan* - *Soorah* al-Maa.idah, *Aayah* 2

18 Majmoo' Fataawa wa Maqaalaat *Mutana*wwi'ah - 5/77

152

mons is beneficial for *Muslims*, and whoever carries this out in order to benefit the *ummah* shall be rewarded. It is upon them to anticipate this reward and be patient no matter what they are accused of, taking the example of the Messenger and other exemplary people before him.

There is nothing wrong with selling tapes containing the aforementioned issues while trying to maintain low prices that are not burdensome for people; by doing so the vendor can support his business and benefit others through his work by spreading knowledge and broadening the benefit.

I also advise people to obtain good and beneficial tapes. I advise them to buy and benefit from them only if they are appropriate; because not all tapes are appropriate and not every speaker has something beneficial to say that is worthy of being recorded.

It is imperative for students of knowledge to select tapes by reputed people of knowledge who are known for analysing issues so that they may benefit from them along with their families, brothers and colleagues. It is also upon the students of knowledge to beware of recording that which harms them and is of no benefit to them.

Shaykh 'Abdul-'Azeez ibn Baaz

5. Is the Masjid the Only Place for Da'wah?

Question: Some people hold the opinion that calling to Allaah can only be carried out in a *masjid*. What is your opinion, and what available mediums and opportunities can a caller to the Religion of Allaah take advantage of?[19]

---

19 Majmoo' Fataawa wa Maqaalaat Mutanawwi'ah - Volume 5, Page 264

Response: Giving *da'wah* is not specific to only the *masjid*; there are other mediums that can be employed in order to call to Allaah. There is no doubt that *masaajid* are a means for giving *da'wah*; such as through the *jumu'ah khutbah*, sermons after the congregational prayers and in circles of knowledge which are the foundation with which knowledge and religion is propagated.

But the *masjid* is not the only place where *da'wah* can be carried out. The caller to Allaah can give *da'wah* in other places as well, such as during gatherings and special occasions; a believer should take advantage of such situations and call to the Religion of Allaah. The media can also be employed in order to perform *da'wah*, as well as authoring books; all of these are mediums of giving *da'wah*. A wise person takes advantage of every time and place to call to Allaah. If he finds that Allaah has brought him together with others at any time or place and he finds an opportunity to give *da'wah*, he calls to the Religion of Allaah with *hikmah*, kind words and an excellent manner.

Shaykh 'Abdul-'Azeez ibn Baaz

Chapter 6
The Caller

1. The Obligations upon the Caller

Question: We want to encourage the callers and students of knowledge to establish classes and lectures all around the country. We noticed that there are areas void of any activity due to the presence of few callers, laziness from the part of the students of knowledge or due to them refraining from giving lessons and lectures. This in turn causes the propagation of ignorance of the *Sunnah* as well as the propagation of *shirk* and innovations.[1]

Response: It is imperative for the scholars, wherever they may be, to propagate the truth, spread the *Sunnah* and teach the people. They should not abstain from carrying out this task; rather it is compulsory for them to propagate the truth by giving lessons in the *masaajid* around them, even if they were not the appointed *Imaams* of those particular *masaajid*. It is upon every one to pay particular attention to the *jumu'ah khutbah* and seek to solve people's needs.

---

1 Majalatul-Buhooth al-Islaamiyyah - Volume 36, Page 127

It is upon those responsible for seminars and lectures to likewise search for what people are in need of and explain to them the religious issues that may be unknown to them. They should also explain the issues that are binding upon them; in relation to the rights of their brothers, including neighbours, issues pertaining to ordering them with good, forbidding them from evil and calling them to Allaah. They must teach the ignorant with gentleness and wisdom. If the scholars remain silent and do not direct and advise the people, the ignorant will speak, misguide the people and be misguided themselves. In an authentic *hadeeth*, the Prophet of Allaah (*sal-Allaahu 'alayhi wa sallam*) said:

> *"Allaah does not take knowledge away by removing it from the chests of men; rather He takes it away through the death of the scholars. When no more scholars remain, people will take the ignorant as leaders; when they are questioned they would respond without knowledge and in turn misguide people as well as be misguided."*

We ask Allaah for safety from all evil, for us as well as all our *Muslim* brothers.

Due to this, it becomes clear that it is obligatory upon the people of knowledge, wherever they may be; whether in villages, towns or cities, within this country or elsewhere, to teach the people and direct them to the sayings of Allaah (*Subhaanahu wa Ta'aala*) and His Messenger (*sal-Allaahu 'alayhi wa sallam*). It is imperative for them to return to the Book of Allaah, the *Sunnah*, and the sayings of the people of knowledge regarding problematic issues.

A scholar continues to learn and gain knowledge until he dies; he studies in order to learn issues that are unclear to him. He must return to the sayings of the people of knowledge that are supported by evidence, in order to give religious verdicts to the people, teach and call them to Allaah upon insight.

A person is in need of gaining knowledge until he dies, even if he were from the Companions (*radhi-yAllaahu 'anhum*). Everybody is in need of seeking knowledge and gaining understanding of the religion; in order to learn and then teach. They should read the Noble *Qur.aan* and ponder over its meanings; read authentic *ahaadeeth* with their explanations; and read the sayings of the people of knowledge in order to benefit and have the issues that are problematic to them clarified. Furthermore, they should teach the people the knowledge that Allaah has taught them, whether in their homes, in a school, college, university, in the *masaajid* around them, in a car, plane, in every time and place; even at the graveyard, if one attends a burial and people are still waiting, he should remind them of Allaah, as the Messenger (*sal-Allaahu 'alayhi wa sallam*) used to.

The point is that the scholar should take advantage of every opportunity in all suitable places and all suitable gatherings. He should not let an opportunity pass by, rather he should take advantage of it; remind and teach the people with kind words and a fine manner, while being upon certainty and being wary of saying things about Allaah without knowledge.

Shaykh 'Abdul-'Azeez ibn Baaz

2. Calling to Allaah Alone

Question: Is it necessary for every *Salafee* to call to *Salafiyyah* within a *Salafee* group, or can one call to Allaah by himself without being attached to a *Salafee* group?[2]

Response: Our Lord says:

وَكُونُواْ مَعَ ٱلصَّـٰدِقِينَ

...and be with those who are truthful (in speech and deeds).[3]

The Messenger of Allaah (*sal-Allaahu 'alayhi wa sallam*) said:

"Allaah's Hand is upon the Jamaa'ah."

He (*sal-Allaahu 'alayhi wa sallam*) also said:

"It is upon you to be with the Jamaa'ah, for indeed the wolf only devours the stray sheep."

We know through experience as well as by understanding the legislated texts, that whoever claims to be *Salafee* in his *'aqeedah* but does not want to affiliate himself with a group, wanting to call by himself as stated in the question, that the outcome would be that he will be alone in calling to Allaah; this is because if Allaah said to Moosaa, may peace be upon him, as has been related in the *Qur.aan*:

سَنَشُدُّ عَضُدَكَ بِأَخِيكَ

"We will strengthen you through your brother..."[4]

---

2   al-Haawee min Fataawa *Shaykh* al-Albaanee - Page 486

3   The Noble *Qur.aan* - *Soorah* at-Towbah, *Aayah* 119

4   The Noble *Qur.aan* - *Soorah* al-Qasas, *Aayah* 35

So this is a man whom Allaah has spoken to and chosen to convey His Message, so how about a single *Muslim*? Isn't he in need of being strengthened by his brothers? No doubt the answer is yes.

Due to this it is incumbent upon the *Salafee* to join the *Jamaa'ah* in his country so long as his call is the same as theirs, because there is strength in this as the aforementioned verse indicates. If he persists in distancing himself from the *Jamaa'ah* then there is no doubt that the wolves will devour him as the previous *hadeeth* confirms. Meaning that the other groups will adopt and pull him towards them; due to this he would deviate from the path whether realising this or not.

In conclusion, I say that Allaah says:

$$وَكُونُوا۟ مَعَ ٱلصَّـٰدِقِينَ$$

...and be with those who are truthful (in words and deeds)[5]

There is no doubt that whoever wants to be by himself in his call is in clear loss.

Shaykh Muhammad Naasiruddeen al-Albaanee

3. Calling to a Deed You Are Unable to Practice

Question: If a *daa'iyah* is calling to something that he himself is unable to practice after struggling to do so, believing that others may be able to practice that certain deed; should he call them to it?[6]

---

5 The Noble *Qur.aan* - *Soorah* at-Towbah, *Aayah* 119

6 Kitaab ad-Da'wah - Volume 2, Page 171

Response: This caller, who is calling to a good deed, should call others to it even if he is unable to practice that certain deed himself. For example; a man advises people to perform the night prayer, but he himself is unable to get up and pray it. We shouldn't say to him that if you are unable to establish the night prayer then don't advise others to practice it.

Another person may call people to spend in charity while he himself is unable to and may not own anything to give in charity; we tell to him to call to it.

However if he is calling to something that he is able to practice and yet does not, then there is no doubt that this is foolishness as well as misguidance in the religion.

Shaykh Muhammad ibn Saalih al-'Uthaymeen

4. Co-operation between the Du'aat

Question: There is no doubt that co-operation between the callers to Allaah is vital for their success and for their call to be accepted. The question is:

There are alot of *Muslim* callers, each of them has his own method in calling to Allaah, and they may differ in important issues such as *'aqeedah*. What are the regulations that you deem fit for working and co-operating with these callers? The *da'wah* is in need of your advice in this issue, may Allaah grant you success.[7]

Response: No doubt that the ruling concerning this sort of differing is to

---

7 Kitaab ad-Da'wah - Volume 2, Page 160

return to what Allaah (*Subhaanahu wa Ta'aala*) has instructed in His saying:

يَتَأَيُّهَا ٱلَّذِينَ ءَامَنُوٓا۟ أَطِيعُوا۟ ٱللَّهَ وَأَطِيعُوا۟ ٱلرَّسُولَ وَأُو۟لِى ٱلْأَمْرِ مِنكُمْ فَإِن تَنَٰزَعْتُمْ فِى شَىْءٍ فَرُدُّوهُ إِلَى ٱللَّهِ وَٱلرَّسُولِ إِن كُنتُمْ تُؤْمِنُونَ بِٱللَّهِ وَٱلْيَوْمِ ٱلْءَاخِرِ ذَٰلِكَ خَيْرٌ وَأَحْسَنُ تَأْوِيلًا

O you who believe! Obey Allaah and obey the Messenger (Muhammad), and those of you who are have authority. (And) if you differ in anything amongst yourselves, then refer it to Allaah and His Messenger, if you believe in Allaah and in the Last Day. That is better and more suitable for final determination. [8]

His (*Subhaanahu wa Ta'aala*) saying as well:

وَمَا ٱخْتَلَفْتُمْ فِيهِ مِن شَىْءٍ فَحُكْمُهُۥٓ إِلَى ٱللَّهِ

And whatsoever you differ in, the decision thereof is with Allaah (He is the ruling Judge). [9]

So it is compulsory to clarify and explain the truth to those who contradict it, whether this contradiction is related to 'aqeedah, to actions, or knowledge. If they accept and return to the truth, this is from the blessings of Allaah upon them, but if they don't return to the truth, then this is an affliction from Allaah (*Subhaanahu wa Ta'aala*) upon them. Furthermore it is upon us to clarify the error that they fell into and warn

---

8 The Noble *Qur.aan* - *Soorah* an-Nisaa, *Aayah* 59

9 The Noble *Qur.aan* - *Soorah* ash-Shooraa, *Aayah* 10

against it according to each individual's ability. Along with this we should not give up on them, for indeed Allaah (*Subhaanahu wa Ta'aala*) has allowed people who were upon immense innovations to return to the truth and become from *Ahlus-Sunnah*.

Alot of us know the story of Abul-Hassan al-Ash'aree, may Allaah have mercy upon him. He was with the *Mu'tazilah* sect for forty years; he then straightened out a bit for a while, afterwards Allaah (*Subhaanahu wa Ta'aala*) guided him to the Straight Path, to the methodology of *Imaam* Ahmad ibn Hanbal, may Allaah have mercy upon him, which is the methodology of *Ahlus-Sunnah*.

In conclusion, the affairs of *'aqeedah* are extremely important and it is essential that we advise each other in issues relating to it, just as it is essential that we advise each other in issues related to actions.

The amount of differing between the people of knowledge in issues that relate to actions is greater than the differing between them in the issues relating to *'aqeedah*.

In general there has been no differing in *'aqeedah*, even though there were some minor differences concerning it such as the issue of whether the Hellfire will cease to exist or not; the punishment of the grave; the scales on the Day of Judgement and what will be weighed on those scales, and other issues. But if we compare these differences to the differing that took place in issues that relate to actions, then, we find that it is minimal and all praise is due to Allaah. However, it is imperative that we advise and clarify the truth to those who differ with us in the issues that relate to *'aqeedah* as well as actions.

Shaykh Muhammad ibn Saalih al-'Uthaymeen

5. The Successful Caller

Question: What should a successful caller be like, and what are the characteristics that should be present in a caller in order for him to have a greater effect upon those he is calling?[10]

Response: A successful caller is one who pays a great deal of attention to evidence; one who is patient during the harms that afflict him; one who exerts all his efforts in calling to the Religion of Allaah, no matter how great the diverse temptations become, and no matter how tired he gets. He must not weaken when afflicted by harm or upon hearing displeasing comments, rather he must be patient and exert all his efforts in calling to the Religion of Allaah, using all possible mediums while paying a great deal of attention to the evidences, as well as using the finest manner so that his call is built upon the firm foundation that Allaah, His Messenger and the believers are pleased with.

He must beware of being lenient in order to avoid saying something about the Religion of Allaah that he has no knowledge of; thus he must pay a great deal of attention to legislated evidences. He must be patient upon hardship while calling to the Religion of Allaah through the media or by teaching. This is the successful caller who deserves praise and elevated levels with Allaah - if he is sincere to Allaah in that.

Shaykh 'Abdul-'Azeez ibn Baaz

6. Prohibiting the Callers to Falsehood from Calling

Question: Alot of brothers would agree that it is the people upon false-

---

10 Majmoo' Fataawa wa Maqaalaat Mutanawwi'ah - Volume 5, Page 267

hood who are to be disallowed from calling to Allaah, not the callers to the truth; they are not to be prohibited from calling to the Religion of Allaah in order for them to benefit people.[11]

Response: There is no doubt that it is compulsory to disallow the callers to falsehood from calling. They are the ones who contend with the people of virtue and knowledge, which may lead the latter being prohibited from calling in *masaajid* because of the callers to falsehood.

If callers to falsehood are disallowed from giving *da'wah*, the correct path would be made clear and there would be ample opportunity to call to the truth. So it is compulsory for the rulers to disallow the people of falsehood from spreading their falsehood by all legislated means, whether these people are communists, polytheists, Christians, innovators or people who are ignorant of rulings of the purified legislation of *Islaam*.

It is essential for the *Muslim* rulers to prohibit the aforementioned people from propagating their falsehood, and it is upon them to aid the callers to the truth; those who call the people to the Book of their Lord and the *Sunnah* of His Messenger (*sal-Allaahu 'alayhi wa sallam*); teach them what Allaah has obligated upon them in terms of knowledge and understanding; teach them the Rights of Allaah; the rights of His servants; the rights of the rulers, and the rights that every *Muslim* has upon his brother. They are the ones who should be aided, and whoever deviates from the path and calls to something other than the Legislation of *Islaam* should be disallowed from doing so.

Shaykh 'Abdul-'Azeez ibn Baaz

---

11 Majmoo' Fataawa wa Maqaalaat Mutanawwi'ah - Volume 5, Page 292

7. Advice for the Youth

Question: Noble *Shaykh*, I want to advise my brothers in this summer break, especially the teachers. Is it better for them to travel and support their brothers, whether in the east or west, or is it better for them to join the summer camps that preserve the youth, or is it better for them to travel to the scholars to benefit from their teachings? We would also like you to advise those who waste their time in other than the aforementioned affairs?[12]

Response: Firstly: We should not call this vacation a 'break' because there are no breaks in a *Muslim*'s life, rather not in a non-*Muslim*'s life either; everyone continuously works, Allaah (*Subhaanahu wa Ta'aala*) said:

$$ يَٰٓأَيُّهَا ٱلْإِنسَٰنُ إِنَّكَ كَادِحٌ إِلَىٰ رَبِّكَ كَدْحًا فَمُلَٰقِيهِ $$

O mankind! Indeed you are traveling towards your Lord [with your deeds and actions (good or bad)], and you will meet Him.[13]

Yes, it is a break from school, but it is better to call it a vacation.

Secondly: In relation to your question: 'Is it better for teachers to travel east and west to aid their brothers, to seek knowledge, to direct the youth or to call to the Religion of Allaah?' This depends on each individual and on the circumstances.

A person who is a carrier of knowledge, one who can memorise as well as understand it, we say to this person; it is better for you to stay in your

---

12 Liqaa.aat al-Baab al-Maftooh - No.898

13 The Noble *Qur.aan* - *Soorah* al-Inshiqaaq, *Aayah* 6

165

country and seek knowledge, because seeking knowledge - as *Imaam* Ahmad stated - has no equal. It is better than *jihaad* in the Cause of Al-laah, if *jihaad* is not an obligation at the time. Allaah (*Subhaanahu wa Ta'aala*) said in His Book:

وَمَا كَانَ ٱلْمُؤْمِنُونَ لِيَنفِرُواْ كَآفَّةً فَلَوْلَا نَفَرَ مِن كُلِّ فِرْقَةٍ مِّنْهُمْ طَآئِفَةٌ

And it is not (proper) for the believers to go out to fight (jihaad) all together. Of every troop of them, only a group should go forth...[14]

Meaning a group should stay behind.

لِّيَتَفَقَّهُواْ

...so that they may get instructions...[15]

Meaning the group that stayed behind.

فِى ٱلدِّينِ وَلِيُنذِرُواْ قَوْمَهُمْ إِذَا رَجَعُوٓاْ إِلَيْهِمْ لَعَلَّهُمْ يَحْذَرُونَ

...in the religion and warn their people when they re-turn to them in order that they may beware (of evil)[16]

So Allaah (*Subhaanahu wa Ta'aala*) made staying behind in order to gain understanding in the Religion equal to *jihaad* in the Cause of Al-

---

14 The Noble *Qur.aan* - *Soorah* at-Towbah, *Aayah* 122

15 The Noble *Qur.aan* - *Soorah* at-Towbah, *Aayah* 122

16 The Noble *Qur.aan* - *Soorah* at-Towbah, *Aayah* 122

laah. Rather, it is better than *jihaad*, because *jihaad* is needed at times and not at others, but knowledge is needed by people in all their affairs; their worship, their manners and in their dealings with others.

As for *jihaad* in the Cause of Allaah; people need it when either defending their lands and religion or in order to make the Religion of Allaah uppermost, because *jihaad* is either in defence or attack, but it is only a specific part of life. Knowledge however is needed in all aspects of life. *Imaam* Ahmad said:

"There is nothing equal to knowledge, for those who have the correct intention."

As for a person who cannot hold knowledge; a person who wouldn't understand anything if he were to sit in the circles of knowledge, but is knowledgeable in the affairs of *jihaad*, is physically fit and has strong determination then *jihaad* is better for this person.

A third person who isn't good at either of the two, but is good at convincing people and has a good method in calling to Allaah and delivering sermons, he wins over peoples' hearts with his technique and sermons, he softens them and causes tears to flow; we say to this type of person; travel! Call the people in other countries, because countries need students of knowledge and *du'aat* to teach the people and help them understand the religion. We have heard that alot of countries are in a state of ignorance and are in need of students of knowledge to teach them.

During the vacation some students of knowledge travelled south; the people there were extremely happy about that, they followed the students everywhere, learning from them. This was the case when they were only students; so what would happen if someone of a higher level travelled to them? He would benefit them tremendously without a doubt.

As for the youth, then I advise them to make use of their time; they shouldn't get used to being lazy and idle. They should keep good company; people who would correctly advise them and safeguard their religion and manners. The Messenger of Allaah (*sal-Allaahu 'alayhi wa sallam*) said:

> *"A righteous companion is like a perfumer; he is either going to gift you some perfume, sell you some, or at least you would smell a pleasant fragrance from him. An evil companion is like a blacksmith; he would either set your clothes on fire or you would smell a wretched smell from him."*

It was also narrated that the Messenger of Allaah (*sal-Allaahu 'alayhi wa sallam*) said:

> *"A man is upon the religion of his most beloved friend; so each of you should take a look at whom he takes as a most beloved friend."*

So my advice to the youth is that they should be keen on befriending good, intelligent, sensible people. They should beware of evil companions, for indeed evil companions are like fire; it burns ones cloth bit by bit until it reaches the body and consumes it.

It is upon them to enrol in summer camps that are run by people who are trustworthy in their religion and manners, trustworthy in their train of thought and advice.

They should also join *Qur.aan* memorisation programmes in order to memorise some of the Book of Allaah during their vacation. Indeed the best of books that is most worthy of time is the Book of Allaah (*Subhaanahu wa Ta'aala*).

We ask Allaah to grant everyone success, and grant us to be amongst those who spend their time in what Allaah (*Subhaanahu wa Ta'aala*) is pleased with.

Shaykh Muhammad ibn Saalih al-'Uthaymeen

8. Shaykh Ibn 'Uthaymeen's Advice to the Du'aat

Indeed the callers of evil wish that the callers to the truth are in a state of division, because they know that their unity and co-operation is a cause for their success, and their division is a cause for failure.[17]

Indeed every one of us is liable to make mistakes, so if one of us sees that his brother has fallen into an error, he should hasten to get in contact with him to confirm the affair; because we may think that something is a mistake, but in reality it is not.

It is also impermissible to make an error that a caller may have fallen into, a reason to slander and chase people away from him. This is not from the signs of the believers, let alone being from the signs of the callers to Allaah (*Subhaanahu wa Ta'aala*).

The *da'wah* which is intended is the *da'wah* that is upon knowledge as Allaah (*Subhaanahu wa Ta'aala*) said:

---

17 Kitaab ad-Da'wah - Volume 2, Page 174

قُلْ هَٰذِهِۦ

سَبِيلِىٓ أَدْعُوٓا۟ إِلَى ٱللَّهِ عَلَىٰ بَصِيرَةٍ أَنَا۠ وَمَنِ ٱتَّبَعَنِى وَسُبْحَٰنَ

ٱللَّهِ وَمَآ أَنَا۠ مِنَ ٱلْمُشْرِكِينَ

Say (O Muhammad): "This is my way; I call to Al-laah (i.e. to the Oneness of Allaah - Islaamic Mono-theism) upon Baseerah, I and whomsoever follows me. And Glorified and Exalted is Allaah (above all that they associate as partners with Him). And I am not of the Mushrikoon (polytheists)."[18]

Baseerah is applied in:

1   What a person is calling to;

2   The state of the people he is calling;

3   The method of calling them.

Baseerah in what a person is calling to requires one to have knowledge. One should not speak except while having knowledge or a reasonable doubt that what he is saying is the truth, and this is if it is permitted to have a reasonable doubt in that particular issue that he is calling to. But for one to call while in a state of ignorance, indeed this person would ruin more than he would build, as well as having fallen into a great sin. Allaah (*Subhaanahu wa Ta'aala*) says:

وَلَا تَقْفُ مَا لَيْسَ لَكَ بِهِۦ عِلْمٌ

إِنَّ ٱلسَّمْعَ وَٱلْبَصَرَ وَٱلْفُؤَادَ كُلُّ أُو۟لَٰٓئِكَ كَانَ عَنْهُ مَسْـُٔولًا

---

18 The Noble *Qur.aan* - *Soorah* Yoosuf, *Aayah* 108

And follow not (O man, i.e., say not or do not or witness not) what you have no knowledge of. Indeed the hearing, sight and the heart, one will be questioned of all of those (by Allaah).[19]

From the requirements of having *baseerah* about the state one is calling, is differentiating between the ignorant, the proud and defiant.

Baseerah in the method of calling to Allaah is knowing how to call people; should one call them forcefully, harshly and by vilifying what they are upon? Or should he call them with lenience and kindness while adorning what he is calling them to without making what they are upon look hideous.

Shaykh Muhammad ibn Saalih al-'Uthaymeen

9. Shaykh Muqbil's Advice to the Callers in America

Question: It is essential for one to call to *Islaam* in America; so what are the correct methods and what are the rules and regulations for calling to Allaah, keeping in mind that the society is known for corruption and decay, among other issues?[20]

Response: Before this, we advise the caller to increase in beneficial knowledge for Allaah (*Subhaanahu wa Ta'aala*) says:

قُلْ هَٰذِهِۦ

سَبِيلِىٓ أَدْعُوٓا۟ إِلَى ٱللَّهِ عَلَىٰ بَصِيرَةٍ أَنَا۠ وَمَنِ ٱتَّبَعَنِى

---

19 The Noble *Qur.aan* - *Soorah* al-Israa, *Aayah* 36

20 Tuhfatul-Mujeeb - Page 68

Say (O Muhammad): "This is my way, I call to Allaah
with sure knowledge, I and those who follow me"[21]

He should then call to the correct *'aqeedah*; we do not call the people
away from worshipping the Messiah (Jesus\'Eesaa ibn Maryam), and
then call them to worshipping graves, as the *Soofee*s do.

Shaykh Muqbil ibn Haadee al-Waadi'ee

10. Shaykh Muqbil's Final Advice to Students of Knowledge

<u>Question</u>: O, *Shaykh*, can you please advise the students of knowledge
in this country (America)?[22]

<u>Response</u>: We advise them with the same advice that Allaah advised His
servants with, and it is: *taqwaa* of Allaah (*Subhaanahu wa Ta'aala*), as
Allaah (*Subhaanahu wa Ta'aala*) says:

$$وَلَقَدْ وَصَّيْنَا الَّذِينَ أُوتُواْ الْكِتَبَ$$
$$مِن قَبْلِكُمْ وَإِيَّاكُمْ أَنِ اتَّقُواْ اللَّهَ$$

And indeed We have recommend to the people of
the Scripture before you, and to you (O Muslims)
that you (all) have Taqwaa of Allaah.[23]

We also advise them to be sincere to Allaah (*Subhaanahu wa Ta'aala*):

---

21 The Noble *Qur.aan - Soorah* Yoosuf, *Aayah* 108

22 Tuhfatul-Mujeeb - Page 156
26-6-1421 - corresponding to 25-9-2000

23 The Noble *Qur.aan - Soorah* an-Nisaa, *Aayah* 131

أَلَا لِلَّهِ ٱلدِّينُ ٱلْخَالِصُ

*Surely, the religion (i.e. worship and obedience) is
for Allaah only.*[24]

وَمَآ أُمِرُوٓا إِلَّا لِيَعْبُدُوا ٱللَّهَ مُخْلِصِينَ لَهُ ٱلدِّينَ حُنَفَآءَ

*And they were not commanded except to worship
Allaah, and worship none but Him Alone (abstaining from ascribing partners to Him*[25]

al-Bukhaaree and *Muslim* reported the *hadeeth* of Jundub ibn 'Abdullaah that the Messenger of Allaah (*sal-Allaahu 'alayhi wa sallam*) said:

**"Whosoever seeks to be heard, Allaah will make
him be heard, and whosoever seeks to show off,
Allaah will make it that he is seen."**

We advise you to be serious about, and exert all your efforts in gaining
beneficial knowledge. The caller to Allaah cannot be successful unless
he has an ample portion of knowledge, the Lord of Graciousness said to
His Messenger, Muhammad:

وَقُل رَّبِّ زِدْنِي عِلْمًا

...and say: "My Lord! Increase me in knowledge.[26]

It is not befitting for one to give up on himself and say: 'I have become
old and can't understand.' Allaah is the granter of ease, and being serious

---

24 The Noble *Qur.aan - Soorah* az-Zumar, *Aayah* 3

25 The Noble *Qur.aan - Soorah* al-Bayyinah, *Aayah* 5

26 The Noble *Qur.aan - Soorah* Taha, *Aayah* 114

about gaining knowledge will make the difference.

We said that indeed Allaah is the granter of ease; this is because Allaah says in His Book:

وَلَقَدْ يَسَّرْنَا ٱلْقُرْءَانَ لِلذِّكْرِ فَهَلْ مِن مُّدَّكِرٍ

And We have indeed made the Qur.aan easy to understand and remember, is there then anyone who will remember (or receive admonition)?[27]

The Messenger of Allaah (*sal-Allaahu 'alayhi wa sallam*) said:

"I was sent with 'al-Hanafeeyah as-Samhaa' (the beautiful upright way)."

He also said in the *hadeeth* of Abu Hurayrah which was collected in *Saheeh* al-Bukhaaree:

"Indeed this religion is easy, and no one would try to overcome it except that it would defeat him."

We also advise them to call to Allaah with lenience and gentleness, for indeed we live within a community, whether in Yemen or here in America where the caller to Allaah has no authority over the people to compel them to do anything; and even if he were to compel them they would not respond, except through the guidance of Allaah (*Subhaanahu wa Ta'aala*).

لَّسْتَ عَلَيْهِم بِمُصَيْطِرٍ

You (O Muhammad) are not a dictator over them.[28]

---

27 The Noble *Qur.aan* - *Soorah* al-Qamar, *Aayah* 15

28 The Noble *Qur.aan* - *Soorah* al-Ghaashiyah, *Aayah* 22

Another issue I advise my brothers with, especially in countries like this; is that we should combine between mixing with people and being secluded. We should not mix with evil people or attend evil gatherings, even if there were a festival there or whatever:

$$وَالَّذِينَ لَا يَشْهَدُونَ الزُّورَ$$

And those who do not witness falsehood... [29]

It is not befitting for you to attend such gatherings.

We should also mix with people in order to call them to the Religion of Allaah and teach them; this is the best course of action. This does not mean that we blend with people such as the *Ikhwaan al-Muslimeen* do, in order to call them to Allaah. They may even shave their beards and do other such things, but at the same time we should not isolate ourselves from the people, indeed it is not permissible to be isolated, the *Muslims* are in need of those who will teach them their religion.

This is what I have to say, and I ask Allaah to grant you as well as myself success, and all praise is due to Allaah Lord of the worlds.

Shaykh Muqbil ibn Haadee al-Waadi'ee

11. The Qualifications of the Caller

Question: At present, many people affiliate themselves to *da'wah*, which makes it necessary to know who the esteemed people of knowledge are; those who direct the *ummah* and its youth to the true and correct *Manhaj*. So which scholars do you advise the youth to benefit from; attend

---

29 The Noble *Qur.aan - Soorah* al-Furqaan, *Aayah* 72

their lessons and listen to their recordings? Who should they turn to regarding important affairs, and at times of tribulations?[30]

Response: Calling to Allaah is an affair that must be carried out; the Religion was established through *da'wah* and *jihaad*, after gaining beneficial knowledge. Allaah (*Subhaanahu wa Ta'aala*) said:

$$\text{وَٱلْعَصْرِ ۝ إِنَّ ٱلْإِنسَـٰنَ لَفِى خُسْرٍ ۝ إِلَّا ٱلَّذِينَ ءَامَنُواْ}$$
$$\text{وَعَمِلُواْ ٱلصَّـٰلِحَـٰتِ وَتَوَاصَوْاْ بِٱلْحَقِّ وَتَوَاصَوْاْ بِٱلصَّبْرِ ۝}$$

By the time, indeed mankind is in a state of loss, except those who believe, do righteous deeds, advise one another with the truth and advise one another with patience.[31]

'Belief' is the knowledge of Allaah (*Subhaanahu wa Ta'aala*), His Names, Attributes and His worship. Righteous actions are a branch of knowledge, because actions must be based upon knowledge. Calling to Allaah, ordering good and mutual advice between *Muslim*s must be practiced, but not just anyone is suited to undertake such duties. These affairs must only be carried out by the people of knowledge and rational reasoning, because these affairs are very important; no one should undertake them except those who are qualified to do so.

It is a calamity these days that the field of *da'wah* has become wide-ranging; everyone enters into it and calls it '*da'wah*,' even ignorant individuals who are not suited to call to Allaah, and so they corrupt more affairs than they rectify. Due to their eagerness they embark upon affairs hastily

---

30 al-Ajwibah al-Mufeedah - Question No.114

31 The Noble *Qur.aan* - *Soorah* al-'Asr

and recklessly, and as a result, more evil is produced than good. They do not even intend to rectify affairs. Rather they may affiliate themselves to the *da'wah* but have ulterior motives that they call to and wish to realise at the expense of the *da'wah*; they trouble the minds of the youth in the name of the *da'wah* and earnest concern for the religion. In reality they intend the opposite, such as deviating the youth and drawing them away from their communities, rulers and scholars. They outwardly approach them by advising and calling them to Allaah, like the hypocrites in this *ummah*; those who present evil to the people in the form of goodness.

Consideration is not given to ones' affiliation or outward appearance; rather it is the reality and the consequences of affairs that are considered. One must examine these individuals who affiliate themselves to the *da'wah*; where did they study? Where did they attain their knowledge? Where were they raised? What is their *'aqeedah*? Allaah (*Subhaanahu wa Ta'aala*) said:

$$ أَمْ لَمْ يَعْرِفُوا رَسُولَهُمْ فَهُمْ لَهُ مُنكِرُونَ $$

**Or is it that they did not recognise their Messenger,
so they deny him?**[32]

Their actions must also be looked into as well as the effect they have upon the people; the good they have produced. What effect have their actions had in terms of rectification? So you must examine their state before you rely upon their statements and outward appearance. This must be looked into, especially during these times in which there are many callers to *fitnah*.

The Prophet (*sal-Allaahu 'alayhi wa sallam*) described the callers to

---

32 The Noble *Qur.aan* - *Soorah* al-Mu'minoon, *Aayah* 69

fitnah as being from amongst us, speaking our language, and when he (*sal-Allaahu 'alayhi wa sallam*) was asked about the *fitnah*, he said:

> **"Callers at the gates of the Hellfire; whoever follows them would be thrown into it because of them."**

He (*sal-Allaahu 'alayhi wa sallam*) called them 'callers', so we must be aware of this and not include everyone who says that he calls to Allaah, or every group that calls to Allaah in the *da'wah*. We must look into the reality of the affair, the reality of each individual and each group. For indeed Allaah (*Subhaanahu wa Ta'aala*) restricted *da'wah* to being the call to Allaah and to His Way; Allaah (*Subhaanahu wa Ta'aala*) said:

$$قُلْ هَٰذِهِۦ سَبِيلِىٓ أَدْعُوٓاْ إِلَى ٱللَّهِ$$

Say (O Muhammad): "This is my way, I call to Allaah..."[33]

This indicates that there are people who call to other than Allaah. Shaykh-ul Islaam Muhammad ibn 'Abdul-Wahhaab, may Allaah have mercy upon him, commented on this verse saying:

$$هَٰذِهِۦ سَبِيلِىٓ أَدْعُوٓاْ إِلَى ٱللَّهِ$$

"This is my way, I call to Allaah..."[34]

'This signifies sincerity, for indeed many people only call to themselves, they do not call to Allaah (*Subhaanahu wa Ta'aala*).'

Shaykh Saalih ibn Fowzaan al-Fowzaan

---

33 The Noble *Qur.aan* - *Soorah* Yoosuf, *Aayah* 108

34 The Noble *Qur.aan* - *Soorah* Yoosuf, *Aayah* 108

Chapter 7
Concerning Women

1. Women's Classes

Question: O, noble *Shaykh*, what is your opinion of establishing classes' specific to women that are carried out by noble female students of knowledge; classes that direct and assist women upon gaining knowledge and making them mentors to themselves, their children and all those who they are responsible for?[1]

Response: I say there is no harm in this; that a facility is established in which women study and are taught by pious women with knowledge, but with the condition that this does not cause other prohibited activities to take place from another angle. For example, that the assembly of women in this place becomes a cause for the foolish to roam around, or that there is no order. Girls' schools these days are organised; everyone comes and calls for his daughter or for whom he is responsible for with a microphone. So if this is accomplished and it is free from prohibitions then there is no harm in it.

Shaykh Muhammad ibn Saalih al-'Uthaymeen

---

1 Liqaa.aat al-Baab al-Maftooh - No.498

2. Facilitating the Opportunities for Female Du'aat

<u>Question</u>: Is there any way to facilitate opportunities for *da'wah* for the female callers to Allaah?[2]

<u>Response</u>: I do not know of anything to prevent this. Whenever there is a woman present who is qualified to give *da'wah* to Allaah (*Subhaanahu wa Ta'aala*), she should be aided and requested to provide guidance to women, because they are in need of female advisors of their own kind.

The presence of a female caller amongst women may be more beneficial in conveying *da'wah* to the path of truth to them than that of a man. Women may be too shy to tell a man about issues that concern them, or there may be something that prevents them from listening to the *da'wah* from a man. This is not the case when they are with a female caller because they intermingle with her, relate to her issues that they are concerned with and they are also affected by a female caller more than a male.

So it is imperative upon those who have knowledge from amongst women to perform what is *waajib* upon them in relation to performing *da'wah* and directing other women to everything that is good according to the best of their abilities, as Allaah (*Subhaanahu wa Ta'aala*) says:

$$ ٱدۡعُ إِلَىٰ سَبِيلِ رَبِّكَ بِٱلۡحِكۡمَةِ وَٱلۡمَوۡعِظَةِ ٱلۡحَسَنَةِ وَجَٰدِلۡهُم بِٱلَّتِي هِيَ أَحۡسَنُ $$

"Call (mankind, O Muhammad) to the Way of your Lord with wisdom (i.e. with the Divine Inspiration

---

2 Majmoo' Fataawa wa Maqaalaat Mutanawwi'ah - Volume 7, Page 325

and the Qur.aan), fair preaching and debate with them in a way that is best."[3]

He (*Subhaanahu wa Ta'aala*) also says:

قُلْ هَٰذِهِۦ سَبِيلِىٓ أَدْعُوٓاْ إِلَى ٱللَّهِ عَلَىٰ بَصِيرَةٍ أَنَا۠ وَمَنِ ٱتَّبَعَنِى

"Say (O Muhammad): "This is my way; I call to Al-laah (i.e. to the Oneness of Allaah – Islaamic Mon-otheism) with sure knowledge, I and those who follows me."[4]

He says as well:

وَمَنْ أَحْسَنُ قَوْلًا مِّمَّن دَعَآ إِلَى ٱللَّهِ وَعَمِلَ صَٰلِحًا وَقَالَ إِنَّنِى مِنَ ٱلْمُسْلِمِينَ

"And who is better in speech than he who [says: "My Lord is Allaah (believes in His Oneness)," and then stands firm (acts upon His Order)], calls to Allaah's (Islaamic Monotheism), does righteous deeds and says: "I am one of the Muslims"."[5]

His saying:

فَٱتَّقُواْ ٱللَّهَ مَا ٱسْتَطَعْتُمْ

---

3 The Noble *Qur.aan* - *Soorah* an-Nahl, *Aayah* 125

4 The Noble *Qur.aan* - *Soorah* an-Nahl, *Aayah* 125

5 The Noble *Qur.aan* - *Soorah* an-Nahl, *Aayah* 125

"So keep your duty to Allaah and fear Him as much as you can."[6]

The verses of this like are plentiful and they are general to both men and women and Allaah is the granter of success.

Shaykh 'Abdul-'Azeez ibn Baaz

---

6 The Noble *Qur.aan - Soorah* an-Nahl, *Aayah* 125

Chapter 8
Seeking Knowledge

1. Which is Better: Seeking Knowledge or Giving Da'wah?

Question: Which is better: seeking knowledge or calling to Allaah?[1]

Response: One should firstly gain knowledge, because it is not possible for one to call to Allaah without knowledge. If an individual does not have knowledge he would not be able to call to Allaah, and if he were to give *da'wah*, indeed his errors would be greater in number than his correct stances. So it is a condition to have knowledge before embarking on *da'wah*:

$$\text{قُلْ هَـٰذِهِۦ}$$

$$\text{سَبِيلِىٓ أَدْعُوٓاْ إِلَى ٱللَّهِ عَلَىٰ بَصِيرَةٍ أَنَا۠ وَمَنِ ٱتَّبَعَنِى وَسُبْحَـٰنَ}$$

"Say: "This is my way, I call to Allaah upon knowledge, I and whoever follows me."[2]

---

1 al-Ajwibah al-Mufeedah - Question No.54

2 The Noble *Qur.aan* - *Soorah* Yoosuf, *Aayah* 8

183

There are some well-known affairs that even a common person has the ability to call to, such as establishing the prayer, the prohibition of abandoning it in congregation, establishing it in ones' household and ordering the children to establish it. These affairs are well-known; both a common person and a student of knowledge know about them. As for affairs that require understanding and knowledge, affairs that are associated with permissible and impermissible issues, affairs of *tawheed* and *shirk*; these affairs must be based on knowledge.

Shaykh Saalih ibn Fowzaan al-Fowzaan

2. Seeking Knowledge for Beginners

Question: What guidance and advice can you provide for students who are at the preliminary stages of gaining knowledge?[3]

Response: My advice to students who are at the preliminary stages of gaining knowledge is to study under scholars who are trusted in regards to their *'aqeedah*, knowledge and counsel. They should start with small, summarised books in different sciences, memorise them and gradually study their explanations from their scholars. They should pay particular attention to the curriculums found in the institutions of knowledge and in *Islaam*ic colleges, as they consist of curriculums that have gradual knowledge for the student, where they gradually learn it and thereby achieve alot of good.

If however a student is not enrolled in a school or college, it is upon him to attend the lessons of the scholars in the *masaajid* regularly, whether the lessons are in *fiqh*, Arabic grammar, *'aqeedah*, and so on.

---

3 al-Ajwibah al-Mufeedah - Question No.51

As for what some youth do now, beginning with lengthy and detailed books, or you find that one of them buys books and sits in his house and reads them, this is incorrect and it is not learning, rather it is deception and vanity.

This is what led some people to speak about affairs of knowledge, issue religious verdicts as well as speak about Allaah without knowledge; due to not building themselves upon a firm foundation.

So it is essential for one to sit in front of the scholars in the circles of knowledge as well as have patience and endurance. *Imaam* ash-Shaafi'ee, may Allaah have mercy upon him, said:

"Whoever does not taste the humility of learning for some time, shall drink from the cup of ignorance for the rest of his life."

Shaykh Saalih ibn Fowzaan al-Fowzaan

3. Beneficial Books

Question: O, *Shaykh*, can you tell us the names of some books that are upon the methodology of the *Salaf* that are necessary for a young *Salafee* to acquire and add to his book collection?[4]

Response: The books that are necessary for a student of knowledge to acquire are the books of *hadeeth* such as the 'Six main books of *hadeeth*': al-Bukhaaree, Muslim, Abu Daawood, at-Tirmidhee, an-Nasaa.ee, Ibn Maajah and the *Musnad* of *Imaam* Ahmad.

---

4 al-Fataawaa al-Jaliyyah 'anil-Manaahij ad-Da'wiyyah - Page 18

Likewise, one should obtain *Saheeh* al-Jaami' as-Sagheer by *Shaykh* al-Albaanee, and the books of the earlier scholars of *hadeeth*.

A student of knowledge should also acquire the books of Muhammad ibn 'Abdul-Wahhaab, the books of his grandchildren, the books of the scholars of his time and those who came after them.

Likewise the books of *Salafee* scholars during present times, such as the books of *Shaykh* 'Abdul-'Azeez ibn 'Abdullaah ibn Baaz, *Shaykh* 'Abdul-'Azeez ibn 'Abdullaah Aal ash-*Shaykh*, *Shaykh* 'Abdullaah ibn 'Abdur-Rahmaan al-Ghudayyaan, *Shaykh* Saalih ibn Fowzaan al-Fowzaan, *Shaykh* Saalih al-Luhaydaan, the scholars of Madeenah such as *Shaykh* Rabee' ibn Haadee al-Madkhalee, *Shaykh* Saalih ibn Sa'd as-Suhaymee, *Shaykh* 'Alee ibn Naasir al-Faqeehee, *Shaykh* Muhammad ibn Haadee al-Madkhalee, *Shaykh* 'Abdul-Muhsin al-'Abbaad and his son 'Abdur-Razzaaq, *Shaykh* Muhammad ibn Rabee' al-Madkhalee and other *Salafee* scholars.

As well as the books of *Shaykh* Zayd ibn Muhammad al-Madkhalee and similar books; all of these are good and beneficial books. The books of the *Salafee*s in every time and place are good and beneficial and all praise is due to Allaah. However what is feared for the student of knowledge are the books of the *hizbee*s.

Shaykh Ahmad ibn Yahyaa an-Najmee

4. Da'wah without Knowledge

Question: O, noble *Shaykh*, which of the two is better; spending time calling to Allaah (*Subhaanahu wa Ta'aala*) or spending it gaining knowledge?[5]

---

5 Kitaabul-'Ilm - Page 145

<u>Response</u>: Gaining knowledge is better and takes precedence over giving *da'wah*. It is possible for a student of knowledge to carry out *da'wah* while gaining knowledge. There is no way that one could give *da'wah* without knowledge; Allaah (*Subhaanahu wa Ta'aala*) said:

$$\text{قُلْ هَٰذِهِۦ سَبِيلِىٓ أَدْعُوٓاْ إِلَى ٱللَّهِ عَلَىٰ بَصِيرَةٍ}$$

"Say (O Muhammad): "This is my way, I call to Allaah with sure knowledge..."."[6]

So how could there be *da'wah* without knowledge? No one has ever given *da'wah* in the past without knowledge; never, and whoever gives *da'wah* without knowledge will not be successful.

Shaykh Muhammad ibn Saalih al-'Uthaymeen

8

---

6 The Noble *Qur.aan - Soorah* Yoosuf, *Aayah* 8

Chapter 9
The Media

1. Working With the Media

Question: How would you explain the fact that some callers abstain from co-operating with the media, and how can we overcome the gap between the callers and the media and bring about an open channel between the two?[1]

Response: There is no doubt that some of the people of knowledge may be negligent in this affair, either because of being busy in worldly affairs, being weak in knowledge, being ill or other reasons that they are mistaken in. For example, one may see that he is not qualified, or that others are carrying out this task and have relieved him of this duty and other reasons.

My advice to the students of knowledge is that they shouldn't be negligent in calling to Allaah claiming that this task is for other than them. Rather they must call to Allaah according to their abilities and knowl-

---

1 Majmoo' Fataawa wa Maqaalaat Mutanawwi'ah - Volume 5, Page 265

edge. They shouldn't involve themselves in affairs that they are unable to accomplish, rather they should call the people according to their knowledge, strive to speak with evidence and abstain from speaking about Allaah without knowledge. One should not belittle himself as long as he has knowledge and understanding in the religion. He must co-operate in practicing good, using all possible methods, whether it be the media or other than that. One shouldn't say: 'This is for other than me,' because if everyone depended on others saying that the task is for other than them, the call would come to a halt, the callers would be few in number and all that would remain would be ignorant people remaining upon their ignorance, and evils remaining in their same state. This is a grave error, rather it is obligatory for the people of knowledge to co-operate in calling to Allaah wherever they may be, whether on the ground, in the air, in trains, cars or ships. Whenever there is an opportunity, the student of knowledge must take advantage of it to call and direct the people. As long as he involves himself in *da'wah* then he is upon alot of good. Allaah (*Subhaanahu wa Ta'aala*) said:

$$\text{وَمَنْ أَحْسَنُ قَوْلًا مِّمَّن دَعَآ إِلَى اللَّهِ وَعَمِلَ صَلِحًا وَقَالَ إِنَّنِى مِنَ الْمُسْلِمِينَ}$$

And who is better in speech than he who [says: "My Lord is Allaah (believes in His Oneness)", and then stands firm (acts upon His Order), and] calls to Allaah (Islaamic Monotheism), and does righteous deeds, and says: "I am one of the Muslims."[2]

Allaah (*Subhaanahu wa Ta'aala*) says: 'There is no speech that is better than this.' The verse here implicates negation, meaning: There is no one

---

2 The Noble *Qur.aan* - *Soorah* Fussilat, *Aayah* 33

that is better in speech than one who calls to Allaah. So this is a tremendous benefit and a great virtue for the callers to Allaah (*Subhaanahu wa Ta'aala*). The Messenger of Allaah (*sal-Allaahu 'alayhi wa sallam*) said:

> **"Whoever directs the people to good attains an equal reward to those who practice that good."**

He (*sal-Allaahu 'alayhi wa sallam*) also said:

> **"Whoever calls to guidance attains the same reward as those who follow him [in practicing it] without that decreasing their rewards at all."**

He said to 'Alee (*radhi-yAllaahu 'anhu*) when he sent him to Khaybar:

> *"By Allaah, if Allaah guides a single person through you, this is better for you than the best of camels."*

So it is not befitting for a scholar to be disinterested and negligent in this affair, with the reasoning that others are carrying it out. Rather it is compulsory for the people of knowledge to co-operate and exert all their efforts in calling to Allaah, wherever they may be. The whole world is in need of *da'wah*, whether they are *Muslims* or not. As for the *Muslims*, it will increase their knowledge, and as for non-*Muslims*, then Allaah may guide them and bless them to accept *Islaam*.

Shaykh 'Abdul-'Azeez ibn Baaz

2. Not Co-operating with Politically-Inclined Media Agencies

Question: Some of the callers to *Islaam* refrain from co-operating with the media, rejecting the policies of newspapers and magazines that purposefully promote marketing based on sales. What is your opinion on this issue?[3]

Response: Those who run newspapers must fear Allaah and beware of publishing things that harm people, whether in daily, weekly or monthly papers. Authors should likewise fear Allaah in relation to what they write, they should only write or publish books that benefit people, call them to good and warn them from evil. As for publishing pictures of women on front covers or within magazines and newspapers, then this is a great evil and an abominable act that leads to corruption.

Likewise circulating misguiding secular ideologies or subjects that lead to sins like fornication, unveiled women, drinking alcohol or anything that Allaah has prohibited, all of this is a great evil. Those who run newspapers must beware of this and whenever they publish such issues they earn the same amount of sin as those who are affected by them. So the owner of a newspaper which publishes evil affairs, whether it is the editorial president or whoever he takes orders from, earns an equal amount of sin as all those who are misguided or affected by such subjects. Just as those who publish good things as well as call to them attain an equal portion of reward as those who are affected by those issues.

Due to this, it is compulsory for all *Muslim*-owned media outlets to remove everything that Allaah has forbidden and beware of spreading

---

3 Majmoo' Fataawa wa Maqaalaat Mutanawwi'ah - Volume 5, Page 266

and broadcasting affairs that harm the society. The media must focus on propagating things that benefit people both in their religious and worldly affairs. They should also beware of being a cause of corruption and a channel in the propagation of evil due to what they circulate in the media. Everyone with authority involved in the media is accountable for this according to his ability.

It is also compulsory for the callers to *Islaam* to take advantage of this opportunity and participate in this field with what they write and propagate. They must beware of what Allaah (*Subhaanahu wa Ta'aala*) has forbidden. This is obligatory for them in their sermons and gatherings with people. All their gatherings should be gatherings of *da'wah*; wherever they are they should call to *Islaam*, whether in their homes, while visiting their brothers or when meeting people. It is compulsory upon them to take advantage of this medium; the mass media, and propagate good through it; not avoid it.

Shaykh 'Abdul-'Azeez ibn Baaz

3. The Media

Question: The mass media is currently directing this generation in whichever direction it sees fit. Television and the radio air a variety of shows and programmes that are designed to establish the ideas and principles of those who produce them. If we do not produce such programmes and leave this matter to others, they would ruin our children, and if we advise our children to study and understand these skills in order to rectify them *Islaam*ically, they become apprehensive.[4]

---

4 Majalatul-Buhooth al-Islaamiyyah - Volume 23, Page 118

<u>Response</u>: Those responsible in *Islaam*ic countries must fear Allaah when it comes to the *Muslim* public. They should only give the responsibility of such affairs to the scholars of guidance and truth. The scholars must not refrain from clarifying the truth through the media; they must not leave this affair to the ignorant or atheists, rather the people of *eemaan*, piety and wisdom should take on this responsibility.

They should direct the media in an *Islaam*ic direction so that nothing remains in it that may harm the *Muslim*s, whether young or old, male or female. It is also the responsibility of the scholars to provide sufficient responses to whatever the media airs until righteous people are able to assume its responsibility and take over. It is also upon *Islaam*ic countries to grant this task to righteous people only, in order to spread good and plant virtuous values in the public.

<u>Question</u>: Does this mean that you advise the *Muslim* youth to study these mediums in order to take control of the areas which are currently in the control of the evildoers?

<u>Response</u>: Yes, the scholars should not leave these affairs for the ignorant and should take responsibility of propagating virtuous issues through all mediums.

However, there is the issue of acting; I advise people not to get involved in acting. It is upon the scholars to just clarify the rulings of Allaah and His Messenger to the people. As for a person taking the name and personality of someone else and saying: 'I am 'Umar,' or, 'I am 'Uthmaan,' then this is lying and is impermissible.

Shaykh 'Abdul-'Azeez ibn Baaz

Chapter 10
Muslim Minorities

1. Certificates Indicating That a Person is Muslim

Question: Foreign *Muslim*s in Europe are given written certificates indicating that they are *Muslim* which they obtain from *Islaam*ic organisations. I know that such certificates were never given to *Muslim*s before in the history of *Islaam*. Is it not sufficient to have two trustworthy *Muslim* witnesses along with the affirmation of the European himself that he is indeed *Muslim*? Isn't this considered to be an innovation?[1]

Response: All praise is due to Allaah alone and may the *salaah* and *salaam* be upon the Messenger, his family and his Companions.

*Muslim*s are not in need of these certificates to prove their faith; this is between the individulal and his Lord. However one may need such certificates in relation to his own rights, rights between him and others in general and rights between him and governments. This is why a person may need a form of identification that states his religion; whether it is an ID card, a passport or birth certificate.

Fataawa al-Lajnah ad-Daa.imah - No.7212

194

His inner belief may not be sufficient at all times, such as in cases where one needs to travel to other countries where he is unknown for example. Or if a person dies somewhere far from his country and companions, and no one is able to identify him except by his passport, ID card or a certificate like the one mentioned. There is usually no sign of the religion that an individual is practicing in such cases. Based upon this, there is no problem in acquiring these certificates even if they are innovated, because they are not an innovation in the religion and it is innovating in the religion that was prohibited in the saying of the Prophet (*sal-Allaahu 'alayhi wa sallam*):

> **"Whoever innovates something in our religion will have it rejected."**

This *hadeeth* clarifies that the innovations that are rejected are those that are in the religion.

Allaah is the granter of success, and may the *salaah* and *salaam* be upon our Prophet Muhammad, his family and his Companions.

The Permanent Committee for Islaamic Research and Verdicts

2. Living in an Ignorant Community Void of Scholars

Question: What role should a faithful *Muslim* who lives in an ignorant community void of scholars or *Islaam*ic groups have, keeping in mind that he is unable to differentiate between different groups in order to follow the one that adheres to the Book of Allaah and the *Sunnah*? What should he do in such a state of helplessness, living amongst wolves?[2]

---

2 Fataawa al-Lajnah ad-Daa.imah - No.4250

Response: All praise is due to Allaah alone, and may the *salaah* and *salaam* be upon His Messenger, his family and Companions.

To Proceed:

A *Muslim* should learn the affairs which would enable him to have knowledge and insight of his religion. He should call the people to good according to his ability. It is not binding upon him to do what he is incapable of doing, due to the general evidences that indicate that the legislation of *Islaam* is undemanding, from amongst these evidences is the saying of Allaah (*Subhaanahu wa Ta'aala*):

$$ مَا يُرِيدُ ٱللَّهُ لِيَجْعَلَ عَلَيْكُم مِّنْ حَرَجٍ $$

"Allaah does not want to place you in difficulty."[3]

His (*Subhaanahu wa Ta'aala*) saying also:

$$ فَٱتَّقُوا ٱللَّهَ مَا ٱسْتَطَعْتُمْ $$

"So keep your duty to Allaah and fear Him as much as you can..."[4]

It is obligatory upon him to co-operate with the people of knowledge that are closest to him. If he is unable to find any, then it becomes compulsory upon him to migrate, if he is able, to a country where he can co-operate with others in learning his religion and establishing its rituals.

The Permanent Committee for Islaamic Research and Verdicts

---

3 The Noble *Qur.aan* - *Soorah* al-Maa.idah, *Aayah* 6

4 The Noble *Qur.aan* - *Soorah* al-Maa.idah, *Aayah* 6

3. Concealing One's Religion out of Fear

Question: I embraced *Islaam* approximately six months ago and am very pleased with the changes that took place in my life since then. However I did not officially register myself as a *Muslim* because I plan to be a teacher in the future, and so I face a big problem: Germany does not welcome *Muslim* teachers, so because of this it would not be possible for me to get a job in the future.

My question is: Is it permissible for me to conceal the fact that I am *Muslim* until I get a job? Is it possible for me to worship Allaah secretly without notifying any government authorities that I have converted to *Islaam*?[5]

Response: All praise is due to Allaah, I asked our *Shaykh*; the noble *Shaykh* Muhammad ibn Saalih al-'Uthaymeen, may Allaah have mercy upon him, this question and he said that it is not obligatory for him to inform them that he embraced *Islaam.* There is also no harm in him concealing his religion if he fears for himself. Allaah knows best.

10

---

5 al-Mowsoo'ah - No.8593

Chapter 11
Non-Muslims

1. The Ten Commandments

Question: Is there anything in the *Qur.aan* similar to the Ten Commandments in the *Injeel* (Bible)?[1]

Response: All praise is due to Allaah. Thank you for directing this question to us, indicating your interest in the *Qur.aan*. We would be delighted to provide you with an answer.

There are verses in the *Qur.aan* that were called the 'Ten Commandments' or the 'Ten Instructions' by some scholars due to them containing ten great commandments to mankind by Allaah. These verses can be found in two places in the *Qur.aan*:

The First: In *Soorah* al-An'aam, Allaah (*Subhaanahu wa Ta'aala*) says:

$$\text{قُلْ تَعَالَوْاْ أَتْلُ مَاحَرَّمَ رَبُّكُمْ عَلَيْكُمْ}$$

---

1 al-Mowsoo'ah - No.2273

'Say (O Muhammad): "Come, I will recite what your Lord has prohibited you from:

أَلَّا تُشْرِكُوا بِهِ شَيْئًا

[1] Join not anything in worship with Him;

وَبِالْوَالِدَيْنِ إِحْسَانًا

[2] Be good and dutiful to your parents;

وَلَا تَقْتُلُوا أَوْلَادَكُم مِّنْ
إِمْلَاقٍ نَّحْنُ نَرْزُقُكُمْ وَإِيَّاهُمْ

[3] Kill not your children because of poverty" – We provide sustenance for you and for them –

وَلَا تَقْرَبُوا الْفَوَاحِشَ مَا ظَهَرَ مِنْهَا وَمَا بَطَنَ

[4] "Come not near al-Fawaahish (great sins and illegal sexual intercourse) whether committed openly or secretly;

وَلَا تَقْتُلُوا النَّفْسَ الَّتِي
حَرَّمَ اللَّهُ إِلَّا بِالْحَقِّ ذَٰلِكُمْ وَصَّاكُم بِهِ لَعَلَّكُمْ تَعْقِلُونَ

[5] And kill not anyone whom Allaah has forbidden except for a just cause (according to Islaamic Law). This He has commanded you with that you may understand.

وَلَا تَقْرَبُواْ مَالَ ٱلْيَتِيمِ إِلَّا بِٱلَّتِي هِيَ أَحْسَنُ حَتَّىٰ يَبْلُغَ أَشُدَّهُ

*[6] And come not near to the orphan's property
except to improve it until he or she attains the age
of full strength;*

وَأَوْفُواْ ٱلْكَيْلَ وَٱلْمِيزَانَ بِٱلْقِسْطِ لَا نُكَلِّفُ نَفْسًا إِلَّا
وُسْعَهَا

*[7] And give full measure and full weight with jus-
tice" – We burden not any person, but that which
they can bear –*

وَإِذَا قُلْتُمْ فَٱعْدِلُواْ وَلَوْ كَانَ ذَا قُرْبَىٰ

*[8] "And whenever you give your word (i.e. judge
between men or give evidence), say the truth even
if a near relative is concerned,*

وَبِعَهْدِ
ٱللَّهِ أَوْفُواْ ذَٰلِكُمْ وَصَّىٰكُم بِهِۦ لَعَلَّكُمْ تَذَكَّرُونَ

*[9] And fulfil the Covenant of Allaah. This He com-
mands you, that you may remember."*

وَأَنَّ هَٰذَا صِرَٰطِي مُسْتَقِيمًا فَٱتَّبِعُوهُ وَلَا تَتَّبِعُواْ ٱلسُّبُلَ
فَتَفَرَّقَ بِكُمْ عَن سَبِيلِهِۦ ذَٰلِكُمْ وَصَّىٰكُم بِهِۦ لَعَلَّكُمْ
تَتَّقُونَ ۝

*[10] "And verily, this (i.e. Allaah's Commandments
mentioned in the above two verses) is my straight
path, so follow it, and follow not (other) paths, for*

they will separate you from His path. This He has ordained for you that you may become al-Mut-taqoon (the pious).'"

The second: In *Soorah* al-Israa, it is as if it is an explanation of the previous verses. Allaah (*Subhaanahu wa Ta'aala*) said:

وَقَضَىٰ رَبُّكَ أَلَّا تَعْبُدُوٓاْ إِلَّآ إِيَّاهُ

[1] 'And your Lord has decreed that you worship none but Him.

وَبِٱلْوَٰلِدَيْنِ إِحْسَٰنًا إِمَّا يَبْلُغَنَّ عِندَكَ ٱلْكِبَرَ أَحَدُهُمَآ أَوْ كِلَاهُمَا فَلَا تَقُل لَّهُمَآ أُفٍّ وَلَا تَنْهَرْهُمَا وَقُل لَّهُمَا قَوْلًا كَرِيمًا ۝ وَٱخْفِضْ لَهُمَا جَنَاحَ ٱلذُّلِّ مِنَ ٱلرَّحْمَةِ وَقُل رَّبِّ ٱرْحَمْهُمَا كَمَا رَبَّيَانِي صَغِيرًا ۝ رَّبُّكُمْ أَعْلَمُ بِمَا فِي نُفُوسِكُمْ إِن تَكُونُواْ صَٰلِحِينَ فَإِنَّهُۥ كَانَ لِلْأَوَّٰبِينَ غَفُورًا ۝

[2] And that you be dutiful to your parents. If one or both of them attain old age in your life, say not to them a word of disrespect, nor shout at them but address them in terms of honour. And lower to them the wing of submission and humility through mercy, and say: "My Lord! Bestow upon them Your Mercy as they did bring me up when I was young." Your Lord knows best what is in your inner-selves. If you are righteous, then, verily, He is Ever Most Forgiving to those who turn to Him again and again in obedience, and in repentance.

وَءَاتِ ذَا ٱلْقُرْبَىٰ حَقَّهُۥ

وَٱلْمِسْكِينَ وَٱبْنَ ٱلسَّبِيلِ وَلَا تُبَذِّرْ تَبْذِيرًا ﴿٢٦﴾ إِنَّ ٱلْمُبَذِّرِينَ
كَانُوٓاْ إِخْوَٰنَ ٱلشَّيَٰطِينِ وَكَانَ ٱلشَّيْطَٰنُ لِرَبِّهِۦ كَفُورًا ﴿٢٧﴾
وَإِمَّا تُعْرِضَنَّ عَنْهُمُ ٱبْتِغَآءَ رَحْمَةٍ مِّن رَّبِّكَ تَرْجُوهَا فَقُل لَّهُمْ قَوْلًا
مَّيْسُورًا ﴿٢٨﴾ وَلَا تَجْعَلْ يَدَكَ مَغْلُولَةً إِلَىٰ عُنُقِكَ وَلَا تَبْسُطْهَا
كُلَّ ٱلْبَسْطِ فَتَقْعُدَ مَلُومًا مَّحْسُورًا ﴿٢٩﴾ إِنَّ رَبَّكَ يَبْسُطُ ٱلرِّزْقَ
لِمَن يَشَآءُ وَيَقْدِرُ إِنَّهُۥ كَانَ بِعِبَادِهِۦ خَبِيرًۢا بَصِيرًا ﴿٣٠﴾

*[3] And give to the kinsman his due and to the mis-
keen (needy) and to the wayfarer. But spend not
wastefully (your wealth) in the manner of a spendthrift. Verily, the spendthrifts are brothers of the
Shayaateen (devils), and the Shaytaan (Devil-Sa-
tan) is ever ungrateful to his Lord. And if you turn
away from them (kindred, needy, wayfarer and
have no wealth at the time they ask you) and are
awaiting a mercy from your Lord for which you
hope, then speak to them a soft, kind word (i.e. Allaah will provide for me and I shall give you). And
let not your hand be tied (like a miser) to your
neck, nor stretch it forth to its utmost reach (like a
spendthrift), so that you become blameworthy and
in severe poverty. Truly, your Lord increases the
provision for whom He wills and straitens it (for
whom He wills). Verily, He is Ever Well-Acquainted,
All-Seer of His slaves.*

وَلَا تَقْتُلُوٓا۟ أَوْلَٰدَكُمْ خَشْيَةَ إِمْلَٰقٍ نَّحْنُ نَرْزُقُهُمْ وَإِيَّاكُمْ إِنَّ قَتْلَهُمْ كَانَ خِطْـًٔا كَبِيرًا

[4] And kill not your children for fear of poverty. We shall provide for them as well as you. Surely, killing them is a great sin.

وَلَا تَقْرَبُوا۟ ٱلزِّنَىٰٓ إِنَّهُۥ كَانَ فَٰحِشَةً وَسَآءَ سَبِيلًا

[5] And come not near to unlawful sex. Verily, it is a faahishah (i.e. anything that transgresses its limits: a great sin), and an evil way (that leads one to Hell unless Allaah forgives him).

وَلَا تَقْتُلُوا۟ ٱلنَّفْسَ ٱلَّتِى حَرَّمَ ٱللَّهُ إِلَّا بِٱلْحَقِّ وَمَن قُتِلَ مَظْلُومًا فَقَدْ جَعَلْنَا لِوَلِيِّهِۦ سُلْطَٰنًا فَلَا يُسْرِف فِّى ٱلْقَتْلِ إِنَّهُۥ كَانَ مَنصُورًا

[6] And do not kill anyone whose killing Allaah has forbidden except for a just cause. And who-ever is killed wrongfully (intentionally with hostil-ity and oppression and not by mistake), We have given his heir the authority [to demand Qisaas, Law of Equality in punishment – or to forgive, or to take the diyah (blood money)]. But let him not exceed the limits in the matter of taking life (i.e. he should not kill anyone except the killer). Verily, he is aided (by the Islaamic Law).

وَلَا تَقْرَبُوا۟ مَالَ ٱلْيَتِيمِ إِلَّا بِٱلَّتِى هِىَ أَحْسَنُ حَتَّىٰ يَبْلُغَ أَشُدَّهُۥ

[7] And come not near to the orphan's property except to improve it, until he attains the age of full strength.

وَأَوْفُوا۟ بِٱلْعَهْدِ إِنَّ ٱلْعَهْدَ كَانَ مَسْـُٔولًا

[8] And fulfil (every) covenant. Verily, the covenant will be questioned about.

وَأَوْفُوا۟ ٱلْكَيْلَ إِذَا كِلْتُمْ وَزِنُوا۟ بِٱلْقِسْطَاسِ ٱلْمُسْتَقِيمِ
ذَٰلِكَ خَيْرٌ وَأَحْسَنُ تَأْوِيلًا

[9] And give full measure when you measure, and weigh with a balance that is straight. That is good (advantageous) and better in the end.

وَلَا تَقْفُ مَا لَيْسَ لَكَ بِهِۦ عِلْمٌ
إِنَّ ٱلسَّمْعَ وَٱلْبَصَرَ وَٱلْفُؤَادَ كُلُّ أُو۟لَـٰٓئِكَ كَانَ عَنْهُ مَسْـُٔولًا ﴿٣٦﴾
وَلَا تَمْشِ فِى ٱلْأَرْضِ مَرَحًا إِنَّكَ لَن تَخْرِقَ ٱلْأَرْضَ وَلَن تَبْلُغَ
ٱلْجِبَالَ طُولًا ﴿٣٧﴾

[10] And follow not (O man, i.e., say not or do not or witness not) that of which you have no knowledge. Verily, the hearing, the sight and the heart, each of those ones will be questioned (by Allaah). And walk not on the earth with conceit and arrogance. Verily, you can neither rend nor penetrate the earth nor can you attain a stature like the mountains in height.

$$كُلُّ ذَٰلِكَ كَانَ سَيِّئُهُۥ عِندَ رَبِّكَ مَكْرُوهًا$$

All the bad aspects of these (the above mentioned things) are hateful to your Lord.

$$ذَٰلِكَ مِمَّآ أَوْحَىٰٓ إِلَيْكَ رَبُّكَ مِنَ ٱلْحِكْمَةِ وَلَا تَجْعَلْ مَعَ ٱللَّهِ إِلَٰهًا ءَاخَرَ فَتُلْقَىٰ فِى جَهَنَّمَ مَلُومًا مَّدْحُورًا$$

This is (part) of al-Hikmah (wisdom, good manners and high character) which your Lord has revealed to you (O Muhammad). And set not up with Allaah any other ilaah (god) lest you should be thrown into Hell, blameworthy and rejected (from Allaah's Mercy).'

After you closely examine these verses O, questioner, we hope that you attain a better perception of the *Qur.aan*, one which is a lot better than the one that preceded it, a stance that opens a way for you to make fundamental changes in your life; a noble way that enables you to embrace the religion of *Islaam*. We wish you continuous success, and may peace be upon those who follow guidance.

2. Non-Muslims Entering the Masjid

Question: It is imperative upon every *Muslim* to call his heedless brothers to Allaah as well as those who indulge in different forms of entertainment and temptations. We, here in Algeria, organise outings wherein we bring people to the *masjid* in order to remind them of Allaah; acting upon the saying of Allaah (*Subhaanahu wa Ta'aala*):

$$فَذَكِّرْ إِن نَّفَعَتِ ٱلذِّكْرَىٰ$$

***Therefore remind, it may be that the reminder
benefits (the believers).***[2]

We do this in order to draw them out of the heedless state they are
drowned in, with the Permission of Allaah. However some scholars in
Algeria claim that it is impermissible to bring people who are in a state
of impurity into the *masjid*. We hope that you can respond as soon as
possible by either negating or affirming this claim while citing the evidences for that.[3]

Response: All praise is due to Allaah alone and may the *salaah* and *salaam* be upon the Messenger, his family and Companions.

To proceed:

Calling to Allaah is the way of the messengers, the last of them being
Muhammad (*sal-Allaahu 'alayhi wa sallam*). Allaah (*Subhaanahu wa
Ta'aala*) says:

$$قُلۡ هَٰذِهِۦ$$

$$سَبِيلِيٓ أَدۡعُوٓاْ إِلَى ٱللَّهِ عَلَىٰ بَصِيرَةٍ أَنَا۠ وَمَنِ ٱتَّبَعَنِيۖ$$

***Say (O Muhammad): "This is my way; I call to Al-
laah (i.e. to the Oneness of Allaah – Islaamic Monotheism) with sure knowledge, I and whomsoever
follows me.***[4]

Da'wah should be given to individuals as well as groups, in *masaajid*,

---

2 The Noble *Qur.aan - Soorah* al-A'laa, *Aayah* 9

3 Fataawa al-Lajnah ad-Daa.imah - No.3778

4 The Noble *Qur.aan - Soorah* Yoosuf, *Aayah* 108

universities, schools and other public places where people gather. It is general for all people; to be given to non-*Muslims*, sinners and believers. Non-*Muslims* may forsake their disbelief and embrace the truth; a sinner may forsake his sin and a believer would increase in knowledge, understanding and *eemaan*.

There is no problem in non-*Muslims* entering the *masjid* for a legislated benefit, such as hoping that they may embrace *Islaam* if they hear the reminder or attend a circle of knowledge. It has been authentically reported that the Messenger (*sal-Allaahu 'alayhi wa sallam*) ordered that Thumaamah ibn Athal al-Hanafee be tied to a pole in his *masjid* while he was a disbeliever; Allaah then guided him and he embraced *Islaam*.

Allaah is the granter of success and may the *salaah* and *salaam* be upon our Prophet Muhammad, his family and his Companions.

The Permanent Committee for Islaamic Research and Verdicts

3. Interacting with Non-Muslims

Question: Noble *Shaykh*, may Allaah forgive you, some of the youth harass non-*Muslims* in pathways, and may also harm them; is this permissible?[5]

Response: Harming non-*Muslims* who have a covenant and treaty with us is prohibited; however honouring them and making room for them is what the Messenger of Allaah (*sal-Allaahu 'alayhi wa sallam*) prohibited when he said:

---

5 Liqaa.aat al-Baab al-Maftooh - No.819

"Do not initiate the greeting of Salaam with Jews and Christians and if you pass by them in walk-ways, then force them to the narrower side."

This does not mean that one harms them or pushes them against the wall or the likes of this. Jews used to be present at the time of the Messenger (*sal-Allaahu 'alayhi wa sallam*) in Madeenah and he never used to treat them in this harmful way, rather he used to treat them according to what the treaty entailed.

Shaykh Muhammad ibn Saalih al-'Uthaymeen

4. Calling a Non-Muslim Servant

Question: Someone has a non-*Muslim* servant, is it binding upon him to call him to *Islaam*?[6]

Response: Yes, it is compulsory upon him to call his servant to *Islaam*, except if someone else is carrying out this task, but usually no one will carry this out in his house except him. The proof that this is obligatory is the saying of Allaah (*Subhaanahu wa Ta'aala*):

$$ ٱدۡعُ إِلَىٰ سَبِيلِ رَبِّكَ بِٱلۡحِكۡمَةِ وَٱلۡمَوۡعِظَةِ ٱلۡحَسَنَةِ وَجَٰدِلۡهُم بِٱلَّتِي هِيَ أَحۡسَنُ $$

Call (mankind, O Muhammad) to the way of your Lord (i.e. Islaam) with wisdom (i.e. with the Divine Revelation and the Qur.aan) and fair preaching,

---

6 Kitaab ad-Da'wah - Volume 2, Page 164

and debate with them in a manner that is best.[7]

The Messenger of Allaah (*sal-Allaahu 'alayhi wa sallam*) said to Mu'aadh when he sent him to Yemen:

"Call them to Islaam."

This is also clear from the spread of *Islaam* in its early period. The virtues of calling to *Islaam* are known to everyone, and if a person were to be guided through you then you attain an equal reward as he does through his actions. This is because the one who calls to good is like the one who practices that good. The Prophet (*sal-Allaahu 'alayhi wa sallam*) said to 'Alee ibn Abee Taalib (*radhi-yAllaahu 'anhu*):

"If Allaah guides a single person through you, this is better for you than the best of camels."

Shaykh Muhammad ibn Saalih al-'Uthaymeen

5. Calling Christians

Question: Noble *Shaykh*, workers who are mostly Christians or Hindus come and reside in parts of Saudi Arabia; students of knowledge may be their neighbours. However, these students do not call them to *Islaam* nor do they treat them well, and this may go on for years. These people come to the lands of the *Muslim*s and the *Muslim*s do not call them to *Islaam*, while if *Muslim*s were to travel abroad, Christians exert efforts in calling and advising them.[8]

---

7 The Noble *Qur.aan* - *Soorah* an-Nahl, *Aayah* 125

8 Liqaa.aat al-Baab al-Maftooh - No.955

209

Response: My advice is that calling to the Religion of Allaah is compulsory upon every *Muslim*, but it is *fardh kifaayah*; if a sufficient group carries it out, the obligation is absolved from the rest. This is due to the saying of Allaah (*Subhaanahu wa Ta'aala*):

$$ادْعُ إِلَىٰ سَبِيلِ رَبِّكَ بِالْحِكْمَةِ وَالْمَوْعِظَةِ الْحَسَنَةِ وَجَادِلْهُم بِالَّتِي هِيَ أَحْسَنُ$$

Call (mankind, O Muhammad) to the Way of your Lord with wisdom (i.e. with the Divine Inspiration and the Qur.aan), fair preaching and debate with them in the finest manner.[9]

Allaah (*Subhaanahu wa Ta'aala*) also said:

$$قُلْ هَٰذِهِ سَبِيلِي أَدْعُو إِلَى اللَّهِ عَلَىٰ بَصِيرَةٍ أَنَا وَمَنِ اتَّبَعَنِي$$

Say (O Muhammad): "This is my way; I call to Allaah (i.e. to the Oneness of Allaah – Islaamic Monotheism) with sure knowledge, I and those who follow me.[10]

Meaning: I call everyone to Allaah, I and those who follow me. So the more intent a person is in following the Messenger (*sal-Allaahu 'alayhi wa sallam*), the more intent you would find him in calling to his legislation.

---

9 The Noble *Qur.aan - Soorah* an-Nahl, *Aayah* 125

10 The Noble *Qur.aan - Soorah* Yoosuf, *Aayah* 108

There is no doubt that these brothers are neglectful, those who have non-*Muslims* neighbours, yet they do not call them to the religion of *Islaam*. Rather it is compulsory for them to call them to *Islaam*, even by being friendly to them. It would be nice if they invited them over for a meal, talked to them, called them to *Islaam* and explained its beauty to them. However, some brothers are overcome by jealousy, coupled with ignorance, so they stay away from, abandon or treat them harshly. Non-*Muslims* would be driven away from *Islaam* because of a *Muslim*, thinking that his mannerisms are the mannerisms that *Islaam* orders people to act upon.

If jealousy is of the good type, it is praiseworthy, but if it is not accompanied by wisdom and knowledge it is harmful in reality. So we advise these brothers of ours and others to call to Allaah (*Subhaanahu wa Ta'aala*). Just as you mentioned; Christians expend their wealth in order to call to Christianity, even though it is a false religion that was proven so by *Islaam*. This being the case, they are keen upon calling to it with the inspiration of the *Shaytaan*. They do this even though Christianity is a false religion that has been abrogated by *Islaam*. So how about us, the people of truth and determination; are we to be lazy, to the point that we do not even call our own neighbours, those who have rights upon us? I am not sure about these brothers, whether they give their neighbours their due rights or not; it has been mentioned in a *hadeeth*:

> *"If you cook broth, add water to it and share it with your neighbours."*

In another authentic *hadeeth* it states:

> *"Whoever believes in Allaah and the Last Day must be hospitable to his neighbour."*

The scholars stated: If your neighbour is a non-*Muslim* he has the rights of a neighbour. If he is a *Muslim* he has the rights of a neighbour as well as the rights of a *Muslim*. If he is a *Muslim* relative, then he has the rights of a neighbour, the rights of a *Muslim* and the rights of a relative.

So advise these brothers and tell them; call these people to the Religion, there may be good in calling them; if Allaah were to guide one person through them, this would be better for them than the best of camels. If one of them were to embrace *Islaam*, he may call others to it, as is well-known these days.

Shaykh Muhammad ibn Saalih al-'Uthaymeen

6. Are Jews and Christians Legislatively Pardoned?

Question: When is a person legislatively pardoned for ignorance? The Jews and Christians who are completely ignorant of *Islaam*, are they pardoned for their ignorance?[11]

Response: I believe this question is incorrect or vague. Why do you say 'Jews' if you already know that they are ignorant of the details of *Islaam*? Of course they are. This is something that everyone agrees upon, because even the *Muslim*s are ignorant of the details of *Islaam*. However if you mean that they are ignorant of the fact that *Islaam* calls to *tawheed*; to worshipping Allaah alone and not associating any partners with him, and they are ignorant of the fact that Muhammad was sent to warn all mankind, then this is something that cannot be agreed upon. Especially during these times and especially in relation to those amongst them who live in Arab lands and speak Arabic.

---

11 Fataawaa Shaykh al-Albaanee: 2/43

In any case, if we were to be lenient with this question, then *Muslim* commoners, those who associate partners with Allaah and seek aid from the dead and so on, these people are ignorant. It is established that what makes a person a disbeliever is the fact that he has knowledge of the reality of an affair in the religion and then denies it.

There are people who are known to the scholars as being the people of *'al-Fitrah.'* The people of *'al-Fitrah'* are those whom the *da'wah* has not reached, due to this fact this question is incorrect; are the Jews pardoned for their ignorance? The question should be corrected to read:

'Are the Jews considered to be from the people of *'al-Fitrah'* or not?'

If they are considered to be from the people of *'al-Fitrah,'* they are pardoned, and if they aren't then they are not pardoned. So are the Jews from the people of *'al-Fitrah?'*

Of course not, therefore someone who is from the people of *'al-Fitrah'* is not to be described as a person of ignorance. However, some individuals from amongst the Jews may be oblivious, but as a people, there is no way that we can describe them as being from the people of *'al-Fitrah'* or as being ignorant.

Question: What if the true reality of *Islaam* was not conveyed to them? This is possible.

Response: It has been conveyed to them since the Messenger of Allaah (*sal-Allaahu 'alayhi wa sallam*) was sent to them.

Question: Yes, but the latter generations; there is no doubt that they are astray and do not know the reality.

Response: Let's agree with this statement for arguments sake; what is the benefit? What we are saying is that those whom the *da'wah* has not reached are not held accountable by Allaah as being disbelievers. This is similar to an issue that we have already dealt with, and I thought that you would have understood it. It is the issue of rulers who do not judge by the Legislation of Allaah; it is either that you believe that this form of disbelief is related to actions or to *'aqeedah*. Whether it is this or that we say that what concerns us is the rule of *Islaam*, a wise person once said:

"Establish the sovereignty of *Islaam* within your hearts and it will be established in your lands."

Allaah is the Judge in this issue. It is only a matter of precision to say that such a leader has fallen into a form of disbelief related to actions, or that he has fallen into a form of disbelief related to *'aqeedah*. This leader's affair is up to Allaah; if Allaah knows that the form of disbelief that he has fallen into is related to *'aqeedah* then he will abide in the Hellfire forever with Pharaoh, Hamaan and Qaaroon and their likes. If Allaah knows that he believes in the Legislation of Allaah but did not rule by it, then if Allaah wills He would punish him and if He wills He would forgive him.

Likewise the issue of the Jews; it does not concern us whether the *da'wah* has been conveyed to them or not. If an *Islaam*ic state is established, do not delve into issues such as these because their affair lies with Allaah, as we have already mentioned in regards to the issue of rulers who do not judge by what Allaah has revealed.

If an *Islaam*ic state is established, then it is known that they do not believe in Allaah and His Messenger, neither do the Christians, so what should the *Islaam*ic state do? They should re-enact the *Seerah*; what did the Messenger of Allaah (*sal-Allaahu 'alayhi wa sallam*) do?

Shaykh Muhammad Naasiruddeen al-Albaanee

214

7. Giving a Sermon about Islaam in a Church

Question: A *Muslim* was asked to give a talk about *Islaam* in a church, should he do so?[12]

Response: All praise is due to Allaah. We asked the noble *Shaykh* Muhammad ibn Saalih al-'Uthaymeen this question and his response was:

This is a doubtful matter that needs to be investigated. The place (church) is not suitable except from a point of view that is hard to believe, and it is that the *Muslims*, due to their strength, are promoting their religion in Christian centres. Meaning that the *Muslims* have subjected themselves to the point where they speak about their religion in the church. Due to this I believe that it should not be done in order to avoid this harm and Allaah knows best.

Shaykh Muhammad ibn Saalih al-'Uthaymeen

8. Embracing Islaam while Having a Non-Muslim Husband

Question: We face a problem in *Islaam*ic centres while calling non-*Muslim* women to *Islaam*. It is the attachment of these women, who want to embrace *Islaam*, to their husbands, while their husbands do not. It is difficult for them to sacrifice their marriage, especially if they have children and their husbands are well-mannered, and so their love for their husbands takes precedence. We know that it is not permissible for a woman who embraces *Islaam* to stay under the guardianship of a non-*Muslim* man due to the saying of Allaah (*Subhaanahu wa Ta'aala*):

$$ لَاهُنَّ حِلٌّ لَّهُمْ وَلَاهُمْ يَحِلُّونَ لَهُنَّ $$

---

12 al-Mowsoo'ah - No.11232

***They are not lawful (wives) for the disbelievers nor
are the disbelievers lawful (husbands) for them.*** [13]

So how do we deal with this problem? Is it permissible for us to concentrate on converting them to *Islaam* and leaving off the rest of the
issue? [14]

All praise is due to Allaah. We asked the noble *Shaykh* Muhammad ibn
Saalih ibn 'Uthaymeen this question:

A woman is asking: 'I would like to embrace *Islaam* but I have a good
husband and I do not want to get separated from him, so what should
I do?'

Response: She has to get separated from him. However, is it possible
for her to call him to *Islaam* saying: 'I want to become *Muslim*, but our
marriage contract will be nullified unless you embrace *Islaam*'? If she
mentions this to him he may agree to become *Muslim*.

Question: If she becomes *Muslim*, should she call him to Allaah at home
or is she to leave the house?

Response: If she hopes that he will become *Muslim*, then she should
stay in his house until her *'iddah* period expires.

Question: Is she to veil herself from him during the *'iddah* period or
not?

---

13 The Noble *Qur.aan* - al-Mumtahinah, *Aayah* 10

14 al-Mowsoo'ah - No.4036

Response: It is safer that she does not expose herself, because it is not guaranteed that he will accept *Islaam*.

Question: How about being alone with him?

Response: She shouldn't even be alone with him.

Question: If telling her this would turn her away from *Islaam*, is it permissible for us to keep the second part of this answer hidden from her and say: 'Embrace *Islaam* first, and we will tell you about the ruling of staying with your husband later'?

Response: No, and if you were to do this she may become an apostate, then the problem would be even greater. This is why the Prophet (*sal-Allaahu 'alayhi wa sallam*) said to 'Alee when he sent him to Khaybar:

"Call them to *Islaam* and inform them of the Rights of Allaah that are obligated upon them in regards to it."

Question: So if this woman stays with her husband after she converts to *Islaam*, she is considered to be performing a major sin, correct?

Response: Yes, but is it permissible to keep practicing fornication (by remaining with him after she embraces *Islaam*)?

Question: In summary, what do we say to her?

Response: We say to her: 'Embrace *Islaam* and know that if you become *Muslim* and your husband does not, your marriage contract will be nullified.' That's it.

When speaking to women who go through this issue, you should con-

217

centrate on the following points while explaining them fully:

- Giving precedence to the love of Allaah and His Messenger over everyone else;

- If she is sincere in calling her husband to *Islaam* and in performing Du'aa for him, Allaah may guide him through her;

- Whoever forsakes something for the Pleasure of Allaah, Allaah will replace it with something better than it;

- Allaah will not forsake a servant of His who has sacrificed something that they love for His Pleasure.

You should also strive to solve problems like these. If a woman embraces *Islaam* and is consequently separated from her husband, then a brother should step forward and present himself to marry her and unite her with her children, or find someone from amongst the wealthy *Muslim*s to provide for her and her children.

We ask Allaah for guidance, success and pertinence, and may the *salaah* be upon our Prophet Muhammad.

Shaykh Muhammad ibn Saalih al-'Uthaymeen

9. Children Out of Wedlock

Question: We would like your advice on a certain issue: A French man came to the *masjid* to proclaim that he is *Muslim*; with him was a *Muslim* sister who says that she brought him to the *masjid* in order for him to embrace *Islaam* and then marry him. She herself does not pray nor wear *hijaab*, and is far from any family members or relatives. The gentleman himself affirms that he would like to embrace *Islaam* because he wishes to be *Muslim*.

What do you advise us to do in this situation, and what should we do if they have already been married for a year or two and had children while the gentleman was a non-*Muslim*?

Is his entry into *Islaam* accepted, and is the fact that he has been away from her for one or two menstrual periods to be considered for the marriage to take place?

How can we rectify their marriage while the sister doesn't even have a legal guardian in France at all?

What is the ruling of their children, are they considered to be 'children due to fornication'?[15]

<u>Response</u>: All praise is due to Allaah alone and may the *salaah* and *salaam* be upon the Messenger, his family and his Companions.

<u>Firstly</u>: The gentleman is to be told of how pleased you are that he is converting to *Islaam* and that this is the greatest obligation upon him, the greatest blessing that anyone can be congratulated for.

<u>Secondly</u>: The 'Pillars of *Islaam*' are to be explained to him along with the foundations of *eemaan*, the meaning of the *shahaadah*, the meaning of 'believing in the Last Day' and the Divine Decree. The falseness of the Christian belief in relation to 'Eesaa is to be explained and clarified to him along with the fact that it is upon him to believe that 'Eesaa is a servant and Messenger of Allaah, just like the rest of the messengers, and that he is not a son of Allaah. High above is Allaah indeed from the sayings of the Christians. It is to be explained to him that Muhammad (*sal-*

---

15 Fataawa al-Lajnah ad-Daa.imah - No.5377

Allaahu 'alayhi wa sallam) is the 'Seal' of the prophets and messengers and his message is universal to all mankind whether they are Arabs or non-Arabs, and to the *jinn* as well. Likewise all this is to be explained to the lady and she is to be asked to accept *Islaam* from anew, because abandoning the prayer is disbelief.

Thirdly: If the lady does not have a legal guardian at all, then the head of the *Islaam*ic centre amongst you should be her guardian for the marriage contract, because he takes the place of a legal guardian in situations like this due to the saying of the Messenger of Allaah (*sal-Allaahu 'alayhi wa sallam*):

> **"The Sultan is a legal guardian for those who have no guardian."**

The head of an *Islaam*ic centre has this authority in his area because of the lack of a *Muslim* judge in his vicinity.

Fourthly: There is no need for them to be away from each other for any period of time if his past relationship with her was in the name of a marriage. Their children are to be attributed to him as they are attributed to the father in the case of 'intercourse due to misconception' in a false marriage.

Allaah is the granter of success, and may the *salaah* and *salaam* be upon our Prophet Muhammad, his family and his Companions.

The Permanent Committee for Islaamic Research and Verdicts

10. Accepting the Invitation of a Non-Muslim

Question: Calling to *Islaam* requires establishing personal relationships with non-*Muslims* in order to familiarise ourselves with them and pre-pare to call them to Allaah. If one of them invites us for a permissible drink or meal such as cheese, fish or tea, is it permissible for us to eat it? Is it permissible to eat from their dishes if there is a possibility that they previously used these dishes for cooking pork or alcohol and then washed them with soap and water?[16]

<u>Response</u>: There are different types of relationships. If a relationship consists of love, affection and brotherhood, it is impermissible for a *Muslim* to have such a relationship with a non-*Muslim*, and it may even be a form of disbelief. Allaah (*Subhaanahu wa Ta'aala*) said:

لَّا تَجِدُ قَوْمًا يُؤْمِنُونَ بِٱللَّهِ وَٱلْيَوْمِ ٱلْأَخِرِ يُوَآدُّونَ مَنْ حَآدَّ ٱللَّهَ وَرَسُولَهُۥ وَلَوْ كَانُوٓاْ ءَابَآءَهُمْ أَوْ أَبْنَآءَهُمْ أَوْ إِخْوَٰنَهُمْ أَوْ عَشِيرَتَهُمْ أُوْلَـٰٓئِكَ كَتَبَ فِى قُلُوبِهِمُ ٱلْإِيمَٰنَ وَأَيَّدَهُم بِرُوحٍ مِّنْهُ وَيُدْخِلُهُمْ جَنَّـٰتٍ تَجْرِى مِن تَحْتِهَا ٱلْأَنْهَٰرُ خَٰلِدِينَ فِيهَا رَضِىَ ٱللَّهُ عَنْهُمْ وَرَضُواْ عَنْهُ أُوْلَـٰٓئِكَ حِزْبُ ٱللَّهِ أَلَآ إِنَّ حِزْبَ ٱللَّهِ هُمُ ٱلْمُفْلِحُونَ ﴿٢٢﴾

You (O Muhammad) will not find a people who believe in Allaah and the Last Day, having friendship with those who oppose Allaah and His Messenger (Muhammad), even if they were their fathers, their sons, their brothers or their kindred (people). For such He has written Faith in their hearts, and strengthened them with Ruh (proofs, light and true guidance) from Himself. And He will admit them into

---

16 Fataawa al-Lajnah ad-Daa.imah - Volume 12, Page 254

Gardens (Paradise) under which rivers flow to dwell therein (forever). Allaah is pleased with them, and they with Him. They are the party of Allaah. Verily, it is the party of Allaah that will be the successful.[17]

The verses and *ahaadeeth* of this like are plentiful.

However if the relationship is that of buying and selling, accepting an invitation to a permissible meal or accepting a permissible gift, while not having an effect upon the *Muslim*, this is permissible.

Eating and drinking permissible forms of food and drink presented by non-*Muslims* is permissible, even if the dishes that the food is served in were previously used for pork, alcohol and so on, as long as they have been washed until all impurities have been completely removed from them. You are rewarded if this aids in calling to *Islaam* and facilitates its acceptance and communication between you and them.

The Permanent Committee for Islaamic Research and Verdicts

11. Giving Non-Muslims a Book that Contains Verses of the Qur.aan

Question: Is it permissible for me to leave books with non-*Muslims* that contain noble verses from the *Qur.aan* that establish the Oneness of Allaah (*Subhaanahu wa Ta'aala*), written in Arabic and translated into English?[18]

---

17 The Noble *Qur.aan* - *Soorah* al-Mujaadalah, *Aayah* 22

18 Fataawa al-Lajnah ad-Daa.imah - Volume 12, Page 251

<u>Response</u>: All praise is due to Allaah. Yes, it is permissible to give them books that contain verses of the *Qur.aan* that are evidence for rulings, *tawheed* and so on, whether they are in Arabic or whether their meanings are translated into another language. Rather we are grateful for this, because giving or lending them these books is a way of calling to the Religion of Allaah and one who does so is rewarded if he is sincere.

The Permanent Committee for Islaamic Research and Verdicts

12. Is the Presence of Christians among Muslims Sufficient for Da'wah?

<u>Question</u>: You mentioned in a previous response that those whom the message of Muhammad has reached from amongst the Jews and the Christians, those who know of it but do not follow it because they are non-*Muslim*, they are to be treated as disbelievers in relation to the life of this world and the next. You are aware that there are alot of Christians and followers of other religions in our country. Is their presence in this *Muslim* country sufficient in conveying the message to them?[19]

All praise is due to Allaah; their presence amongst the *Muslims* necessitates that they are considered to be amongst those whom the message of Muhammad (*sal-Allaahu 'alayhi wa sallam*) has reached, and the rulings of that are to be applied to them, because Allaah (*Subhaanahu wa Ta'aala*) says:

$$\text{وَأُوحِىَ إِلَىَّ هَٰذَا ٱلْقُرْءَانُ لِأُنذِرَكُم بِهِۦ وَمَنۢ بَلَغَۚ}$$

This Qur.aan has been revealed to me that I may

---

19 Fataawaa al-Lajnah ad-Daa.imah - Volume 12, Page 252

therewith warn you and whomsoever it reaches.[20]

The Messenger of Allaah (*sal-Allaahu 'alayhi wa sallam*) said:

"By Him in Whose Hands my soul lies in, nobody from amongst this ummah, whether Jewish or Christian, would hear of me and then die without believing in what I was sent with, except that they would be from the people of the Hellfire."

The Permanent Committee for Islaamic Research and Verdicts

13. Giving the Qur.aan to a Christian

Question: If a Christian asks me for a copy of the *Qur.aan*, should I give one to him?[21]

Response: You should not give it to him; you should read the *Qur.aan* to him, let him hear it, call him to Allaah and pray that Allaah guides him due to the saying of Allaah (*Subhaanahu wa Ta'aala*) in His Book:

وَإِنْ أَحَدٌ مِّنَ ٱلْمُشْرِكِينَ ٱسْتَجَارَكَ فَأَجِرْهُ حَتَّىٰ يَسْمَعَ كَلَٰمَ ٱللَّهِ ثُمَّ أَبْلِغْهُ مَأْمَنَهُ

And if any of the Mushrikoon (polytheists) seeks your protection then grant him protection so that he may hear the Word of Allaah (the Qur.aan) and

---

20 The Noble *Qur.aan* - *Soorah* al-An'aam, *Aayah* 19

21 Majmoo' Fataawa wa Maqaalaat Mutanawwi'ah - Volume 6, Page 372

then escort him to where he can be secure...[22]

Also, the saying of the Messenger:

"Do not travel with the Qur.aan to the lands of the enemies, so that they do not touch it."

This indicates that a non-*Muslim* is not to be given a copy of the *Qur.aan* for fear that he will demean or fool around with it. However he should be taught; the *Qur.aan* should be read to him, he should be advised and supplicated for. If he embraces *Islaam*, he is to be given a copy of the *Qur.aan*.

There is no problem in giving him an explanation of the *Qur.aan*, a book of *hadeeth* or a translation of the meanings of the *Qur.aan* if he wants to benefit from that.

Shaykh 'Abdul-'Azeez ibn Baaz

14. Non-Muslims Entering the Masjid

Question: In relation to non-*Muslim*s such as polytheists and Communists entering the *masjid*; some claim that they are permitted to enter the *masaajid*, perhaps Allaah will guide them; others say that this is impermissible. We hope that you will benefit us with the correct opinion, may Allaah benefit you.[23]

Response: It is not permissible for non-*Muslim*s to enter *al-Masjid al-*

---

22 The Noble *Qur.aan* - *Soorah* at-Towbah, *Aayah* 6

23 Fataawa Noor 'alad-Darb - Volume 1, Page 380

Haraam; not Jews, Christians, polytheists or Communists. All disbelievers are prohibited from entering *al-Masjid al-Haraam* due to the saying of Allaah (*Subhaanahu wa Ta'aala*):

$$يَٰٓأَيُّهَا ٱلَّذِينَ ءَامَنُوٓاْ إِنَّمَا ٱلۡمُشۡرِكُونَ نَجَسٞ فَلَا يَقۡرَبُواْ ٱلۡمَسۡجِدَ ٱلۡحَرَامَ بَعۡدَ عَامِهِمۡ هَٰذَآ$$

O you who believe, indeed the Mushrikoon (polytheists) are unpurified so do not let them approach al-Masjid al-Haraam after this year[24]

Thus Allaah prohibited them from entering *al-Masjid al-Haraam*. Jews and the Christians are included amongst the polytheists when this word is mentioned without restriction.

As for the rest of the *masaajid*, there is no harm in non-*Muslim*s entering them if there is a need or a benefit to do so, including the *masjid* of Madeenah. Even though the *masjid* in Madeenah is unique, in this issue it is like other *masaajid* because the Prophet tied a disbeliever to one of the pillars there, allowed the 'Delegation of Thaqeef' to enter it before they accepted *Islaam* and likewise allowed a delegation of Christians to enter his *masjid*.

This proves that it is permissible for polytheists to enter into the Prophet's *masjid* and this is more so the case with the rest of *masaajid* if there is a need to do so, such as asking a question, benefiting by listening to a lesson there or entering to embrace *Islaam* and announcing that and so on.

---

24 The Noble *Qur.aan* - *Soorah* at-Towbah, *Aayah* 28

The point is that it is permissible for them to enter if there is a benefit. However, if there is no benefit, then there is no need for them to enter the *masjid*. Likewise if it is feared that they may act carelessly with the *masjid*'s property, furniture or that they may bring filth and impurities into it then this is prohibited.

Shaykh 'Abdul-'Azeez ibn Baaz

Chapter 12
Converts

1. Circumcision for New Muslims

Question: A Christian man and his wife wanted to accept *Islaam*; they were told to wash their hands, enunciate the *shahaadah* willingly, while accepting and submitting to it, and to perform circumcision. The husband is asking if this is correct and would like you to respond by citing narrations from the *Salaf* concerning this issue as well as explaining how people used to embrace *Islaam* at the time of the Messenger (*sal-Allaahu 'alayhi wa sallam*)?[1]

Response: All praise is due to Allaah alone and may the *salaah* and *salaam* be upon the Messenger, his family and his Companions.

The way of the Messenger (*sal-Allaahu 'alayhi wa sallam*) in calling non-*Muslims* to *Islaam* is that he would order them to bear witness that there is no deity worthy of worship except Allaah and that Muhammad is the Messenger of Allaah. If they accepted this he would then call them

---

1 Fataawa al-Lajnah ad-Daa.imah - Volume 3, Page 1557

to the rest of the *Islaam*ic legislation according to due importance and depending on what the circumstances entailed.

Amongst what has been related in this issue is what al-Bukhaaree and Muslim reported on the authority of Ibn 'Abbaas (*radhi-yAllaahu 'anhu*), that when the Messenger of Allaah (*sal-Allaahu 'alayhi wa sallam*) sent Mu'aadh to Yemen, he said to him:

> *"Indeed you are travelling to a people from amongst the People of the Book; so call them firstly to testify that none has the right to be worshipped except Allaah."*

In another narration:

> *"To single out Allaah in worship. If they accept this from you, inform them that Allaah has enjoined five prayers upon them which are to be performed daily. If they accept that from you, inform them that Allaah has enjoined zakaat upon them which is to be taken from the rich from amongst them and given to the poor from amongst them. If they accept that from you, then beware of taking the best of their wealth and fear the supplication of the oppressed one, for indeed there is no barrier between it and Allaah [i.e. his supplication is answered]."*

Amongst what has been narrated also is what al-Bukhaaree and Muslim reported on the authority of Sahl ibn Sa'd as-Saa'idee, that the Messenger of Allaah said to 'Alee when he handed him the banner:

> *"Proceed with calmness until you reach their land, then call them to Islaam and inform them of*

12

229

what has been obligated upon them in relation to the Rights of Allaah in it. For by Allaah, if Allaah guides a single person through you, this would be better for you than the best of camels."

In another narration:

"Then call them to bear witness that none has the right to be worshipped except Allaah and that Muhammad is the Messenger of Allaah."

The *Salaf* differed in regards to the ruling of *ghusl* in relation to one who embraced *Islaam*. *Imaam* Maalik, Ahmad and Abu Thowr, may Allaah have mercy upon them, stated that it is compulsory due to a narration reported by Abu Daawood and an-Nasaa.ee on the authority of Qays ibn 'Aasim (*radhi-yAllaahu 'anhu*) that he said:

"I came to the Prophet (*sal-Allaahu 'alayhi wa sallam*) wanting to embrace *Islaam*, so he ordered me to perform *ghusl* with water and leaves from a lotus tree."

An order by the Prophet (*sal-Allaahu 'alayhi wa sallam*) to perform *ghusl* necessitates that this is an obligation.

Imaam ash-Shaafi'ee and some *Hanbalee* scholars stated that it is recommended to perform *ghusl* except in the case of one who was in a state of sexual impurity before embracing *Islaam*; in this situation it is obligatory for him to perform *ghusl*.

Abu Haneefah stated that it is obligatory in all circumstances.

In any case it is legislated for a new *Muslim* to perform *ghusl* due to the aforementioned *hadeeth* as well as others that confirm this meaning.

As for circumcision, it is obligatory upon men and considered to be a noble act for women. However, it would be good to delay informing one who desires to enter into *Islaam* about this issue to a later time such that he becomes comfortable with *Islaam* and it becomes firmly established in his heart, for fear that hastily informing him to perform circumcision may chase him away from *Islaam*.

Allaah is the granter of success.

The Permanent Committee for Islaamic Research and Verdicts

2. Enunciating the Shahaadah in the Presence of a Judge

Question: Two non-*Muslims* who wanted to embrace *Islaam* asked a *Muslim* to bring them to the *masjid* to perform prayers and to obtain a translated copy of the meanings of the *Qur.aan* in English. He told them that they would be taken to the hospital to be circumcised, and then they would be taken to a judge in order to enunciate the *shahaadah* in his presence. He advised them to prepare themselves for this. They are asking for advice concerning the obligations they have to carry out.[2]

Response: The way of the Messenger (*sal-Allaahu 'alayhi wa sallam*) in calling non-*Muslims* to *Islaam* is that he would order them to bear witness that there is no deity worthy of worship except Allaah and that Muhammad is the Messenger of Allaah. Ibn 'Abbaas (*radhi-yAllaahu 'an-hum*) narrated that when the Messenger of Allaah (*sal-Allaahu 'alayhi wa sallam*) sent Mu'aadh to Yemen, he said to him:

---

2 Fataawa al-Lajnah ad-Daa.imah - No.1588

"Indeed you are travelling to a People of the Book; so call them firstly to testify that none has the right to be worshipped except Allaah."

In another narration:

"To single out Allaah in worship."

In another narration as well:

· *"Call them to testify that none has the right to be worshipped except Allaah and that I am the Messenger of Allaah. If they accept this from you, inform them that Allaah has enjoined five prayers upon them which are to be performed daily. If they accept that from you, inform them that Allaah has enjoined zakaat upon them which is to be taken from the rich from amongst them and given to the poor from amongst them. If they accept that from you, then beware of taking the best of their wealth and fear the supplication of the oppressed one, for indeed there is no barrier between it and Allaah [i.e. his supplication is answered]."*

al-Bukhaaree and Muslim also reported upon the authority of Sahl ibn Sa'd as-Saa'idee that the Messenger of Allaah said to 'Alee when he handed him the banner at the battle of Khaybar:

"Proceed with calmness until you reach their land, then call them to Islaam and inform them of what has been obligated upon them in relation to the Rights of Allaah in it. For by Allaah, if Al-

laah guides a single person through you, then this is better for you than the best of camels."

In another narration:

"Then call them to bear witness that none have the right to be worshipped except Allaah and that Muhammad is the Messenger of Allaah."

Abu Daawood and an-Nasaa.ee reported on the authority of Qays ibn 'Aasim what proves that *ghusl* is legislated for one who wishes to accept *Islaam*. So the likes of the two people mentioned in the question should practice *ghusl* and then immediately declare that there is no deity worthy of worship except Allaah and that Muhammad is the Messenger of Allaah. They should then be taken to the *masjid* after purifying themselves in the legislated manner. They are then to be taken to an *Islaam*ic court house to officially declare that they are *Muslim*s.

As for circumcision then it is compulsory upon men and a 'recommended act' for women. However it would be good if you were to delay informing those who wish to embrace *Islaam* about circumcision to a latter time when *Islaam* is firmly established in their hearts.

Allaah is the granter of success and may the *salaah* and *salaam* be upon our Prophet Muhammad, his family and his Companions.

The Permanent Committee for Islaamic Research and Verdicts

3. The Obligations upon a New Convert

Question: There is a *Muslim* who recently converted to *Islaam* but didn't proclaim it yet; are the obligations upon all *Muslim*s binding upon him in this period as well?[3]

Response: All praise is due to Allaah alone and may the *salaah* and *salaam* be upon the Messenger, his family and his Companions.

If a person accepts *Islaam* it is compulsory upon him to learn the issues that are legislated for him gradually and according to his ability. He is to act upon that from the instant he accepts *Islaam*.

The Permanent Committee for Islaamic Research and Verdicts

4. Reading the Qur.aan during Prayer for New Muslims

Question: Can a *Muslim* who recently learnt how to recite the Faatihah[4] and the *Qur.aan* recite them in periods during the prayer when *tasbeeh* and invocations must be read? Is there something else that can take their place due to the difficulty of reading them for a new *Muslim* during his early stages?[5]

Response: He is to recite the *Qur.aan* as well as read the invocations during the *salaah* in their respected places according to his ability due to the general saying of Allaah (*Subhaanahu wa Ta'aala*):

$$ لَا يُكَلِّفُ ٱللَّهُ نَفْسًا إِلَّا وُسْعَهَا $$

Allaah burdens not a person beyond his ability.[6]

Allaah burdens not a person beyond his ability.

---

3 Fataawa al-Lajnah ad-Daa.imah - No.5377

4 The Noble *Qur.aan* - *Soorah* al-Faatihah

5 Fataawa al-Lajnah ad-Daa.imah - No.6348

6 The Noble *Qur.aan* - *Soorah* al-Baqarah, *Aayah* 286

He should not read the Faatihah[7] while bowing or during prostrations instead of *tasbeeh* for example.

Allaah is the granter of success, and may the *salaah* and *salaam* be upon our Prophet Muhammad, his family and his Companions.

The Permanent Committee for Islaamic Research and Verdicts

5. Does a New Muslim Make up Past Obligations?

<u>Question</u>: Does a man who embraced *Islaam* at the age of forty make up for lost obligations during past years?[8]

<u>Response</u>: All praise is due to Allaah. A person who embraces *Islaam* does not have to make up obligations that he missed such as prayers, fasting and *zakaat* while he was a disbeliever due to the saying of Allaah (*Subhaanahu wa Ta'aala*):

$$قُل لِّلَّذِينَ كَفَرُوٓا۟ إِن يَنتَهُوا۟ يُغْفَرْ لَهُم مَّا قَدْ سَلَفَ$$

Say to those who have disbelieved, if they cease (from disbelief), their past will be forgiven.[9]

Also due to the saying of the Messenger of Allaah (*sal-Allaahu 'alayhi wa sallam*):

"Islaam erases whatever was before it."

---

7 The Noble *Qur.aan* - *Soorah* al-Faatihah

8 Fataawa al-Lajnah ad-Daa.imah - Volume 6, Page 400

9 The Noble *Qur.aan* - *Soorah* al-Anfaal, *Aayah* 38

This is also because the Messenger of Allaah (*sal-Allaahu 'alayhi wa sallam*) never ordered anyone who embraced *Islaam* to make up for the legislated acts of *Islaam* they missed while they were disbelievers, and there is consensus of the people of knowledge upon that.

The Permanent Committee for Islaamic Research and Verdicts

6. Changing One's Name after Converting to Islaam

Question: Does a person who declared his conversion to *Islaam* have to change his name, such as George, Joseph and so on?[10]

Response: He doesn't have to change his name except if he were called 'the servant (*'Abd*)' of other than Allaah; however changing it to a better name is legislated. It is good as well as suitable to change his name from a non-Arabic name to an *Islaami*c name.

As for it being obligatory to change it, then the answer is no. However if his name is 'Abdul-Maseeh' or a name similar to it that means a person is the 'servant' of other than Allaah, then it is obligatory to change it due to the consensus by the people of knowledge reported by Abu Muhammad Ibn Hazm, that this is a form of devoting worship to other than Allaah, and with Allaah is all success.

Shaykh 'Abdul-'Azeez ibn Baaz

7. A New Muslim Praying while Still Drinking

Question: A man accepted *Islaam* through me and I visit him in order to teach it to him; however he continues to drink alcohol. I visit him in or-

---

der to teach him how to pray and explain *Islaam* to him but sometimes when it's time to pray, I find him drinking, and he doesn't even know how to pray yet. Is it permissible for me to pray with him while he is in this state?[11]

Response: If he does not know what he is saying then you shouldn't pray with him:

$$يَٰٓأَيُّهَا ٱلَّذِينَ ءَامَنُواْ لَا تَقْرَبُواْ ٱلصَّلَوٰةَ وَأَنتُمْ سُكَٰرَىٰ حَتَّىٰ تَعْلَمُواْ مَا تَقُولُونَ$$

O you who believe! Do not approach as-Salaat (the prayers) while you are in a drunken state until you know (the meaning) of what you utter...[12]

If however he does know what he is saying then there is no harm in doing so *inshaa.-Allaah*. This does not mean that the affair of drinking alcohol is a light one; indeed it is a major sin and may lead to other major sins.

Question: What if he is under the influence of drugs; does the same ruling apply?

Response: Like Hasheesh, Shaykhul Islaam Ibn Taymiyyah said that drugs are more dangerous than alcohol; there is no good whatsoever in them, may Allaah bless you.

Question: So he should pray and we teach it to him, even though he uses drugs?

---

11 ar-Rihlah al-Akheerah li-Imaam al-Jazeerah - Page 116

12 The Noble *Qur.aan - Soorah* an-Nisaa, *Aayah* 43

Response: Yes, teach him how to pray and let him pray, it's better than having a Christian or Jew teaching him, may Allaah bless you.

Shaykh Muqbil ibn Haadee al-Waadi'ee

8. Advice to the New Muslim

Question: If Allaah guides someone to *Islaam*, what should he say and what should be said to him?[13]

Response: He should say:

أَشْهَدُ أَلاَّ إِلَهَ إِلاَّ الله،

وَ أَشْهَدُ أَنَّ مُحَمَّداً عَبْدُهُ وَ رَسُولُهُ

I bear witness that there is no deity worthy of worship except Allaah, and that Muhammad is His servant and messenger.

He should then be advised to accompany righteous people, for indeed the Messenger of (*sal-Allaahu 'alayhi wa sallam*) said:

> *"The example of the righteous companion and the evil companion is like the perfumer and the blacksmith. As for the perfumer, he is either going to gift you some perfume, sell you some, or you would at least smell a pleasant fragrance from him. As for the blacksmith, he would either burn your clothes or you would smell a wretched smell from him."*

---

13 Tuhfatul-Mujeeb - Page 65

I was told of a story while I was studying in the *Islaam*ic University of Madeenah; someone embraced *Islaam*, so he moved from the non-*Muslim*s home to live with the *Muslim*s. However, the *Muslim*s that he stayed with didn't even pray, so his *Islaam* was merely moving from one house to another.

So it is essential for one to strive to accompany righteous people, and disbelieve in worshipping the Messiah.

We also advise them to acquire beneficial books such as: Riyaadhus-Saaliheen, Fat.hul-Majeed; the explanation of Kitaabut-Tawheed, Buloogh al-Maraam and Tafseer Ibn Katheer.

Likewise we advise them to learn *Islaam* from the books of *Islaam*, and not from the actions of the *Muslim*s, because their actions are not good. You may find a *Muslim* lying, committing adultery or drinking alcohol while they know that these acts are forbidden. Then non-*Muslim*s use this as evidence against *Muslim*s, so we say to them: We do not call you to this; rather we call you to adhere to the correct religion.

إِنَّ ٱللَّهَ يَأْمُرُ بِٱلْعَدْلِ وَٱلْإِحْسَانِ وَإِيتَآئِ ذِى ٱلْقُرْبَىٰ وَيَنْهَىٰ عَنِ ٱلْفَحْشَآءِ وَٱلْمُنكَرِ وَٱلْبَغْيِ يَعِظُكُمْ لَعَلَّكُمْ تَذَكَّرُونَ

Verily Allaah enjoins al-'Adl (justice), al-Ihsaan (beneficence), helping kin, and forbids al-Fahshaa'(evil), al-Munkar, and al-Baghy (oppression) He admonishes you, in order that you may take heed.[14]

---

14 The Noble *Qur.aan* - *Soorah* an-Nahl, *Aayah* 90

Likewise the issue of trustworthiness, honesty and other issues that the *Muslims* do not abide by, which is in opposition to the Legislation of *Islaam*, these people are not evidence against *Islaam*, rather *Islaam* is a proof against the *Muslims* themselves. So it is important to make this clear to them, so that they do not use the actions of sinful *Muslims* as evidence against *Islaam*, rather we say to them: We do not call you to be like these people, nor to be like those who are corrupt, thieves, those who sell or make alcohol, nor do we call you to become *Soofees*.

A noble brother who studies either in Britain or Germany once visited us, he told us that Allaah guided a woman to *Islaam*. She then saw the *Soofees* dance in the *masaajid*, so she called him and said, 'I saw such and such in the *masjid*, so if this is *Islaam* then there is no difference between it and the religion that I have left.'

So we do not call you to become a *Shee'ee*, a *Soofee* or a *'Ilmaanee*, rather we call you to act upon the Book of Allaah and the *Sunnah* of His Messenger (*sal-Allaahu 'alayhi wa sallam*) even if all the people were to contradict you.

Shaykh Muqbil ibn Haadee al-Waadi'ee

9. Embracing Islaam and Following a Deviant Sect

Question: Noble *Shaykh*, there are alot of Christians who accept *Islaam* and then end up following a methodology other than the methodology of *Ahlus-Sunnah wal-Jamaa'ah*, such as the *Soofiyyah* and *Shee'ah*. Are they considered to be disbelievers due to following a methodology other than that of *Ahlus-Sunnah* and the *Salafus-Saalih* or do we judge them according to the sect they follow?[15]

---

15 Liqaa.aat al-Baab al-Maftooh - No.1081

<u>Response</u>: If a non-*Muslim* embraces *Islaam*, affiliates himself to it and then joins an innovated sect, he then takes the ruling of that sect.

If he involves himself in innovations that are within themselves a form of disbelief, he is considered to be a disbeliever and his conversion from Christianity to this innovation would not have benefited him. If these innovations do not lead to disbelief then he is not considered to be a disbeliever.

However *Ahlus-Sunnah* should search for and properly receive those who embrace *Islaam* on their own. Because it is extremely likely that they accepted *Islaam* due to their own desire, and then an innovator approaches them and harms them by saying: "This innovation is a part of *Islaam*," and so they practice it.

Shaykh Muhammad ibn Saalih al-'Uthaymeen

12

Chapter 13
Opposing Views and Methodologies

1. Abstaining from Speaking about the Tawheed of the 'Names and Attributes' of Allaah

Question: A group affiliated to *Islaam* holds the opinion that the *tawheed* of the 'Names and Attributes of Allaah' should not be addressed because it causes splitting and occupies people from performing their obligations, which is *Islaam*ic *jihaad*. Is this correct?[1]

Response: This opinion is incorrect. Indeed Allaah has clarified His 'Names and Attributes' in His Noble Book. He mentioned them in order to teach them to the believers, and so that they can invoke, describe and praise Him (*Subhaanahu wa Ta'aala*) with them. There are numerous narrations confirming that the Messenger of Allaah (*sal-Allaahu 'alayhi wa sallam*) mentioned the 'Names and Attributes of Allaah' in his sermons and while speaking with his Companions. He praised Allaah with them and encouraged others to do so.

---

1 Majmoo' Fataawa wa Maqaalaat Mutanawwi'ah - Volume 5, Page 102

It is compulsory for the people of knowledge and *eemaan* to propagate Allaah's 'Names and Attributes' and include them in their lectures, books and sermons, because through them Allaah is known and with them He is worshipped. It is impermissible to be ignorant of them or abstain from mentioning them, claiming that some of the commoners may be confused by the issue, or that some of the people of innovations may cause confusion amongst the commoners in this issue. Rather it is obligatory to expose these misconceptions by refuting them and clarifying that it is compulsory to confirm the 'Names and Attributes of Allaah' in a way that is befitting to Allaah (*Subhaanahu wa Ta'aala*) without *tahreef, ta'teel, takyeef* or *tamtheel*, until the ignorant know the ruling of this affair, and the innovator discontinues and refrains from exceeding his limits, and in order to establish the evidence upon them.

Ahlus-Sunnah wal-Jamaa'ah have clarified in their books that it is an obligation upon the *Muslims*, especially the people of knowledge, to convey the verses of the *Qur.aan* and *ahaadeeth* that contain Allaah's Attributes exactly as they were transmitted, while believing that they are true; that they are Names and Attributes that belong to Allaah (*Subhaanahu wa Ta'aala*); that their meanings are true; and that Allaah (*Subhaanahu wa Ta'aala*) is described by them in a way that is befitting to Him, such as *ar-Rahmaan, ar-Raheem, al-'Azeez, al-Hakeem, al-Qadeer, as-Samee'* and *al-Baseer*, and other than that.

It is compulsory to convey the 'Names and Attributes' of Allaah exactly as they were transmitted while having faith in them and believing that there is nothing similar to Allaah; He has no equal nor is there anything that is comparable to Him, Glorified and Exalted be He.

We do not say or question how these Attributes are, because this is known only to Allaah; none other than Him have knowledge of this. So just like He (*Subhaanahu wa Ta'aala*) has an Essence that is unlike any other, and it is impermissible to say or ask about how it is, likewise He has Attributes that are unlike any other attributes and it is impermissible to question or state how they are.

The Attributes of Allaah retain the same rulings as His Essence and are to be compared to it. This is the position of *Ahlus-Sunnah*, the Companions of the Messenger of Allaah (*sal-Allaahu 'alayhi wa sallam*) and those that came after them. Allaah (*Subhaanahu wa Ta'aala*) said:

$$\text{قُلْ هُوَ ٱللَّهُ أَحَدٌ ۝ ٱللَّهُ ٱلصَّمَدُ ۝ لَمْ يَلِدْ}$$
$$\text{وَلَمْ يُولَدْ ۝ وَلَمْ يَكُن لَّهُۥ كُفُوًا أَحَدُۢ ۝}$$

"Say (O Muhammad): "He is Allaah, (the) One. Allaah, the Self-Sufficient Master, Whom all creatures need, (He neither eats nor drinks)] He begets not, nor was He begotten. And there is none coequal or any one comparable to Him"."[2]

He (*Subhaanahu wa Ta'aala*) also said:

$$\text{لَيْسَ كَمِثْلِهِۦ شَىْءٌ وَهُوَ ٱلسَّمِيعُ ٱلْبَصِيرُ}$$

"There is nothing like Him, and He is the All-Hearer, the All-Seer."[3]

He (*Subhaanahu wa Ta'aala*) said as well:

$$\text{فَلَا تَضْرِبُوا لِلَّهِ ٱلْأَمْثَالَ إِنَّ ٱللَّهَ يَعْلَمُ وَأَنتُمْ لَا تَعْلَمُونَ}$$

---

2 The Noble *Qur.aan* - *Soorah* al-Ikhlaas

3 The Noble *Qur.aan* - *Soorah* ash-Shuraa, *Aayah* 11

"So put not forward similitudes for Allaah (as there is nothing similar to Him, nor does He resemble anything). Truly, Allaah knows and you know not."[4]

He (*Subhaanahu wa Ta'aala*) also said:

وَلِلَّهِ ٱلْأَسْمَآءُ ٱلْحُسْنَىٰ فَٱدْعُوهُ بِهَا

"And (all) the Most Beautiful Names belong to Allaah, so call on Him by them..."[5]

The verses that are of this meaning are plentiful.

Shaykh 'Abdul-'Azeez ibn Baaz

2. War upon the Arabic Language

Question: What is your opinion of 'al-Haadithah'?[6]

After asking for a clarification of what 'al-Haadithah' is, the *Shaykh* replied:

Firstly: 'al-Haadithah,' according to what I have understood, is a war against the Arabic language; the language of the *Qur.aan*, and that some Arabs dislike it. There is no doubt that any intelligent person would not accept this, disliking his own language, whatever it may be. This is why we find that the English are extremely pleased that their language is spoken around most of the world, because using a people's language and keeping it alive means that its people would also remain.

---

4 The Noble *Qur.aan - Soorah* an-Nahl, *Aayah* 74

5 The Noble *Qur.aan - Soorah* al-A'raaf, *Aayah* 180

6 Majmoo' Duroos wa Fataawa al-Haram al-Makkee - Page 113

So these people want to eliminate themselves by eliminating their language, which in turn would eliminate their existence. They would dwell amongst others, unconscious of their nationality and language, the most complete language, since Allaah created the world until now.

Secondly: I also understand that they want to eliminate all religions that descended from the heavens including Judaism and Christianity. They do not accept being *Muslims*, Jews or Christians because this necessitates affiliating oneself to a religion, and they do not want to affiliate themselves to anything from the past, even if it was the Religion and Legislation of Allaah.

There is no doubt that this is utter deviation; they resemble those whom Allaah informed us about:

وَقَالُوٓاْ إِنْ هِىَ إِلَّا حَيَاتُنَا ٱلدُّنْيَا وَمَا نَحْنُ بِمَبْعُوثِينَ

'And they said: "There is no (other life) but our (present) life of this world, and we shall never be resurrected (on the Day of Resurrection)."'[7]

Any intelligent person wouldn't have a doubt that this is apostasy, and whoever is involved in it must be asked to repent; he either repents or is killed due to becoming an apostate. The Messenger of Allaah said:

"Whoever changes his religion must be killed."

Thirdly: I also understand that they want to get rid of all good manners related to the past, because this principle of theirs is applied on everything related to religion, whether it is manners, languages and so forth.

---

7 The Noble *Qur.aan* - *Soorah* al-An'aam, *Aayah* 29

This necessitates that they wipe out all forms of good mannerisms. At this point, the human being would be deprived of his humanity, and would be included in the same category as animals. If a male animal desires to mate with a female, it does so while others of its kind watch; if it desires anything, intelligence would not stop it from engaging in it.

Fourthly: I understand from your evaluation, that 'al-Haadithah' is cloaked with the disguise of hypocrisy; this is the greatest calamity. Al-laah (*Subhaanahu wa Ta'aala*) said concerning hypocrites:

$$هُمُ ٱلۡعَدُوُّ فَٱحۡذَرۡهُمۡۚ قَـٰتَلَهُمُ ٱللَّهُۖ أَنَّىٰ يُؤۡفَكُونَ$$

They are the enemies, so beware of them. May Al-laah curse them! How they deny (or deviate from) the Right Path?[8]

He (*Subhaanahu wa Ta'aala*) said concerning the *Shaytaan*:

$$إِنَّ ٱلشَّيۡطَـٰنَ لَكُمۡ عَدُوٌّ فَٱتَّخِذُوهُ عَدُوًّاۚ$$

"Surely, Shaytaan (Satan) is an enemy to you, so take (treat) him as an enemy."[9]

Those who ponder over these two methods would find that hypocrites are more harmful to the believers than the *Shayaateen*.

So it is upon us, O, *Muslims*, to give *da'wah* to them using the deterrent of *eemaan*, to truthfully and sincerely advise them to return to the Religion of Allaah (*Subhaanahu wa Ta'aala*); the Book of Allaah and

---

8 The Noble *Qur.aan - Soorah* al-Munaafiqoon, *Aayah* 4

9 The Noble *Qur.aan - Soorah* Faatir, *Aayah* 6

the *Sunnah* of His Messenger (*sal-Allaahu 'alayhi wa sallam*); to prove to them that this is absolute disbelief. If they do not respond, then it is upon us as well as the rulers to use the deterrent of authority based upon the Book of Allaah and the *Sunnah* of His Messenger (*sal-Allaahu 'alayhi wa sallam*), in order to stop this deadly poison from spreading within the body of the *Muslim ummah*.

Since we are trying to get rid of drugs, and it is obligatory upon us to do so because drugs destroy meaningful things such as maturity, and cause people to behave with bad manners. It is a higher obligation upon us to get rid of this despicable methodology, higher than getting rid of drugs, alcohol and bad mannerisms.

Educated youth must clarify and explain the hidden meanings that are under the disguise of altered poetry styles, and expose the aforementioned hidden meanings that are behind such a disguise. This matter is very dangerous; it is not just a matter of changing the style of a poem or writing words which have no beginning or end; words that are neither connected in wording nor meaning; neither eloquent nor articulate. Glorified is Allaah! If a heart lapses, it would see faults as being faultless; otherwise whoever reads such poems would see that they are not poems in reality; a whole stanza that consists of only one meaningful word followed by another stanza that consists of ten words! Can this be called poetry? What happened to poems that move people? Tranquil poems that are beloved to the souls? I prefer not to cite a poem that suits this description.

We ask Allaah (*Subhaanahu wa Ta'aala*) to guide them and bring them back to the truth; to protect me as well as yourselves from misguiding afflictions; to grant us to be amongst those who see the truth as it truly is, and follow it, and to see falsehood as it truly is, and avoid it.

Shaykh Muhammad ibn Saalih al-'Uthaymeen

3. Criticising the Rulers Publicly

<u>Question</u>: Is criticising the rulers from the *minbar* from the methodology of the *Salaf*? And what is the methodology of the *Salaf* concerning advising the rulers?[10]

<u>Response</u>: It is not from the methodology of the *Salaf* to publicise the faults of the rulers from the *minbar*; this leads to anarchy and defiance of the rulers when they order with good. It also leads to harmful, unbeneficial debates.

The way of the *Salaf* is to either advise the rulers in person, write to them, or contact scholars who are in touch with them in order for them to direct the rulers to good.

The rebuttal of evil is to be carried out without mentioning those who practice it; so one should rebut fornication, drinking alcohol and usury without mentioning those who practice these sins. It is sufficient to rebut and warn from sins without mentioning those who practice them whether they are rulers or not.

When *fitnah* befell at the time of 'Uthmaan, some people said to Usaamah ibn Zayd (*radhi-yAllaahu 'anhu*): "Will you not rebut 'Uthmaan?"

He said: "I will not rebut him in public, but in private. I will not open a door of evil upon the people."

When they opened [that door] of evil at the time of 'Uthmaan (*radhi-yAllaahu 'anhu*) and rebutted him publicly, the *fitnah*, war and evil be-

---

10 Huqooq ar-Raa'ee war-Raa'iyyah - Page 27

249

gan; the effects of which are still being experienced by people to this day. The *fitnah* continued until it fell between 'Alee and Mu'aawiyah (*radhiyAllaahu 'anhumaa*); 'Uthmaan and 'Alee were killed due to it, along with a great number of Companions and others. All of this occurred due to rebutting [the ruler] publicly; mentioning 'Alee's faults publicly until people started to despise their leader and consequently killed him. We ask Allaah to relieve us from such affairs.

Shaykh 'Abdul-'Azeez ibn Baaz

4. Criticising the Scholars

<u>Question</u>: What is your opinion of youth, including students of knowledge, whose only concern has become criticising others, chasing people away and warning against each other? Is this legislated, and is one rewarded or punished for this?[11]

<u>Response</u>: My opinion is that these actions are prohibited. If it is prohibited to backbite your *Muslim* brother, who is not even a scholar, then how can it be permissible to backbite your brothers from amongst the scholars? It is compulsory for a believer to withhold his tongue from backbiting his brothers. Allaah (*Subhaanahu wa Ta'aala*) says:

يَـٰٓأَيُّهَا ٱلَّذِينَ ءَامَنُوا ٱجۡتَنِبُوا كَثِيرًا مِّنَ ٱلظَّنِّ إِنَّ بَعۡضَ ٱلظَّنِّ إِثۡمٌ وَلَا تَجَسَّسُوا وَلَا يَغۡتَب بَّعۡضُكُم بَعۡضًا أَيُحِبُّ أَحَدُكُمۡ أَن يَأۡكُلَ لَحۡمَ أَخِيهِ مَيۡتًا فَكَرِهۡتُمُوهُ وَٱتَّقُوا ٱللَّهَ إِنَّ ٱللَّهَ تَوَّابٌ رَّحِيمٌ

---

11 Majmoo' Fataawa wa Maqaalaat Mutanawwi'ah - Volume 7, Page 314

"O you who believe! Avoid a lot of suspicion; indeed some suspicions are sins. And spy not, and do not backbite one another. Would any of you like to eat the flesh of his dead brother? You would hate it (so hate backbiting). And fear Allaah. Verily, Allaah is the One Who forgives and accepts repentance, Most Merciful."[12]

A person afflicted with this disease should know that criticising a scholar would cause people to reject the truth that he propagates. So the sin and harms of rejecting the truth would be upon this individual who criticises scholars, because dispraising a scholar in reality, is not a personal critique of that scholar, rather it is a critique of the inheritance of the Messenger, Muhammad (*sal-Allaahu 'alayhi wa sallam*).

Indeed the scholars are the inheritors of the messengers, so criticising and slandering them would cause people to consider their knowledge unreliable, while it is inherited from the Messenger of Allaah (*sal-Allaahu 'alayhi wa sallam*). Therefore people would not trust anything that this particular scholar teaches.

I am not saying that every scholar is errorless; rather everyone is liable to make mistakes. If you see that a scholar is mistaken in an issue then call him and discuss with him. If it becomes clear to you that his stance is correct, it then becomes binding upon you to follow him. If it does not become clear that his stance is correct, but you find that there is sound reasoning behind his opinion, then it is binding upon you to keep silent. If you do not find his reasoning to be acceptable, beware of his opinion, because acknowledging and agreeing over error is impermissible, but do not criticise him if he is a scholar who is known for having good intentions.

13

---

12 The Noble *Qur.aan - Soorah* al-Hujuraat, *Aayah* 12

If we were to criticise scholars who are known for having good intentions, for a mistake in the affairs of *Islaami*c Jurisprudence, then we would criticise all major scholars. However it is binding to follow what I previously mentioned; if you see that a scholar has made a mistake, then speak to him about it. If it becomes clear to you that he is correct then follow him, and if it is you who holds the correct opinion, then he is to follow you. If the truth is not clear, then the difference between the two of you is considered to be from the issues where it is permissible to have a difference of opinion. Therefore it is compulsory for you to withhold your tongue from speaking against him, and you are to present your opinion and allow him to present his.

All praise is due to Allaah; differing has not only occurred during these times, differing has been present since the time of the Companions and has continued to this day of ours. However if the truth is clear, and he (scholar with the incorrect opinion) persists in supporting his opinion then it is obligatory upon you to clarify the error and warn against it; but not with the intention of slandering the man or retribution, because he may have other opinions in other issues that are correct.

Shaykh 'Abdul-'Azeez ibn Baaz

5. The Saved Sect and Different Sects

Question[13]: I came across a noble *hadeeth* related by Shaykh-ul-Islaam Muhammad ibn 'Abdul-Wahhaab in his book: 'Mukhtasarus-Seerah'; it is the saying of the Messenger of Allaah (*sal-Allaahu 'alayhi wa sallam*):

> *"My ummah will split into seventy different sects,*

---

13 Fataawa al-Lajnah ad-Daa.imah - No.830

all of which would be in the Hellfire, except one."

Imaam Muhammad ibn 'Abdul-Wahhaab made a statement in this book that I would like you to clarify, he said:

"This is one of the most important of issues, for whoever understands it is knowledgeable, and whoever acts upon it is *Muslim*. We ask Allaah, the Bountiful, the Gracious, to bless us with understanding it and to act upon it."

I would also like you to answer the following questions in relation to this *hadeeth*:

1   Which is the saved sect that has been mentioned in the *hadeeth*?

2   Are groups other than *Ahlul-Hadeeth* such as the *Shee'ah*, *Shaafi'iyyah*, *Hanafiyyah*, *Tijaaniyyah*, and others included in the seventy-two groups that the noble Messenger cited as being in the Hellfire?

3   If all of these groups are in the Hellfire except one, then how is it that you allow them to visit *al-Masjid al-Haraam*? Was this great *Imaam* mistaken or have you swayed from the upright path.

<u>Response</u>: All praise is due to Allaah alone, and may the *salaah* and *salaam* be upon His Messenger, his family and his Companions.

13

<u>Firstly</u>: The *hadeeth* that *Imaam* Muhammad ibn 'Abdul-Wahhaab, may Allaah have mercy upon him, mentioned in his book: 'Mukhtasarus-Seerah', is only a portion of a well-known authentic *hadeeth*. It was reported by the authors of the 'Four Books of *ahaadeeth*' as well as the *Masaaneed* such as Abu Daawood, an-Nasaa.ee, at-Tirmidhee and others, with different terminology, including:

"The Jews split into seventy-one groups, all of them in the Hellfire except one. My ummah will also split into seventy-three groups, all of them in the Hellfire except one."

In another narration:

"Into seventy three sects."

In one narration the Companions said:

"O, Messenger of Allaah, which is the saved sect?"

He (*sal-Allaahu 'alayhi wa sallam*) said:

"Whoever adheres to what I and my Companions today adhere to."

In another narration he (*sal-Allaahu 'alayhi wa sallam*) said:

"It is the Jamaa'ah; the Hand of Allaah is over the Jamaa'ah."

Secondly: The Messenger of Allaah (*sal-Allaahu 'alayhi wa sallam*) explained which the saved sect was in some narrations of this *hadeeth*, along with its attributes and merits in response to his Companion's question:

"Which is the saved sect?"

He said:

"Whoever adheres to what I and my Companions today adhere to."

In another narration he said:

"It is the Jamaa'ah; the Hand of Allaah is over the Jamaa'ah."

So the Messenger of Allaah (*sal-Allaahu 'alayhi wa sallam*) described it as being the one that adheres to what he (*sal-Allaahu 'alayhi wa sallam*) and the Companions (*radhi-yAllaahu 'anhum*) adhered to in relation to their *'aqeedah*, sayings, actions and manners. So they traverse upon the path of the Book of Allaah and the *Sunnah* in everything that they do as well as everything they don't. They hold fast to the *Jamaa'ah* of the *Muslim*s who are the Companions, being that they followed none other than the Messenger of Allaah (*sal-Allaahu 'alayhi wa sallam*); one who did not speak based on desires, indeed he only spoke due to revelation.

So whoever follows the Book of Allaah, the *Sunnah* and the consensus of the scholars of the *ummah*, without falling victim to false conjecture, misleading desires or false interpretations is amongst them; interpretations that are not accepted by the Arabic language, the language of the Messenger of Allaah (*sal-Allaahu 'alayhi wa sallam*) with which the *Qur.aan* was revealed; interpretations that are rejected by the foundations of the *Islaam*ic Legislation. Whoever is upon that path is from the saved sect; *Ahlus-Sunnah wal-Jamaa'ah*.

13

<u>Thirdly</u>: In regards to an individual who takes his desires as a lord [i.e. follows his desires] and opposes the Book of Allaah and the authentic *Sunnah* with his opinion, the opinion of his *Imaam* or the opinion of whoever he follows blindly, or one who falsely interprets the texts of the *Qur.aan* and the *Sunnah* with interpretations that the Arabic language and the foundations of the *Islaam*ic Legislation reject, then he would have deviated from the saved sect and would be included amongst the

seventy-three sects that the errorless Messenger (*sal-Allaahu 'alayhi wa sallam*) mentioned in the *hadeeth*. Therefore the sign with which these sects are identified is their deviation from the Book of Allaah, the *Sunnah*, the consensus of the scholars and their misinterpretations of the texts; interpretations that are not in accord with the language of the *Qur.aan* or the foundations of the *Islaam*ic Legislation, which would be pardoned if this was the case.

Fourthly: The response to the issue mentioned by the *Imaam* of the *da'wah, Shaykh* Muhammad ibn 'Abdul-Wahhaab, as being one of the most important issues, that whoever understands it has understood the religion and that whoever acts upon it is a *Muslim* has already preceded in the second point of this answer, along with the issue of distinguishing the saved sect from others with what the Prophet, Muhammad (*sal-Allaahu 'alayhi wa sallam*) distinguished it with, and that other sects are unlike it. So whoever distinguishes the saved sect from the destroyed sects according to his (*sal-Allaahu 'alayhi wa sallam*) explanation has understood the religion. He has also distinguished between those whom he must adhere to and hold onto their *Jamaa'ah*, and those whom he must stay away and flee from just as one flees from a lion.

Whoever acts upon this correct understanding and clings onto the *Jamaa'ah* of guidance and truth and their ruler, is a *Muslim*, because the description of the saved sect is applied to him in knowledge, *'aqeedah*, sayings, as well as deeds.

There is no doubt that this is amongst the most important of issues as well as having the greatest and most wide-ranging benefit. So may Allaah have mercy upon the *Imaam, Shaykh* Muhammad ibn 'Abdul-Wahhaab, a man who possessed a commanding insight and a precise understanding of the texts of the religion and its objectives. He drew attention to what concerns the *Muslim*s in their religion with a mere indication at times as he did here, and with thorough explanations at other times as is in alot of his books.

Fifthly: The Messenger of Allaah (*sal-Allaahu 'alayhi wa sallam*) did not name the different groups that affiliate themselves to *Islaam* nor did he explain the signs with which the seventy-two sects would be identified; nor did he give them titles in order to differentiate between them. Indeed the only sign he gave them was their deviation from the Book of Allaah, the *Sunnah*, the consensus of the Rightly Guided Caliphs and the rest of the Companions (*radhi-yAllaahu 'anhu*) as well as following mere speculations, their desires, saying about Allaah what they have no knowledge of due to stubbornly or blindly following leaders other than the Messenger of Allaah (*sal-Allaahu 'alayhi wa sallam*), and showing enmity and making allegiance based upon this. Just as he (*sal-Allaahu 'alayhi wa sallam*) made the sign of the saved sect; *Ahlus-Sunnah wal-Jamaa'ah*, adhering to the Book, the *Sunnah* and holding fast to the *Jamaa'ah* of the *Muslims*. They give precedence to that over their speculations, understanding and desires, for their desires are in accordance with the *Islaam*ic Legislation. They make allegiance as well as show enmity based upon this.

So whoever uses a scale other than the clarification of the Messenger of Allaah (*sal-Allaahu 'alayhi wa sallam*) to distinguish the saved sect from the destroyed sects has indeed spoken without knowledge and judged the groups without insight. By doing so he has committed injustice to himself as well as the groups that affiliate themselves to *Islaam*.

Likewise whoever refers to the explanation of the Messenger of Allaah (*sal-Allaahu 'alayhi wa sallam*) in differentiating the saved sect from others, ruled justly. He knows that there are different levels of groups in this *ummah*, amongst them are those who are the most intent on following the *Islaam*ic Legislation and submitting to it as well as being

257

the farthest away from innovating in the religion and distorting its texts by either making additions or deductions. They are the most worthy of people to be from the saved sect.

Amongst the scholars of *hadeeth* and *Islaam*ic Jurisprudence are those who are qualified to perform *ijtihaad* and are keen on adhering to the *Islaam*ic Legislation and submitting to it. However they may falsely interpret some of the texts mistakenly and are therefore pardoned for their mistakes due to their qualification in practicing *ijtihaad*. There are also those who reject some of the texts of the legislation, either because they are new converts or were brought up in the outer reaches of the *Islaam*ic world and have no knowledge of the texts they reject. Amongst them as well are those who innovate or practice sins that do not remove them from the fold of *Islaam*; they are considered to be believers who are obedient to Allaah due to the forms of obedience they practice, and sinful due to the sins or innovations they commit. They are under the Will of Allaah, if He Wills He shall forgive them, and if He Wills He shall punish them. Allaah (*Subhaanahu wa Ta'aala*) says:

إِنَّ ٱللَّهَ لَا يَغْفِرُ أَن يُشْرَكَ بِهِۦ وَيَغْفِرُ مَا دُونَ ذَٰلِكَ لِمَن يَشَآءُ

"Verily, Allaah does not forgive that partners are associated with Him (in worship), but He forgives anything else other than that for whom He wills."[14]

He (*Subhaanahu wa Ta'aala*) also says:

وَءَاخَرُونَ ٱعْتَرَفُوا بِذُنُوبِهِمْ خَلَطُوا عَمَلًا صَٰلِحًا
وَءَاخَرَ سَيِّئًا عَسَى ٱللَّهُ أَن يَتُوبَ عَلَيْهِمْ إِنَّ ٱللَّهَ غَفُورٌ رَّحِيمٌ

---

14 The Noble *Qur.aan* - *Soorah* an-Nisaa, *Aayah* 48

258

"And (there are) others who have acknowledged their sins, they have mixed a deed that was righteous with another that was evil. Perhaps Allaah will turn to them in forgiveness. Surely, Allaah is Oft-Forgiving, Most Merciful."[15]

So these people are not disbelievers due to their erroneous misinterpretations or rejection of some of the texts, rather they are pardoned and are considered to be from the saved sect even though they are not considered to be from the best level.

Amongst them are those who reject something that is 'known in the religion by necessity' after the truth has become apparent to them and follow their desires without guidance from Allaah, or misinterpret some of the texts of the *Islaam*ic Legislation in a way that is far from correct and is in opposition to the interpretations of the *Muslim* scholars before them. When the truth is clarified to them and the proofs are established for them through debates and so on, they do not accept the truth. They are considered to be disbelievers, apostates, even if they claim to be *Muslim*s and have exerted great efforts in calling the people to their *'aqeedah* and their way such as the *Qaadiyaaniyyah al-Ahmadiyyah*. They reject that Muhammad (*sal-Allaahu 'alayhi wa sallam*) is the final Messenger. They claim that Ghulaam Ahmad al-Qaadiyanee is a prophet and a messenger of Allaah, or that he is al-Maseeh, 'Eesaa ibn Maryam, or that his spirit or the spirit of Muhammad (*sal-Allaahu 'alayhi wa sallam*) has transmigrated into his body so he has their status in prophethood.

Sixthly: *Ahlus-Sunnah wal-Jamaa'ah* have solid principles founded upon evidences with which they build secondary issues upon. They re-

---

15 The Noble *Qur.aan - Soorah* at-Towbah, *Aayah* 102

turn to these principles when proving secondary issues and when implementing rulings over themselves and others such as; that *eemaan* is composed of sayings, actions, and *'aqeedah*; it increases through obedience and decreases through sinning. So whenever a *Muslim* increases in obedience, he increases his *eemaan*, and whenever he is negligent in his obedience or commits sins, his *eemaan* would therefore decrease, and this is if that particular sin does not lead to manifest disbelief.

So *eemaan* according to *Ahlus-Sunnah* has different levels, and the saved sect also has different levels, some being higher than others depending on evidence and on the goodness they have earned in relation to deeds and sayings.

Amongst their principles is that they do not declare a certain individual or group of individuals to be disbelievers if they are from the people of the *qiblah*. They steer clear away from this due to the Prophet (*sal-Allaahu 'alayhi wa sallam*) reprimanding Usaamah ibn Zayd ibn Haarithah when he killed a man from the disbelievers after he had uttered the testimony of faith, saying that there was no deity worthy of worship except Allaah. He (*sal-Allaahu 'alayhi wa sallam*) did not accept Usaamah's excuse that he killed him because he only said it in order to save himself, rather he said to him:

"Did you open his heart to see if he said it or not."

Meaning if he said it sincerely from his heart or not.

With the exception, of course, if an individual fell into a clear form of disbelief such as rejecting something that is 'known in the religion by necessity', opposing the consensus of the scholars or misinterpreting clear texts in a manner that is unacceptable and not returning to the truth after it has been clarified and explained to him.

The *Shaykh*, Muhammad ibn 'Abdul-Wahhaab, may Allaah have mercy upon him, held fast to the methodology of *Ahlus-Sunnah* wal-*Jamaa'ah* and acted on their principles. He did not declare particular individuals or groups amongst the people of the *qiblah* to be disbelievers based upon sins, false interpretations, or innovations except if there was evidence establishing that they fell into disbelief and after explanations and clarifications had been conveyed to them.

The government of Saudi Arabia, may Allaah guard and support it, does not differ from this method in its dealings with its citizens and its verdicts over them. Nor does it differ in its stance with all the *Muslim*s in general, especially those who arrive to visit the House of Allaah, *al-Masjid al-Haraam* to fulfil the ceremonies of *hajj* and *'umrah*. The government thinks positively of the *Muslim*s and considers them to be brothers in the religion; it co-operates with them in everything that supports and protects their rights. It returns their stolen property to them; it welcomes those who visit it and carries out all possible measures to facilitate the procedure of their ceremonies for them or whatever business they have here in the best possible way, with affection and kindness. This can be seen by examining its state of affairs; the efforts that it exerts and the money it spends in the cause of rectifying the general affairs of the *Muslim*s and providing comfort for the pilgrims of the House of Allaah, *al-Masjid al-Haraam*.

It is for this reason that it allows different *Muslim* groups to visit the House of Allaah, *al-Masjid al-Haraam* without investigating their hidden beliefs acting upon what is apparent, and Allaah is the Guardian of all secrets. If it becomes clear to the government that a certain individual or certain sect have fallen into disbelief, like the *Qaadiyaaniyyah* for example, while this is ascertained by scholars from *Islaam*ic countries, then it has no choice except to forbid those whose disbelief has been established and apostates from performing *hajj* or *'umrah*. This is in order

261

to protect to the House of Allaah from being approached by those who have filth in their hearts, acting upon the saying of Allaah (*Subhaanahu wa Ta'aala*):

يَـٰٓأَيُّهَا ٱلَّذِينَ ءَامَنُوٓاْ إِنَّمَا ٱلْمُشْرِكُونَ نَجَسٌ فَلَا يَقْرَبُواْ ٱلْمَسْجِدَ ٱلْحَرَامَ بَعْدَ عَامِهِمْ هَـٰذَآ

"O you who believe. Verily, the Mushrikoon (poly-theists, pagans, idolaters, disbelievers in the One-ness of Allaah, and in the Message of Muhammad) are Najas (impure). So let them not come near al-Masjid al-Haraam (at Makkah) after this year..."[16]

His saying as well:

وَطَهِّرْ بَيْتِيَ لِلطَّآئِفِينَ وَٱلْقَآئِمِينَ وَٱلرُّكَّعِ ٱلسُّجُودِ

"And sanctify My House for those who circumambu-late it, and those who stand up (for prayer), and those who bow (submit themselves with humility and obedi-ence to Allaah), and make prostration (in prayer)."[17]

The great importance of the issue in question, the issue that the *Imaam* of the *da'wah* of his time; *Shaykh* Muhammad ibn 'Abdul-Wahhaab al-luded to, has been clarified in what has preceded. Just as it becomes clear that he, may Allaah have mercy upon him, traversed upon the sound path, being that he adhered to the principles of *Ahlus-Sunnah wal-Jamaa'ah*. The government of Saudi Arabia, in its dealing with the *Muslim*s of the world, has not deviated from this upright path, rather it

---

16 The Noble *Qur.aan* - *Soorah* at-Towbah, *Aayah* 28

17 The Noble *Qur.aan* - *Soorah* al-Hajj, *Aayah* 26

also adheres to the principles of *Ahlus-Sunnah* wal-*Jamaa'ah*, just as the *Imaam* of the *da'wah* did. It treats *Muslims* according to their apparent state and does not investigate what is in their hearts. In doing so it is tolerant with those whose state is hidden and is harsh upon those whose inner beliefs have been exposed while insisting upon them after the truth has been constantly clarified to them in a number of debates.

Success is granted by Allaah, and may the peace and blessings be upon our Prophet Muhammad, his family and his Companions.

The Permanent Committee for Islaamic Research and Verdicts

6. Differing is a Cause of Failure

Question: Noble *Shaykh*, the differing within the circle of the callers to Allaah causes failure and weakness; alot of it arises due to ignorance concerning the manners of differing. Can you give a word regarding this issue?[18]

Response: Yes, I advise all my brothers amongst the people of *da'wah* and knowledge to select the best manner and be lenient when debating with each other or studying issues that contain differing. Jealousy or isolation should not cause an individual to say something inappropriate which may in turn lead to division, differing, hatred and detachment between the *du'aat*. Rather it is upon the caller to Allaah, teachers and those who advise people to select beneficial methods and use soft words in order for their advice to be accepted and so that they do not chase people away from them as Allaah (*Subhaanahu wa Ta'aala*) said to His Messenger (*sal-Allaahu 'alayhi wa sallam*):

13

---

18 Majmoo' Fataawa wa Maqaalaat Mutanawwi'ah - Volume 5, Page 105

فِمَا رَحْمَةٍ مِّنَ
ٱللَّهِ لِنتَ لَهُمْ وَلَوْ كُنتَ فَظًّا غَلِيظَ ٱلْقَلْبِ لَٱنفَضُّوا مِنْ حَوْلِكَ

"And by the Mercy of Allaah, you dealt with them gently. And had you been severe and harsh hearted, they would have dispersed from around you..."[19]

He (*Subhaanahu wa Ta'aala*) said to Moosaa and Haaroon when He sent them to Pharaoh:

فَقُولَا لَهُ قَوْلًا لَّيِّنًا لَّعَلَّهُ يَتَذَكَّرُ أَوْ يَخْشَىٰ

"And speak to him mildly, perhaps he may accept admonition or fear Allaah."[20]

He (*Subhaanahu wa Ta'aala*) also says:

ٱدْعُ إِلَىٰ سَبِيلِ رَبِّكَ بِٱلْحِكْمَةِ
وَٱلْمَوْعِظَةِ ٱلْحَسَنَةِ وَجَٰدِلْهُم بِٱلَّتِي هِيَ أَحْسَنُ

"Call (mankind, O Muhammad) to the way of your Lord (i.e. Islaam) with wisdom (i.e. with the Divine Revelation and the Qur.aan) and fair preaching, and debate with them in a manner that is better."[21]

He (*Subhaanahu wa Ta'aala*) says:

---

19 The Noble *Qur.aan - Soorah* Aal-'Imraan, *Aayah* 159

20 The Noble *Qur.aan - Soorah* Taha, *Aayah* 44

21 The Noble *Qur.aan - Soorah* an-Nahl, *Aayah* 125

وَلَا تُجَٰدِلُوٓاْ أَهۡلَ ٱلۡكِتَٰبِ إِلَّا بِٱلَّتِى هِىَ أَحۡسَنُ إِلَّا ٱلَّذِينَ ظَلَمُواْ مِنۡهُمۡۖ

"And do not debate with the people of the book except in a manner that is best except with those of them who do wrong..."[22]

The Messenger of Allaah (*sal-Allaahu 'alayhi wa sallam*) said:

"Indeed gentleness is not practiced in any affair except that it beautifies it, and it is not removed from any affair except that it ruins it."

He (*sal-Allaahu 'alayhi wa sallam*) also said:

"Whoever is deprived of gentleness is deprived of everything that is good."

So the caller to Allaah and teachers must carefully select beneficial methods and avoid using harshness and force because this may lead to the rejection of the truth and to extreme differing and separation between brothers. The goal is to clarify the truth and be eager for its acceptance and benefiting the *da'wah*; not merely conveying the *da'wah* of Allaah in order for the people to benefit from your talks. So it is upon them to use methods that will facilitate the acceptance of the *da'wah*, just as it is upon them to beware of the methods that cause it to be rejected or unaccepted.

Shaykh 'Abdul-'Azeez ibn Baaz

---

22 The Noble *Qur.aan* - *Soorah* al-'Ankaboot, *Aayah* 46

Question: How can *Muslim* societies resist both the Eastern and Western ideologies which they face during current times?[23]

Response: There is no doubt that the most dangerous affair that *Islaam-*ic societies face during current times is what is called 'Ideological warfare' which is waged with a variety of weapons such as books, television, newspapers, magazines and so on. This is because colonisation in recent times has changed its previous methods due to its failure and results, as well as nations fighting and risking their lives to defend their religion, lands and heritage. Taking over through power, force and terrorism is something that is naturally rejected and hated, especially during present times when everybody is more aware due to communication between people. There are also alot of organisations these days that defend each country's rights and reject colonisation through force; they demand that each nation have the right to decide its own path; that it is every nation's natural right to rule their own land and reap the benefits of their own resources. They also facilitate the process of leadership in each country according to its people's inclinations and aspirations in life, and according to whatever religion they practice as it relates to their beliefs, ideologies and the different methods each country implements in ruling themselves.

This forced colonisers to leave colonised lands after severe battles, armed clashes and countless bloody wars. Before leaving however, they thought up alot of methods, and started implementing well thought out, carefully studied plans. They extensively studied the effects such plans would have on the public and calculated the necessary steps needed to

---

23 Majmoo' Fataawa wa Maqaalaat Mutanawwi'ah - Volume 5, Page 259

be taken in order to further their goals. These goals could be summed up in that they would establish school curriculums that are weakly connected to religion; an extremely cunning deception geared to further their goals, spread their ideologies, and firmly establish awe in the hearts of the masses for their industrial and materialistic achievements, until their hearts absorb and admire its external glitter and are amazed at their worldly accomplishments and wonderful inventions, especially young students.

Groups of students captivated by the sorcery of this culture chose to complete their education abroad in European and American universities where they would face a string of doubtful ideas and lustful acts at the hands of Orientalists and atheists in an organised and well thought out manner, using twisted methods in the highest degree of slyness and deception. They would face a Western way of life; a life of decay, squandering of wealth and immodesty; a way of life where every forbidden act is permitted. Few are able to safely escape from the traps and harms of such weapons when combined with deception and encouragement, without any form of religious or legal restraint. These students, those amongst them whom the colonisers trusted, returned to their countries after completing their education. The colonisers then transferred the trust of implementing their vile plans to these students, and so they did with the utmost precision, rather they used methods that were even harsher than those used by the colonisers, as has taken place in many of the countries that have been afflicted by colonisation or had a strong bond to it.

As for the means of salvation from this danger and escaping from its evils and harms, then this can be summarised in the following; establishing a variety of universities, colleges and institutions that are specialised in all fields in order to avoid sending students abroad. All forms of sciences should be taught in these facilities, while paying special attention to religious subjects and *Islaam*ic ideology in order to safeguard the *'aqeedah* of the students and preserve their manners for fear for their future, and in order for them to contribute to the progression of their society upon the light of *Islaam*ic education, according to the needs and requirements of the *Muslims*. It is also compulsory to restrict sending students abroad and only permit it for specific fields that are unavailable locally.

Shaykh 'Abdul-'Azeez ibn Baaz

8. Playing the Roles of the Companions

Question: Noble *Shaykh*, what is the ruling concerning acting out the roles of the Companions and the *Taabi'oon* and similar activities that take place in Summer camps?[24]

Response: Acting out the roles of the Companions, the *Taabi'oon* and other than them is impermissible because this leads to scorning and ridiculing them, especially if the person who is playing their roles is not a righteous person; like someone who shaves his beard for example. He wears a fake beard and plays the role of one of them, this is not permissible.

Acting should be avoided altogether, but if it does not consist of impermissible issues and is carried out in order to solve a problem, then I pray that there is nothing wrong with that. However, if it consists of an impermissible issue, then there is a *hadeeth* that states:

> *"Woe to one who lies in order to entertain people, woe to him, woe to him."*

Shaykh Muhammad ibn Saalih al-'Uthaymeen

---

24 Liqaa.aat al-Baab al-Maftooh - No.909

9. Are the Rightly Guided Khulafaa Free from Error?

<u>Question</u>: Noble *Shaykh*, upon mentioning the saying of the Messenger:

> *"It is upon you to follow my Sunnah, and the Sunnah of the Rightly Guided Caliphs, hold onto it tightly as if you were biting on to it with your molars."*

A *Soofee Shaykh* commented: "The Messenger of Allaah raised the rank of the four Rightly Guided Caliphs to the level of perfection by ordering the *Muslims* to follow their guidance. Could it be that he ordered us to follow their *Sunnah* while knowing that they fall into error? What is the meaning of 'rightly guided'? Does it not mean that Allaah safeguards them from falling into error?"

What do you think?[25]

<u>Response</u>: The Prophet (*sal-Allaahu 'alayhi wa sallam*) said:

> *"It is upon you to follow my Sunnah, and the Sunnah of the Rightly Guided Caliphs who come after me."*

He (*sal-Allaahu 'alayhi wa sallam*) started off with his *Sunnah* first; this means that if the *Sunnah* of the Rightly Guided Caliphs contradicts his *Sunnah*, we do not follow it. This is why Ibn 'Abbaas (*radhi-yAllaahu 'anhu*) said:

"I fear that boulders from the sky may rain down upon you, I tell you that the Messenger of Allaah (*sal-Allaahu 'alayhi wa sallam*) said such and

---

25 Majalatul-Buhooth al-Islaamiyyah - Volume 23, Page 993

such, and you tell me 'Abu Bakr and 'Umar said!'"

Whoever studies the opinions of the Rightly Guided Caliphs would find that some of their opinions are derived from *ijtihaad* and may not be in accord with the *Sunnah*. This is known by studying their opinions, and this proves that they are not free from error. However, if there is an issue which has no evidence in the *Sunnah*, then there is no doubt that their *Sunnah* is the closest to the truth and that their opinions are considered to be binding evidence as *Imaam* Ahmad, may Allaah have mercy upon him, has stated. This does not mean, however, that all their opinions, actions or judgements are free from error.

As for them being rightly guided, then guidance is for them as well as others; but their guidance is better because they are the Rightly Guided Caliphs who took leadership in place of the Prophet (*sal-Allaahu 'alayhi wa sallam*) after he passed away, in *'aqeedah*, actions and *da'wah*. In addition he described them as being rightly guided, and it is known that if a person makes an error in an issue, he would not be rightly guided in that issue, but he would be forgiven for it if it was due to *ijtihaad*.

Shaykh 'Abdul-'Azeez ibn Baaz

10. Is the Salafee Da'wah Harsh?

Question: *Salafiyy*ah according to some people means harshness. Some callers hold the opinion that we should not address certain forbidden issues in recent times such as music, picture-taking, shaving the beard and eating strangled (dead) chicken with the reasoning that these issues distance people from the *da'wah*. This is taking place because they consider *Salafiyy*ah to be harsh. If what they are saying is correct, shouldn't we at least bring these issues up within the circles of the callers themselves so that they may avoid such issues as well?[26]

Response: As far as them describing *Salafees* as being harsh, then this does not concern us, because every individual from amongst the *Muslims* is either, harsh, lenient or moderate. What concerns us is the *Salafee da'wah* itself; do they understand it correctly in its true form; that it is based upon the *Qur.aan* and the *Sunnah*? If this is the case then it does not concern us what they say; that it is obligatory to forsake the aforementioned issues; that it is obligatory to refrain from speaking about shaving the beard, television, taking pictures and eating forbidden forms of meat, which are prohibited based on the texts of the Book and the *Sunnah*. This *da'wah* of theirs is not a call to *Islaam* as a whole; rather it is a call to just a portion of *Islaam* and this verse is enough proof that they have deviated from *Islaam*:

$$ إِنَّ ٱلدِّينَ عِنـدَ ٱللَّهِ ٱلْإِسْلَـٰمُ $$

"Truly, the religion with Allaah is Islaam."[27]

All of *Islaam* and not just a portion of it, this is why we say that these callers are mistaken. They want the *Salafees* to avoid addressing these issues because they want to please certain people who some callers may mix with, as has been mentioned in the question, which shows that one who lacks a certain thing can not provide it to others. In reality these callers themselves need to be called to *Islaam* and made to understand it with the correct understanding before calling others, so that they become eager on calling to it correctly before calling others to it.

Question: But we see that a great number of people turn to the *Islaam*ic

---

26 al-Haawee min Fataawa Shaykh al-Albaanee - Page 493-494

27 The Noble *Qur.aan* - *Soorah* Aal-'Imraan, *Aayah* 19

groups which hold this opinion and prefer to remain silent about the likes of these forbidden issues. Do you not believe that in doing so, a greater benefit may be achieved at the expense of a minor one?

Response: What benefit is there in gathering masses who do not understand *Islaam* around callers who also do not understand *Islaam*? Who from amongst the people of knowledge understood that we must practice a portion of *Islaam* and postpone another portion to a latter time, especially if the issues in question are forbidden or compulsory? As for issues that are not compulsory then this saying of a Bedouin is sufficient:

"I will not perform any deeds in addition to those that have been obligated upon me, nor will I come up short of practicing them."

So the Messenger of Allaah (*sal-Allaahu 'alayhi wa sallam*) said: "He will be successful if he is truthful."

"He will be successful if he is truthful."

As for them saying that we should delay addressing important issues that *Islaam* has ordered us to carry out, such as growing the beard, or issues that *Islaam* has prohibited us from practicing; this means that we have been afflicted with the same calamity that the Christians have been afflicted with, as it relates to changing and altering their Book.

Furthermore it is not from amongst our objectives that the ends justify the means, or to increase numbers around us. Having a few people around us who properly understand the *'aqeedah* is more beloved to us than having a majority who have no understanding of the religion. Therefore we must forget the idea of trying to be with the majority of the masses, which is by getting comfortable with and inclining towards numbers while we know that the texts of the Book and the *Sunnah* both condemn the majority and that it is the few who are successful:

$$وَقَلِيلٌ مِّنْ عِبَادِيَ ٱلشَّكُورُ$$

'But few of My slaves are grateful.'[28]

Question: Their evidence is a *hadeeth* in which a non-*Muslim* came to the Messenger and embraced *Islaam* with the condition that he would only pray one prayer a day instead of five. The Messenger (*sal-Allaahu 'alayhi wa sallam*) agreed to this in order for him to embrace *Islaam* and be saved. Is this *hadeeth* authentic, and can it be used as evidence for this issue?

Response: The *hadeeth* is authentic but with the condition that he prays twice a day and not once. As for using it as evidence to justify their case then it is not, because what we are talking about here is the methodology of *da'wah*. Did the Messenger (*sal-Allaahu 'alayhi wa sallam*) call the people to perform two daily prayers or five? Of course he called them to perform five. They want to change the methodology of *da'wah*; they want us to stop clarifying to the people what Allaah has obligated upon them.

If a man who does not pray and wears a gold ring at the same time approaches you for example, it isn't that they want you to start with the issue of establishing the prayers first and delay the issue of wearing the gold ring to a latter time. If this is what they want we would agree with them in that, but what they want is to change the methodology of *da'wah*. So we say to them; this *da'wah* that you are calling the people to is not *Islaam*. It is *Islaam* yes, but what is the understanding of

---

28 The Noble *Qur.aan* - *Soorah Saba*, *Aayah* 13

this *Islaam*? Is it in establishing the five daily prayers and prohibiting all forms of evil?

As for dealing with a particular individual then yes, an individual should be treated in a way that is specific to his situation. So using this *hadeeth* as evidence for their claim is incorrect; *da'wah* is one thing and the method of dealing with individuals who are being called to this *da'wah* is another.

Question: How come the Messenger (*sal-Allaahu 'alayhi wa sallam*) approved for this man to pray only twice a day instead of five times?

Response: This is the methodology of giving *da'wah*, and there is another *hadeeth* that is a suitable response to this question, and it is:

"If they are truthful, they will be good Muslims and strive in the Cause of Allaah."

Meaning that if we accept a little from these people while they are polytheists or disbelievers, then practicing a little will lead to practicing a lot of what has been obligated upon them. This is 'legislated strategy', but it is to be implemented on individuals and not on the *da'wah* itself. *da'wah* is to be conducted in the same way in which it was revealed, without making any deductions from it. As for individuals, then they are to be dealt with according to their situations.

This is why I object to a story that some people tell; about a century ago, more or less, a group of rulers wanted to embrace *Islaam*, however, they said that they couldn't abandon alcohol because their countries were extremely cold, so they sent couriers to ask the *Mufti* of Istanbul who responded by saying that this was unacceptable. I believe this is incorrect due to the aforementioned *hadeeth*. We should convey the *da'wah* to them and inform them that alcohol is prohibited and that it is upon them to try and minimise this sin. We should first tell them to testify that there is no deity worthy of worship except Allaah and that Muhammad (*sal-Allaahu 'alayhi wa sallam*) is the Messenger of Allaah; to pray; fast and so on; and to try to minimise what they are afflicted with as much as they possibly can. This is called 'legislated strategy'.

As for concealing the *Sharee'ah* and telling people that they don't have to pray five daily prayers but merely two then this is not *da'wah*. We must differentiate between calling to *Islaam* and dealing with individuals; an individual must be treated according to his situation in order to draw him closer to *Islaam*.

Shaykh Muhammad Naasiruddeen al-Albaanee

11. Establishing the Proof on Deviant Relatives

Question: O, noble *Shaykh*, may Allaah preserve you, a group of us travelled to South Yemen in order to visit our relatives. These relatives of ours were brought up by *Soofee* scholars. Amongst the issues they taught them was that if anyone from Hijaaz, Najd or anyone who practices *tawheed* comes to them, then they are to be considered *Wahhaabees* and nothing should be accepted from them. We called them to *tawheed* but they did not accept the *da'wah* from us; are the proofs considered to be established upon them? Also, is understanding the evidence a condition for establishing the proof upon someone?[29]

Response: There is no doubt that if they were told of the truth and that this is the Book of Allaah and the *Sunnah* of the Messenger of Allaah

---

29 Liqaa.aat al-Baab al-Maftooh - No.1001

(*sal-Allaahu 'alayhi wa sallam*) as evidence to prove it, then by doing so the proof has been established upon them. Because they are Arabs, they understand by merely listening [to Arabic]. However if they were non-Arabs and you were speaking to them in Arabic while they do not understand, then the proof has not been established upon them because they don't understand what you are saying. But if they know what you are saying and you use the Book of Allaah and the *Sunnah* as evidence, but yet they persist [upon falsehood] and say: "We will follow our scholars," then indeed the proof has been established upon them and they are similar to those whom Allaah has said in regards to:

وَكَذَٰلِكَ مَآ أَرْسَلْنَا مِن قَبْلِكَ فِي قَرْيَةٍ مِّن نَّذِيرٍ إِلَّا قَالَ مُتْرَفُوهَآ
إِنَّا وَجَدْنَآ ءَابَآءَنَا عَلَىٰٓ أُمَّةٍ وَإِنَّا عَلَىٰٓ ءَاثَٰرِهِم مُّقْتَدُونَ

And similarly, We have not sent a warner before you (O Muhammad) to any town (people) except that the prosperous ones among them said: "We found our fathers following a certain way and religion, and we will indeed follow in their footsteps."[30]

Therefore we say [to them]: call us whatever you like; *Wahhaabiyyah*, *Hanaabilah*, *Najdiyyah* or *Hijaaziyyah*; whatever you wish. Do you not believe in Allaah and His Messenger? Do you not consider the *Qur.aan* and the *Sunnah* to be authentic evidences? Go ahead [answer].

However it seems that some of those who give *da'wah* chase people away, and if it is said to one of them; "We do not take from you, you are a *Wahhaabee*," he turns away from them in aversion or responds to them in a similar manner and says; "You people are misguided, you have such

---

30 The Noble *Qur.aan* - *Soorah* az-Zukhruf, *Aayah* 23

and such innovations." So *da'wah* with wisdom would not have been achieved by this individual.

Shaykh Muhammad ibn Saalih al-'Uthaymeen

12. Criticising some of the Du'aat

<u>Question</u>: Some students of knowledge have directed certain criticisms towards a specific group of callers who made some errors related to *manhaj*; is this considered to be backbiting?[31]

<u>Response</u>: It is obligatory for *da'wah* to be based on the way that Allaah (*Subhaanahu wa Ta'aala*) defined it to His Prophets in His saying:

> **And indeed we have sent a Messenger to every nation ordering them [the people], to worship Allaah alone and to stay away from false deities.**

He (*Subhaanahu wa Ta'aala*) also defined it to His Prophet Muhammad (*sal-Allaahu 'alayhi wa sallam*) who is the last of the Messengers; Allaah said:

قُلْ هَٰذِهِۦ سَبِيلِىٓ أَدْعُوٓا۟ إِلَى ٱللَّهِ عَلَىٰ بَصِيرَةٍ أَنَا۠ وَمَنِ ٱتَّبَعَنِى وَسُبْحَٰنَ ٱللَّهِ وَمَآ أَنَا۠ مِنَ ٱلْمُشْرِكِينَ

> **"Say (O Muhammad): "This is my way; I call to Allaah (i.e. to the Oneness of Allaah - Islaamic Monotheism) upon Baseerah, I and whomsoever follows**

13

---

31 al-Fataawaa al-Jaliyyah 'anil-Manaahij ad-Da'wiyyah - Question No.8, Page 12

me. And Glorified and Exalted is Allaah (above all that they associate as partners with Him). And I am not of the Mushrikoon (polytheists)."[32]

Therefore whoever brings a *manhaj* that opposes the *manhaj* of the Messenger, or a way that opposes the way of the Messenger (*sal-Allaahu 'alayhi wa sallam*) then indeed it is obligatory for the scholars to clarify their errors. Whosoever does not clarify errors while knowing them is indeed sinful, unless a sufficient group have already embarked upon clarifying their errors. Doing so is '*Fardh Kifaa.ee*'; if a sufficient group of people carry it out then the obligation is absolved from the rest.

If the person who is clarifying the mistakes of some of the callers is in need of help and support, it then becomes binding upon everyone to aid and support him, and whoever claims that it is not permissible to speak about individuals who have established a *manhaj* that is in opposition to the *manhaj* and the way of the Messenger of Al-laah (*sal-Allaahu 'alayhi wa sallam*) is a *mubtil*; one who intends to invalidate the 'promotion of good,' the 'forbidding of evil,' the clarification of the truth, and co-operation upon righteousness and piety. If that is not his intention, then he has indeed blindly followed one who has such intentions and has consequently been deceived.

Therefore it is obligatory for him to return to the truth and abandon what he is upon in saying that it is not permissible to denounce those who have erred in their *manhaj* or the legislated way of giving *da'wah*.

Shaykh Ahmad ibn Yahyaa an-Najmee

---

32 The Noble *Qur.aan* - *Soorah* Yoosuf, *Aayah* 108

Chapter 14
Groups and Sects

1. The Ruling Regarding Groups in Islaam

Question: What is the ruling concerning initiating groups, and is it permissible to have different groups such as *Hizbut-Tahreer* and *al-Ikhwaan al-Muslimoon* in *Islaam*?[1]

Response: All praise is due to Allaah alone, and may the *salaah* and *salaam* be upon the Messenger, his family and his Companions.

To Proceed:

It is not permissible for *Muslims* to split up into sects and groups and engage in cursing and fighting one another. Indeed Allaah has forbidden splitting; He admonished those who start it as well as those who follow them, and promised them a terrible torment. Allaah and His Messenger freed themselves from splitting. Allaah (*Subhaanahu wa Ta'aala*) says:

$$وَٱعۡتَصِمُواْ بِحَبۡلِ ٱللَّهِ جَمِيعٗا وَلَا تَفَرَّقُواْ$$

---

1 Fataawa al-Lajnah ad-Daa.imah - No.1674

279

*And hold fast, all of you together, to the Rope of
Allaah (i.e. this Qur.aan), and be not divided
amongst yourselves...*[2]

To His saying:

وَلَا تَكُونُوا كَالَّذِينَ تَفَرَّقُوا وَاخْتَلَفُوا مِنْ بَعْدِ مَا جَاءَ
هُمُ الْبَيِّنَاتُ وَأُولَٰئِكَ لَهُمْ عَذَابٌ عَظِيمٌ

*...and be not like those who divided and differed
among themselves after the clear proofs had come to
them. It is they for whom there is an awful torment.*[3]

Allaah (*Subhaanahu wa Ta'aala*) also said:

إِنَّ الَّذِينَ فَرَّقُوا دِينَهُمْ وَكَانُوا شِيَعًا لَّسْتَ
مِنْهُمْ فِي شَيْءٍ إِنَّمَا أَمْرُهُمْ إِلَى اللَّهِ ثُمَّ يُنَبِّئُهُم بِمَا كَانُوا يَفْعَلُونَ
﴿١٥٩﴾ مَن جَاءَ بِالْحَسَنَةِ فَلَهُ عَشْرُ أَمْثَالِهَا وَمَن جَاءَ بِالسَّيِّئَةِ
فَلَا يُجْزَىٰ إِلَّا مِثْلَهَا وَهُمْ لَا يُظْلَمُونَ ﴿١٦٠﴾

*"Verily, those who split their religion and break
up into sects (all kinds of religious sects), you (O
Muhammad) are not from them in the least. Their
affair is only with Allaah, Who will then tell them
of what they used to do. Whoever brings a good
deed (Islaamic Monotheism and deeds of obedience to Allaah and His Messenger) shall have ten*

---

2 The Noble *Qur.aan* - *Soorah* Aal-'Imraan, *Aayah* 103

3 The Noble *Qur.aan* - *Soorah* Aal-'Imraan, *Aayah* 105

times the like thereof to his credit, and whoever brings an evil deed (polytheism, disbelief, hypocrisy, and deeds of disobedience to Allaah and His Messenger) shall have only the recompense of the like thereof, and they will not be wronged."[4]

It has been confirmed that the Messenger of Allaah said:

"Do not revert to disbelief after me, striking at each others' necks."

The verses in the *Qur.aan* and the *ahaadeeth* that admonish splitting in the religion are plenty.

However, it is legislated for a ruler to organise groups and distribute different duties amongst them, in regards to both religious and daily life affairs in order for each group to carry out its duty in its respected field. Rather it is compulsory upon a *Muslim* ruler to distribute different duties amongst his subjects in relation to religious as well as daily life needs. He may designate a group that occupies itself with the knowledge of *hadeeth*, how it is propagated, collecting it in books and distinguishing what is authentic from what isn't and so on. He may designate another group which concerns itself with collecting and teaching *fiqh*; a third group that concerns itself with the Arabic language, its rules; singular forms, explaining it and unlocking its secrets. A fourth group as well, that occupies itself with *jihaad*; defending the lands of *Islaam*. Another group can be designated to oversee industry, farming, and business and so on.

14

---

4 The Noble *Qur.aan* - *Soorah* al-An'aam, *Aayahs* 159-160

This is from the necessities of the religion; a necessity which the *ummah* could not grow without; *Islaam* will not be protected or propagate except through such means. This is to be done of course while everyone adheres to the Book of Allaah, the guidance of His Messenger and what the Rightly Guided Caliphs and the Righteous Predecessors of this *ummah* were upon. They should have a united goal and work together for *Islaam*'s success; achieving methods with which a blissful life can be established; guiding everyone under the shade of *Islaam*, its banner, upon the upright path of Allaah, while staying away from deviant paths and destructive groups. Allaah (*Subhaanahu wa Ta'aala*) says:

$$وَأَنَّ هَٰذَا صِرَٰطِى مُسْتَقِيمًا فَٱتَّبِعُوهُ وَلَا تَتَّبِعُوا۟ ٱلسُّبُلَ فَتَفَرَّقَ بِكُمْ عَن سَبِيلِهِۦ ذَٰلِكُمْ وَصَّىٰكُم بِهِۦ لَعَلَّكُمْ تَتَّقُونَ$$

And verily, this is my Straight Path, so follow it, and follow not (other) paths for they will separate you away from His Path. This He has ordained for you that you may become al-Muttaqoon (the pious)[5]

The Permanent Committee for Islaamic Research and Verdicts

2. The Correct Stance Concerning Sects

Question: What should a *Muslim*'s stance regarding the differing between the well-known *madhaahib* and different groups and sects be?[6]

Response: It is compulsory for the *Muslim* to adhere to the truth that

---

5 The Noble *Qur.aan* - *Soorah* al-An'aam, *Aayah* 153

6 Majmoo' Fataawa wa Maqaalaat Mutanawwi'ah - Volume 5, Page 157

is supported by the evidences of the *Qur.aan* and the *Sunnah* of the Messenger (*sal-Allaahu 'alayhi wa sallam*), and to practice *walaa* and *baraa* upon that. It is upon him to free himself of every group or *madh.hab* that opposes the truth and is contradictory to the Book and the *Sunnah*.

The Religion of Allaah is one; it is the Straight Path; it is worshipping Al-laah alone and following His Messenger Muhammad (*sal-Allaahu 'alay-hi wa sallam*). So it is obligatory for every *Muslim* to adhere to this truth and be steadfast upon it. It is being obedient to Allaah and acting upon His Legislation, which His Prophet Muhammad (*sal-Allaahu 'alayhi wa sallam*) brought, while being sincere to Allaah in that and abstaining from worshipping other than Him (*Subhaanahu wa Ta'aala*).

So it is compulsory to stay away from and free oneself from every *madh.hab* that is contradictory to this way and every group that does not wor-ship Allaah with this *'aqeedah*. It is obligatory upon them to leniently call their followers to the truth with legislative evidences; carefully se-lecting beneficial methods to teach them the truth.

Shaykh 'Abdul-'Azeez ibn Baaz

3. The Raafidhah Calling to Their Innovations

Question: O, noble *Shaykh*, there are now alot of *Raafidhah* in our neighbourhood who partake in activities with foreign students. They accompany them when going to the markets, see to their needs and participate in other activities with them. What is the solution?[7]

14

---

7 Liqaa.aat al-Baab al-Maftooh - No.821

Response: If they (*Raafidhah*) are eager in participating in activities and calling to their innovations, then you should be even more enthusiastic in participating in such activities and in calling to your *Sunnah*. Because if the truth is practiced and propagated by its people, then Allaah (*Subhaanahu wa Ta'aala*) says in His Book:

$$ بَلۡ نَقۡذِفُ بِٱلۡحَقِّ عَلَى ٱلۡبَـٰطِلِ فَيَدۡمَغُهُۥ فَإِذَا هُوَ زَاهِقٌ $$

***Nay, We fling (send down) the truth (this Qur.aan)
against falsehood (disbelief), so it destroys it, and
behold, it (falsehood) is vanished.*** [8]

If we however, see that the people of innovations are enthusiastic in calling to their innovations, especially the major ones, and then keep quiet or say: 'What should we do?' then this is cowardice. If they call to their innovations, your call should be greater and grander, because you are on the truth and would be rewarded for doing so.

The people of innovations on the other hand acquire sins when calling to their innovations and would carry the burden of practicing such evil. They also acquire the sins of all those they call to their innovation, because the Prophet (*sal-Allaahu 'alayhi wa sallam*) said:

***"Whoever initiates something evil in Islaam, will carry
the weight of that sin as well as the weight of the sins of
all those who act upon it until the Day of Judgment."***

Therefore, I encourage you to have more enthusiasm than them. If they spend a dollar then spend two; if they visit and invite people, then you should be much keener in doing so.

---

8 The Noble *Qur.aan* - *Soorah* al-Anbiyaa, *Aayah* 18

Furthermore, the Prophet (sal-Allaahu 'alayhi wa sallam) has given us a principle to follow, that we treat them in the same manner that they treat us.

Shaykh Muhammad ibn Saalih al-'Uthaymeen

4. Causes of Deviation

Question: What causes alot of youth to deviate and be disinterested in the Religion?[9]

Response: There are alot of reasons that cause alot of youth to deviate and be disinterested in anything related to religion. The most important of these reasons being lack of knowledge, ignorance of the reality of Islaam and its benefits, their disregard for the Qur.aan and the lack of knowledgeable individuals to teach them; individuals with the ability to explain the reality of Islaam to the youth, clarify its benefits to them and explain its objectives in detail, and the goodness that would result from abiding by Islaam in the life of this world and in the hereafter.

There are other reasons such as the community, television, travelling abroad and mixing with people who have false beliefs, bad manners and extreme ignorance. There are also other reasons that cause them to turn away from Islaam and interest them in atheistic beliefs and ideologies that permit everything. Alot of youth have fallen victim to this; their hearts have been drained of beneficial knowledge and the correct 'aqeedah, and filled with alot of misconceptions, doubts, false claims and alluring temptations. The result being what you have mentioned in your question relating to their deviation and disinterest in anything to

---

9 Majmoo' Fataawa wa Maqaalaat Mutanawwi'ah - Volume 5, Page 253

do with *Islaam*. A beautiful proverb was related concerning this matter:

> **Her temptations arrived before I knew what temp-
> tations were – so they encountered a vacant heart
> and established themselves.**

Even more eloquent and superior to this is the saying of Allaah (*Subhaanahu wa Ta'aala*):

$$أَرَءَيْتَ$$

$$مَنِ ٱتَّخَذَ إِلَٰهَهُۥ هَوَىٰهُ أَفَأَنتَ تَكُونُ عَلَيْهِ وَكِيلًا ﴿٤٣﴾$$

$$أَمْ تَحْسَبُ أَنَّ أَكْثَرَهُمْ يَسْمَعُونَ أَوْ يَعْقِلُونَ إِنْ هُمْ إِلَّا$$

$$كَٱلْأَنْعَٰمِ بَلْ هُمْ أَضَلُّ سَبِيلًا ﴿٤٤﴾$$

> **"Have you (O Muhammad) seen the one who has
> taken his own vain desires as his ilaah (god)? Would
> you then be a Wakeel (a disposer of his affairs or
> a watcher) over him? Or do you think that most of
> them hear or understand? They are only like cattle
> – nay, they are even farther astray from the Path
> (i.e. even worse than cattle)."**[10]

The cure, I believe, differs according to different illnesses. The most important cure is to give alot of time to reading the Noble *Qur.aan* and the
biography of the Prophet (*sal-Allaahu 'alayhi wa sallam*), and to have
a good teacher, principles and *manhaj*.

The media in *Muslim* countries also needs to be purified from promot-

---

10 The Noble *Qur.aan* - Soorah al-Furqaan, *Aayah* 43-44

ing all un*islaam*ic things; un*islaam*ic manners, various vices and infidelity. This can be accomplished if those responsible for the media are truthful in their claim that they are *Muslim* and are intent on directing the society and the youth to *Islaam*.

Amongst the solutions as well, is to spend time in rectifying the community and purifying it from what has befallen it. Another solution is to prohibit people from travelling abroad unless it is necessary, and to focus on enlightening people about *Islaam* in an objective and competitive way using the media, teachers, callers and lecturers.

I ask Allaah to bless us with that. I ask Allaah to rectify *Muslim* rulers and to grant them understanding of their religion; to adhere to it as well as fight all that oppose it with sincerity, truthfulness and continuous effort. Indeed He is All-Close and All-Hearing.

Shaykh 'Abdul-'Azeez ibn Baaz

5. Islaamic Groups

<u>Question</u>: How can you explain the emergence of different religious groups, every group having its own way in calling to *Islaam* and each group wanting to be in charge? Are all of these groups or some of them included in the saying of the Messenger of Allaah (*sal-Allaahu 'alayhi wa sallam*):

"My ummah will also split into seventy-three groups, all of them in the hellfire except one."

Also, how can we conciliate between these groups; *al-Ikhwaan al-Muslimoon*, the *Salafees*, the *Khalafees*, *at-Takfeer wal-Hijrah*, *at-Tableegh*,

287

as-Soofiyyah and so on?[11]

Response: All Praise is due to Allaah alone, and may the *salaah* and *salaam* be upon the Messenger, his family and companions.

To Proceed.

The religion of Allaah is one, and the way to it is one, so whoever is acts upon the religion of *Islaam* and what the Messenger of Allaah (*sal-Allaahu 'alayhi wa sallam*) was upon is the correct one.

Success is granted by Allaah, and may the *salaah* and *salaam* be upon our Prophet Muhammad, his family and companions.

The Permanent Committee for Islaamic Research and Verdicts

6. Affiliating Oneself to a Group with a Leader

Question: Is it compulsory for every *Muslim* to be with an *Islaam*ic group that has a leader, even though this leads to the division of the *Muslim*s, the dismantling of their unity and creates disputes between them?[12]

Response: All praise is due to Allaah alone, and may the *salaah* and *salaam* be upon the Messenger, his family and his Companions.

To Proceed:

---

11 Fataawa al-Lajnah ad-Daa.imah - No.6800

12 Fataawa al-Lajnah ad-Daa.imah - No.161

It is compulsory for every *Muslim* to follow everything in the Book of Allaah (*Subhaanahu wa Ta'aala*) and the *Sunnah* of His Messenger (*sal-Allaahu 'alayhi wa sallam*) in deeds, actions, as well as *'aqeedah*. It is also compulsory to love and hate for the Pleasure of Allaah; to have allegiance and show enmity for the Pleasure of Allaah, and to be intent on being the closest person to the truth according to each individual's ability.

Success is granted by Allaah, and may the *salaah* and *salaam* be upon our Prophet Muhammad, his family and his Companions.

The Permanent Committee for Islaamic Research and Verdicts

7. Affiliation to Islaamic Groups

<u>Question</u>: I am a university student who lives in a whirlpool of ideologies, opinions and groups. Each one of these groups claims to be the best and does everything possible to gain supporters. They include: *al-Ikhwaan al-Muslimoon, Jamaa'at at-Tableegh*, those who go out in *khurooj* for forty days or four months, *Jamaa'at Ansaar as-Sunnah* and *al-Jamaa'ah al-Islaahiyyah*, which belongs to 'Abdul Hameed ibn Baadees. Based upon this information, can you direct us to the correct path in which our happiness and the safety in *Islaam* lies; safety from external influences that snap at our bones while we are unaware?[13]

<u>Response</u>: All praise is due to Allaah alone, and may the *salaah* and *salaam* be upon His Messenger, his family and his Companions.

To Proceed:

---

13 Fataawa al-Lajnah ad-Daa.imah - No.4093

It is obligatory for you to hold fast to the truth that is supported by evidences without siding with any particular group. The most worthy of groups to co-operate with is the one that adheres to the correct *'aqeedah* which the scholars of the *Salafus-Saalih (rahima-humullaah)* adhered to, commits itself to, acting upon the Book of Allaah and the *Sunnah* of His Messenger *(sal-Allaahu 'alayhi wa sallam)* and discards whatever has been made up such as innovations and superstitions.

The Permanent Committee for Islaamic Research and Verdicts

8. Obligation of the Scholars towards Splitting & Differing

<u>Question</u>: What are the obligations of the *Muslim* scholars towards the numerous groups and organisations present in alot of *Islaam*ic as well as non-*Islaam*ic countries? There is a great deal of differing between them to the point that each group declares the other to be astray. Wouldn't you agree that it would be appropriate to get involved in such matters by clarifying the correct stance in this differing for fear that it may increase and its harmful effect on *Muslims*?[14]

<u>Response</u>: Indeed our Prophet Muhammad *(sal-Allaahu 'alayhi wa sallam)* showed us only one path, and it is compulsory for all the *Muslims* to follow it; it is the Straight Path of Allaah and the upright *manhaj* of His Religion. Allaah *(Subhaanahu wa Ta'aala)* says:

$$ وَأَنَّ هَٰذَا صِرَٰطِى مُسْتَقِيمًا فَٱتَّبِعُوهُ وَلَا تَتَّبِعُوا۟ ٱلسُّبُلَ فَتَفَرَّقَ بِكُمْ عَن سَبِيلِهِۦ ذَٰلِكُمْ وَصَّىٰكُم بِهِۦ لَعَلَّكُمْ تَتَّقُونَ $$

---

14 Majmoo' Fataawaa wa Maqaalaat Mutanawwi'ah - Volume 5, Page 202

"And verily, this is my straight path, so follow it and follow not (other) paths, for they will separate you away from His path. This He has ordained for you that you may become al-Muttaqoon (the pious)."[15]

The Lord of Might and Majesty forbade the *ummah* of Muhammad (*sal-Allaahu 'alayhi wa sallam*) from splitting and differing because they are amongst the greatest causes of failure and allow the enemy to gain power over them, as is in the saying of Allaah (*Subhaanahu wa Ta'aala*):

وَٱعۡتَصِمُواْ بِحَبۡلِ ٱللَّهِ جَمِيعٗا وَلَا تَفَرَّقُواْ

"And hold fast, all of you together, to the Rope of Allaah (i.e. this Qur.aan), and be not divided amongst yourselves..."[16]

His (*Subhaanahu wa Ta'aala*) saying as well:

شَرَعَ لَكُم مِّنَ ٱلدِّينِ مَا وَصَّىٰ بِهِۦ نُوحٗا وَٱلَّذِىٓ أَوۡحَيۡنَآ
إِلَيۡكَ وَمَا وَصَّيۡنَا بِهِۦٓ إِبۡرَٰهِيمَ وَمُوسَىٰ وَعِيسَىٰٓ أَنۡ أَقِيمُواْ ٱلدِّينَ
وَلَا تَتَفَرَّقُواْ فِيهِۚ كَبُرَ عَلَى ٱلۡمُشۡرِكِينَ مَا تَدۡعُوهُمۡ إِلَيۡهِ

"He (Allaah) has ordained for you the same religion (Islaamic Monotheism) which He ordained for Nooh, and that which We have revealed to you (O Muhammad), and that which We ordained for Ibraaheem, Moosaa and 'Eesaa saying you should establish the religion (i.e. to do what it orders you

14

---

15 The Noble *Qur.aan* - *Soorah* al-An'aam, *Aayah* 153

16 The Noble *Qur.aan* - *Soorah* Aal-'Imraan, *Aayah* 103

to do practically) and make no divisions in it. In-
tolerable for the Mushrikoon is (Islaamic Monothe-
ism) to which you (O Muhammad) call them to..."[17]

This is a Godly *da'wah* to unify the ranks and the hearts. If there are alot
of groups in an *Islaam*ic country for the purpose of spreading good,
helping people, co-operating upon piety and *taqwaa* without its found-
ers differing then this is good and has great benefits. However if every
group declares the other to be misguided and criticises the others actions then the harms would be great and the consequences would also
be harmful. So it is compulsory for the *Muslim* scholars to clarify the
reality of the situation and deliberate with every one of these groups.

We also advise everybody to act upon the path that Allaah (*Subhaanahu
wa Ta'aala*) has drawn out for His servants, the path that our Prophet
Muhammad (*sal-Allaahu 'alayhi wa sallam*) called to. Whoever crosses
these bounds and continues in their obstinacy because of personal gains
or personal goals that only Allaah (*Subhaanahu wa Ta'aala*) has knowledge of, it would then be compulsory for those who know their reality to
warn against them publicly so that people can stay away from their ways
and not join them due to being unaware of the reality of their state. They
should do this to stop them from leading others astray and turning them
away from the Straight Path which Allaah (*Subhaanahu wa Ta'aala*)
ordered us to follow in His saying:

وَأَنَّ هَٰذَا صِرَٰطِى مُسْتَقِيمًا فَٱتَّبِعُوهُ وَلَا تَتَّبِعُوا۟ ٱلسُّبُلَ
فَتَفَرَّقَ بِكُمْ عَن سَبِيلِهِۦ ذَٰلِكُمْ وَصَّىٰكُم بِهِۦ لَعَلَّكُمْ
تَتَّقُونَ

---

17 The Noble *Qur.aan - Soorah* ash-Shooraa, *Aayah* 13

And verily, this is my straight path, so follow it, and follow not (other) paths, for they will separate you away from His path. This He has ordained for you that you may become al-Muttaqoon (the pious). [18]

There is no doubt that that the *Shaytaan* firstly, and the enemies of the *Muslims* secondly, are keen on having many groups and sects in *Islaam*-ic communities; because the conformity of the *Muslims*, their unification and awareness of the danger that threatens them and endeavours to ruin their *'aqeedah* would cause them to be active in struggling against this opposition in a unified rank for the benefit of the *Muslims*, and cause them to fend off this danger from their religion, countries and brothers. The enemies amongst the devils and mankind do not approve of this; this is why they are eager in separating the *Muslims*, dispersing their unity and spreading enmity amongst them.

We ask Allaah to unify the *Muslims* upon the truth, and remove every misguiding *fitnah* from their communities; indeed He is Able to do all things.

Shaykh 'Abdul-'Azeez ibn Baaz

9. Establishing Different Islaamic Groups

<u>Question</u>: Is establishing *Islaam*ic groups in *Muslim* countries in order to cultivate and raise the youth according to *Islaam*, considered to be a positive issue in this time period?[19]

---

18 The Noble *Qur.aan - Soorah* al-An'aam, *Aayah* 103

19 Majmoo' Fataawa wa Maqaalaat Mutanawwi'ah - Volume 5, Page 272

Response: The presence of these *Islaami*c groups is good for *Muslims*, but it is upon them to clarify the truth with evidence and not compete with each other. They should be keen on co-operating with and loving one another as well as advising one another and propagating each others good traits. They should also be keen on abandoning anything that may cause problems between them. There is no problem in having groups if they call to the Book of Allaah and the *Sunnah* of His Messenger (*sal-Allaahu 'alayhi wa sallam*).

Shaykh 'Abdul-'Azeez ibn Baaz

10. Advice to the Youth involved in Islaamic Groups?

Question: What advice can you give to the youth who are involved in these groups?[20]

Response: I advise them to look for and follow the correct path; to return to the people of knowledge in the affairs that confuse them; to co-operate with groups in affairs that benefit the *Muslims* according to the legislated evidences, not with force or ridicule, but with kind words and a fine manner. They should take the Righteous Predecessors as their role models; the truth should be their evidence. They should pay a great deal of attention to the correct *'aqeedah* that the Messenger (*sal-Allaahu 'alayhi wa sallam*) of Allaah and his Companions were upon.

Shaykh 'Abdul-'Azeez ibn Baaz

---

20 Majmoo' Fataawa wa Maqaalaat Mutanawwi'ah - Volume 5, Page 267

11. Islaamic Groups with Rulers

Question: O, noble *Shaykh*, if we look at the *Islaam*ic world today, we find alot of different groups calling to *Islaam*, all of which say: 'We are upon the *manhaj* of the *Salaf*, and the Book of Allaah and the *Sunnah* are in agreement with us.'

What should our stance concerning these groups be, and what is the ruling on pledging allegiance to a leader from one of these groups?[21]

Response: The ruling concerning these groups which claim to be upon the truth is very simple, we ask them: 'What is the Truth?'

The truth is what the Book of Allaah and the *Sunnah* confirm, and returning to the Book and the *Sunnah* resolves differences for those who believe. As for those who follow their desires then nothing you use will benefit them. Allaah (*Subhaanahu wa Ta'aala*) says:

$$فَإِن تَنَٰزَعۡتُمۡ فِی شَیۡءٖ فَرُدُّوهُ إِلَی ٱللَّهِ وَٱلرَّسُولِ إِن كُنتُمۡ تُؤۡمِنُونَ بِٱللَّهِ وَٱلۡیَوۡمِ ٱلۡأٓخِرِۚ ذَٰلِكَ خَیۡرٌ وَأَحۡسَنُ تَأۡوِیلًا$$

"And if you differ in anything amongst yourselves, refer it to Allaah and His Messenger, if you believe in Allaah and in the Last Day. That is better and more suitable for final determination."[22]

So we say to those groups: Gather and let every one of you do away with his own desires and have the intention that he will follow whatever the

21 Liqaa.aat al-Baab al-Maftooh - No.875

22 The Noble *Qur.aan* - *Soorah* an-Nisaa, *Aayah* 59

Qur.aan and the *Sunnah* confirm, with the basis of removing desires, not on the basis of blind following or being tenacious about one's opinion; because understanding the *Qur.aan* and the *Sunnah* based upon a persons own *'aqeedah* and opinions does not benefit at all; one will only reach or confirm his own *'aqeedah*.

This is why the scholars have stated that it is obligatory for a person to look at the evidence first, and subsequently believe in something; not believe first and then look at the evidence. This is because the evidence is the foundation, and a ruling branches off from it.

If one was to believe in something first, before looking at the evidence, he would not have good intentions when looking at the evidences; he would twist the texts of the Book and the *Sunnah* to suit his beliefs, and would therefore remain upon his desires and not follow guidance.

So I say to these groups which claim to be upon the truth; come with good intentions, stripped of desires and tenaciousness. Here lies the Book of Allaah and this is the *Sunnah* of the Messenger (*sal-Allaahu 'alayhi wa sallam*); if they did not contain a solution to differing, Allaah would not have commanded us to refer back to them, for indeed Allaah does not refer to anything except that the benefit lies in it.

"refer it to Allaah and His Messenger (sal-Allaahu 'alayhi wa sallam)"

Disputes that occur by not agreeing upon the Book and the *Sunnah* are due to the absence of the following condition:

"...if you believe in Allaah and in the Last Day."

As for the issue of pledging allegiance to a man then this is impermissible, because allegiance is only to be pledged to the ruler of a country. If we say that one can pledge allegiance to any person, the *ummah* will split. A country that has a hundred districts would have a hundred rulers for each state. This is splitting, so as long as a country has a legislated ruler, it is not permissible to pledge allegiance to anyone.

If the ruler does not judge by the laws that Allaah has revealed, there are different circumstances to this situation. This could be a form of disbelief; a form of transgression or a form of disobedience to Allaah, according to what the legislated texts confirm.

If this ruler is persistent on practicing a form of disbelief which we have evidence for, we must try to get rid of him if we are able to. This does not mean that we battle him with armed forces, because this is in opposition to the legislation of *Islaam* and is in opposition to wisdom. This is why the Messenger (*sal-Allaahu 'alayhi wa sallam*) was not ordered to carry out *jihaad* while he was in Makkah; because he did not have the means to overthrow them. So a small number of people trying to overthrow a government while having no weaponry when compared to the weaponry of a government, there is no doubt that this is in opposition to the Book and the *Sunnah*.

If you see a ruler practicing an apparent form of disbelief in which you have evidence from the Religion of Allaah for, then wait for the fifth condition; the ability to overthrow him, because the Prophet (*sal-Allaahu 'alayhi wa sallam*) did not permit the *ummah* to try and overthrow a leader except with these five conditions; an apparent form of disbelief in which you have evidence from the Religion of Allaah for, and the condition rendering it compulsory is having the ability to overthrow that certain ruler and his government. Without the ability to do so, one must pray to Allaah (*Subhaanahu wa Ta'aala*) for relief and refrain from provoking those who are capable of disposing of him, his group and others.

14

The saying of the Messenger (*sal-Allaahu 'alayhi wa sallam*):

"Unless you see."

Meaning that you see it yourselves; others seeing it and reporting it is not sufficient, because they may report something incorrectly. His saying:

"Disbelief"

Meaning that it is not just disobedience; it is not permissible to overthrow a leader even if he practices the worst forms of disobedience as long as they are not forms of disbelief, such as if he commits fornication, drinks alcohol or unjustly murders people while not believing these acts are impermissible, or doing this out of oppression. It is not permissible to overthrow him due to that. The saying of the Messenger of Allaah:

"Apparent"

Meaning a clear form of disbelief that cannot be due to a misunderstanding; as for a form of disbelief that may have been committed due to a misunderstanding, then the ruler may have committed it due to a misunderstanding. His saying:

"That you have a proof for."

Meaning that we have evidence from the Book and the *Sunnah* for it; not a proof based upon analogy in which one may be mistaken.

These are four conditions; the fifth condition that needs to be met in order to render overthrowing the ruler compulsory is having the ability to do so, and this condition is a condition for every obligation due to the saying of Allaah (*Subhaanahu wa Ta'aala*):

$$\text{لَا يُكَلِّفُ ٱللَّهُ نَفْسًا إِلَّا وُسْعَهَا}$$

Allaah does not burden a person beyond his ability. [23]

His saying as well:

$$\text{فَٱتَّقُوا ٱللَّهَ مَا ٱسْتَطَعْتُمْ}$$

"So have Taqwaa of Allaah as much as you can." [24]

So these brothers want to have different groups, every group with a leader because the ruler according to them is not a legislated ruler, we say to them: It is not permissible for you to split up the *ummah* by having a ruler for every group, this is a tremendous error.

Allaah informed His Prophet (*sal-Allaahu 'alayhi wa sallam*) that he is free from these people. But it is upon them to prepare and build their might in order to remove the ruler who has met the conditions that make it permissible for them to remove him, so that Allaah may strengthen and aid them in overthrowing him.

Shaykh Muhammad ibn Saalih al-'Uthaymeen

12. The Correct Stance towards Islaamic Groups

Question: Noble *Shaykh*, as you already know, from the blessings of Allaah (*Subhaanahu wa Ta'aala*) upon this country is that it is upon the methodology of the Book and the *Sunnah*. However, there are those who are upon other methodologies, some may be misguided, such as

14

---

23 The Noble *Qur.aan* - *Soorah* al-Baqarah, *Aayah* 286

24 The Noble *Qur.aan* - *Soorah* at-Taghaabun, *Aayah* 16

299

the methodology of the *Khawaarij* or other methodologies that split the *Muslim*s. Do you think this is permissible?[25]

<u>Response</u>: The Messenger of Allaah (*sal-Allaahu 'alayhi wa sallam*) clarified during a *jumu'ah khutbah* as well as on other occasions that the best of speech is the Speech of Allaah, and the best of guidance is the guidance of Muhammad (*sal-Allaahu 'alayhi wa sallam*).

If we look at the guidance of the Messenger (*sal-Allaahu 'alayhi wa sallam*), we would find that he wanted this *ummah* to be one unified *ummah* that does not split, differ or have ill-feelings between its individuals. The Messenger (*sal-Allaahu 'alayhi wa sallam*) even abandoned preferable things in order to stop splitting; he (*sal-Allaahu 'alayhi wa sallam*) ordered the public to be patient with the oppression, injustice and selfishness of their rulers, and he informed them that such things would take place. He said to the *Ansaar*:

> **"Indeed you will go through a time period after me in which the rulers will be selfish."**

He (*sal-Allaahu 'alayhi wa sallam*) also said:

> **"Whoever sees something from his ruler that he dislikes must be patient."**

When someone asked him (*sal-Allaahu 'alayhi wa sallam*) about some rulers who demand their own rights but don't give the public their rights, he said:

---

25 Liqaa.aat al-Baab al-Maftooh - No.954

"Listen and obey, for indeed they will be held responsible for their duties and you for yours."

There is no doubt that inciting hatred against the rulers and saying things about them that would cause the public to hate them is in opposition to the guidance of the Prophet (*sal-Allaahu 'alayhi wa sallam*). This is because the *Islaamic ummah* relies on two types of people: the scholars and the rulers; they are the people of authority with regards to whom Allaah (*Subhaanahu wa Ta'aala*) has said the following:

يَـٰٓأَيُّهَا ٱلَّذِينَ ءَامَنُوٓاْ أَطِيعُواْ ٱللَّهَ وَأَطِيعُواْ ٱلرَّسُولَ وَأُوْلِى ٱلۡأَمۡرِ مِنكُمۡ

"O you who believe! Obey Allaah and obey the Messenger (Muhammad, and those amongst you who are in authority."[26]

The scholars who explained this verse said:

"'Those in authority,' in this verse are the scholars and rulers, for the scholars lead this *ummah* with the Legislation of Allaah, and the rulers lead this *ummah* with the authority of Allaah (*Subhaanahu wa Ta'aala*)."

If it weren't for the scholars and the rulers, the *ummah* would not be stable, because the scholars lead the people with the legislation, and the rulers lead the people with authority and law enforcement.

So if someone says things about the rulers or the scholars that cause people to despise them and lowers their status, the *ummah* would be lost because they would not have scholars in whom they could trust;

---

26 The Noble *Qur.aan* - *Soorah* an-Nisaa, *Aayah* 59

thus the legislation of *Islaam* would be lost. They would also not have rulers in whom they could trust, so security would be lost. This is why I think that the behaviour of some individuals in speaking about the rulers and scholars is a gross mistake; they fill people's hearts with hatred towards rulers. If they see the scholars or rulers doing something wrong, it is obligatory for them to advise them, not to talk about and spread that certain act; this is an opposition to the Legislation of *Islaam*.

Of course the scholars and the rulers have errors, whether they are carried out by mistake or deliberately, but the cure to a disease is not by creating a disease that is greater than it, and one does not cure evil with an evil that is greater than the first, never! Nothing has harmed the *Islaam*ic *ummah* more than speaking about its rulers and scholars!

What is it that led to the murder of 'Uthmaan? It was people's criticism of him; they spoke about him saying that he favours his relatives and he did this and that. So people started harbouring negative feelings about him in their hearts. These feelings evolved into abhorrence, hatred and enmity until it reached the point where they murdered him in his house; and the *ummah* split up after that.

What is it that led to the murder of the ruler of the believers, 'Alee ibn Abee Taalib? Nothing other than this same reason; they revolted against him saying that he contradicted the Legislation of *Islaam*; they declared him to be a disbeliever along with the rest of the *Muslim*s, and what happened after that is history.

All praise is due to Allaah, as the questioner stated; we live in a secure, calm country, its provision reaches it with ease from every place. It is the best of *Islaam*ic countries, according to my knowledge, in terms of implementing the Legislation of Allaah. This is something that is apparent, we are not saying that it is perfect, rather it has a lot of shortcomings, and injustice exists in it as well as selfishness; but if you compare the injustice in it to the justice, you would find that it is alot less and it is unjust for someone to notice only the errors and shut his eyes to the good. Since this is the case, then it is upon people to judge with justice; Allaah (*Subhaanahu wa Ta'aala*) says:

يَٰٓأَيُّهَا ٱلَّذِينَ ءَامَنُواْ كُونُواْ قَوَّٰمِينَ بِٱلْقِسْطِ شُهَدَآءَ لِلَّهِ وَلَوْ عَلَىٰٓ أَنفُسِكُمْ أَوِ ٱلْوَٰلِدَيْنِ وَٱلْأَقْرَبِينَ

"O you who believe! Firmly establish justice, as witnesses to Allaah, even if it were against your own selves, your parents or your kin..."[27]

Allaah (*Subhaanahu wa Ta'aala*) also said:

يَٰٓأَيُّهَا ٱلَّذِينَ ءَامَنُواْ كُونُواْ قَوَّٰمِينَ لِلَّهِ شُهَدَآءَ بِٱلْقِسْطِ وَلَا يَجْرِمَنَّكُمْ شَنَئَانُ قَوْمٍ عَلَىٰٓ أَلَّا تَعْدِلُواْ

"O you who believe! Firmly establish justice for Allaah, as just witnesses; and let not the enmity and hatred of others allow you to avoid justice..."[28]

Meaning: do not let your hatred of others cause you to be unjust to them;

Be just: that is closer to piety; and fear Allaah.

I say: All praise and gratitude is due to Allaah, we live in a secure country, the best *Muslim* country in relation to implementing the Legislation of

---

27 The Noble *Qur.aan* - *Soorah* an-Nisaa, *Aayah* 135

28 The Noble *Qur.aan* - *Soorah* al-Maa.idah, *Aayah* 8

Islaam, according to my knowledge. So it is essential for us to stay unified as much as possible and consider the differences that take place between us as *ijtihaad*, where one is rewarded if he has the correct intention; two rewards for the one who reaches the correct opinion, and one reward for the one who is mistaken.

We should discuss issues where we think that someone is mistaken until we reach the truth collectively. If Allaah sees that we want to reach the truth, He will make it easy for us, and make unity easy for us. This is what I wanted to say about this issue, and it is compulsory to stop propagating people's faults, especially the scholars and rulers. It is obligatory to rectify errors according to each person's ability, but in a manner in which we accomplish what is intended without practicing something impermissible.

Shaykh Muhammad ibn Saalih al-'Uthaymeen

13. Helping the Deviated

Question: There are a group of *Muslim*s with incorrect ideas against which they have been advised; however they persisted in their errors and were afflicted with trials, harm and oppression due to their mistakes. Is it permissible to help them in their predicament based on the following *hadeeth*?

> **"The Muslim is the brother of the Muslim; he does not oppress nor let him down."**

Or is it compulsory to assist them; or is it impermissible to assist them because by doing so we may be assisting them in their errors?[29]

---

29 al-Haawee min Fataawa Shaykh al-Albaanee - Page 487

Response: There is no doubt that it is compulsory to assist them in what benefits them in their religious and worldly affairs. The fact that they do not respond to the caller in some issues when he calls them does not mean that one should forsake them. It is upon the caller to assist them and free them from the misguidance they are in, especially since we know, through personal experience, that alot of those who are misguided and are persistent on their misguidance after being called to the truth, they do not do so due to evil intentions, but rather because they believe that they are on the truth, and what they are being called to is misguidance. So it is upon the *Salafee* caller to be patient and not give up hope in that they would return to the truth.

In conclusion we must lend them a helping hand so long as we do not oppose the *Sharee'ah*.

Shaykh Muhammad Naasiruddeen al-Albaanee

14. Numerous Islaamic Groups

Question: What is your opinion on the numerous names to *Muslim* groups in our time, such as *Salafees*, *al-Ikhwaan al-Muslimoon*, *Ahlul-Hadeeth*, *al-Jamaa'ah*, *as-Sunnah* and other than that? May Allaah reward you![30]

Response: As for the numerous groups, then there is no evidence from the Book or the *Sunnah* to support this, not even one letter. Rather the Messenger of Allaah mentioned the *Jamaa'ah*:

> **"Even if they do not have an Imaam or a Jamaa'ah."**

---

30 ar-Rihlah al-Akheerah li-Imaam al-Jazeerah - Page 172

"Indeed the Hand of Allaah is over the Jamaa'ah."

"Whoever abandons obedience [of the ruler] and forsakes the Jamaa'ah."

"Whoever abandons the Jamaa'ah so much as a hand span will die the death of the people of ignorance."

Likewise the Qur.aanic verses:

إِنَّ هَٰذِهِۦٓ أُمَّتُكُمْ أُمَّةً وَٰحِدَةً

"Truly this, your ummah [Sharee'ah or religion (Islaamic Monotheism)] is one religion..."[31]

إِنَّ ٱلَّذِينَ فَرَّقُوا۟ دِينَهُمْ وَكَانُوا۟ شِيَعًا لَّسْتَ مِنْهُمْ فِى شَىْءٍ

"Verily, those who divide their religion and break up into sects (all kinds of religious sects), you (O Muhammad) are not from them in the least."[32]

وَٱعْتَصِمُوا۟ بِحَبْلِ ٱللَّهِ جَمِيعًا وَلَا تَفَرَّقُوا۟

"And hold fast, all of you together, to the Rope of Allaah (i.e. this Qur.aan), and be not divided among yourselves..."[33]

---

31 The Noble *Qur.aan - Soorah* al-Anbiyaa, *Aayah* 92

32 The Noble *Qur.aan - Soorah* al-An'aam, *Aayah* 159

33 The Noble *Qur.aan - Soorah* Aal-'Imraan, *Aayah* 103

تَحْسَبُهُمْ جَمِيعًا وَقُلُوبُهُمْ شَتَّىٰ

*"You would think they were united, but their hearts
are divided."*[34]

As for this partisanship, then the enemies of *Islaam* have prepared a great plot for the *Muslims*. Why? Do they love us? Is this why they spend millions in elections supporting their democratic ideas, which are considered to be a form of disbelief? Because democracy means that a nation judges itself by its own laws, Allaah and His Messenger (*sal-Allaahu 'alayhi wa sallam*) have no jurisdiction, respecting everyone's opinion. What this means is that someone would use a verse from the *Qur.aan* as evidence, and someone else would use his opinion, and there would be no telling which opinion is correct except if one of them agrees with the other. So we haggle with the Book of Allaah and the *Sunnah* of the Messenger (*sal-Allaahu 'alayhi wa sallam*).

As for *Salafiyyah*, *Ahlul-Hadeeth* and *Ahlus-Sunnah*; they are one and the same thing. They indicate that one is holding fast to the Book and the *Sunnah*, upon the understanding of the *Salafus-Saalih*. It is binding upon every *Muslim* to be a Sunni, holding fast to the Book and the *Sunnah*, upon the understanding of the *Salafus-Saalih*.

The point is that this is a conspiracy from the enemies of *Islaam*, and there are many that have fallen victim to it, and the enmity between the people of partisanship is great; each group prepares itself to grab authority and leadership. They want to set the people up in a blazing fire.

It is binding upon the *Muslims* to be only one group; the group of Al-

---

34 The Noble *Qur.aan* - *Soorah* al-Hashr, *Aayah* 14

laah, whether they are Arabs or non-Arabs, black or white, men or women, human or *jinn*.

It is obligatory for all of them to be servants of Allaah (*Subhaanahu wa Ta'aala*) and distance themselves from these groups. Allaah (*Subhaanahu wa Ta'aala*) says:

إِنَّمَا ٱلْمُؤْمِنُونَ إِخْوَةٌ

"The believers are brothers (in Islaam)."[35]

He (*Subhaanahu wa Ta'aala*) also says:

يَـٰٓأَيُّهَا ٱلنَّاسُ إِنَّا خَلَقْنَـٰكُم مِّن ذَكَرٍ وَأُنثَىٰ وَجَعَلْنَـٰكُمْ
شُعُوبًا وَقَبَآئِلَ لِتَعَارَفُوٓا۟ إِنَّ أَكْرَمَكُمْ عِندَ ٱللَّهِ أَتْقَىٰكُمْ

"O mankind! We have created you from a male and a female, and made you into nations and tribes that you may know one another. Verily, the most honorable of you with Allaah is that (believer) who has at-Taqwaa [i.e. he is one of the the pious.]"[36]

They are nothing but games; they appoint a certain minister with a position and another one with another position, and likewise a president and a vice president; nothing is left except playing games with the people. One of the scholars who is in opposition to this said to one of their heads: "Why do you busy the people with these affairs?"

They replied: "Two reasons; the first being that we are pressured by the enemies of *Islaam* to do so, the second being that we receive alot of

---

35 The Noble *Qur.aan* - *Soorah* al-Hujuraat, *Aayah* 10

36 The Noble *Qur.aan* - *Soorah* al-Hujuraat, *Aayah* 13

money from them, millions. We take most of it and distribute a little among the people."

From Allaah alone do we seek assistance.

Yes, games; if a certain group prevails, they quickly change the country, and all the groups disappear and become like scattered dust; it is nothing but games. There are also those in Yemen who are willing to support them with weapons.

So I advise every brother to free himself from this partisanship, and repent to Allaah (*Subhaanahu wa Ta'aala*); and from Allaah alone do we seek assistance.

From the strangest of affairs is that some people say that these groups are good for *Islaam*. Rather it is only a fire that blazes in the lands of the *Muslim*s. Look at Lebanon and what happened to it because of partisanship. Look at what happened in Sudan; how the *al-Ikhwaan al-Muslimoon* used to applaud it saying that it was an *Islaam*ic country. In the end at-Turaabee was removed, an evil man he is; he was removed and then the *al-Ikhwaan al-Muslimoon* started insulting Sudan.

As for us, and all praise is due to Allaah, from the beginning to the end, no one spends money on *Ahlus-Sunnah*, and all praise is due to Allaah. *al-Ikhwaan al-Muslimoon* know more than us about the state of the rulers, but *Ahlus-Sunnah*, due to their adherence to the Book and the *Sunnah* are granted success by Allaah and He defends them:

14

> '*Truly, Allaah defends those who believe. Verily, Allaah likes not any treacherous ingrate to Allaah [those who disobey Allaah but obey Shaytaan (Satan)].*'

Shaykh Muqbil ibn Haadee al-Waadi'ee

15. Who are Ahlus-Sunnah wal-Jamaa'ah?

Question: Who are *Ahlus-Sunnah wal-Jamaa'ah?*[37]

Response: *Ahlus-Sunnah wal-Jamaa'ah* are those who adhere to the *Sunnah*, they unite upon it, not turning to anything other than it; not in affairs of faith nor in affairs related to performing actions. This is why they are called *Ahlus-Sunnah*, because they strictly adhere to it, and they are called '*al-Jamaa'ah*' because they gather and unite upon it.

However, if you were to consider the state of the people of innovations you would find that they differ in what they are upon, in their methodology of belief as well as their methodology in the practical implementation of the religion. This indicates that they are far from the *Sunnah*, and their distance from the *Sunnah* is in accordance to what they have innovated.

Shaykh Muhammad ibn Saalih al-'Uthaymeen

---

37 Fataawa Arkaanul-Islaam - Page 21

Glossary of Arabic Terms

Aadam [آدَم]
Arabic for Adam.

'Abd, pl. 'Ibaad [عَبْد جـ عِبَاد]
A slave or servant. Also used to refer to a man or a human being.

'Aqeedah, pl. 'Aqaa.id [عَقِيْدَة جـ عَقَائِد]
Creed, belief, doctrine.

'Awrah, pl. 'Awraat [عَوْرَة جـ عَوْرَات]
Private parts, genitalia. With respect to a woman, it refers to her whole body, including her hair.

Aayah, pl. Aayaat [آية جـ آيات]
Sign, miracle, verse from the Noble Qur.aan.

Ahlul-Hadeeth [أَهْلُ الـحَدِيْث]
The upholders of Hadeeth (Prophetic tradition), both in belief and action.

Ahlus-Sunnah wal-Jamaa'ah [أَهْلُ السُّنَّة وَ الـجَمَاعَة]
Those who gather upon firm adherence to the Sunnah of the Prophet (sal-Al-laahu 'alayhi wa sallam) and his Companions and follow their path in 'aqeedah, speech and action, and thereby stand firm and upright upon this adherence and avoid innovations.

GAT

al-'Azeez [الْعَزِيْز]

From the Beautiful Names of Allaah, meaning The Exalted in Power.

Ansaar [أَنْصَار]

The inhabitants of Madeenah who helped and supported the Prophet (*sal-Allaahu 'alayhi wa sallam*), upon his migration from Makkah.

al-Baseer [الْبَصِيْر]

From the Beautiful Names of Allaah, meaning The All-Seeing.

Baseerah [بَصِيْرَة]

Insight, foresight, vision and sound knowledge.

Daa'ee, pl. Du'aat [دَاعِي جـ دُعَاة]

One who engages in missionary work to invite all people to worship Allaah as One, without associating any partners with Him; in short - Islaam.

Daawood [دَاوُوْد]

Arabic for David.

Da'wah [دَعْوَة]

Missionary work to invite all people to worship Allaah as One, without associating any partners with Him; in short - Islaam.

Eed al-Fitr [عِيْد الْفِطْر]

The Feast of Breaking the Fast; The Celebration held on the first day of Shawwaal to mark the end of the fast of Ramadhaan.

Eed al-Adh.haa [عِيْدُ الأَضْحَى]

The Feast of Sacrifice; The celebration held on the 10th through to the 13th days of Dhul-Hijjah.

Eemaan [إِيْـمَان]

A firm belief in Allaah, the Angels, the Revealed Books, the Messengers. The Last Day and al-Qadar. It manifests itself in the heart, the tongue, and upon the limbs – and it increases with obedience to Allaah and decreases with disobedience to Him.

'Eesaa [عِيْسَى]

Arabic for Jesus.

Faatihah [فَاتِحَة]

Name of the first Soorah in the Noble Qur.aan.

Fard Kifaayah [فَرْض كِفَايَة]

Collective obligation.

Fatwa, pl. Fataawa [فَتْوَى جـ فَتَاوَى]

Legal ruling based upon the Qur.aan and the Sunnah, passed by a Scholar in response to a question.

Fiqh [فِقْه]

Islaamic jurisprudence.

Fitnah, pl. Fitan [فِتْنَة جـ فِتَن]

Test, affliction, civil strife, disorder, unrest, riot, turmoil, war, or satanic act.

Haaroon [هَارُوْن]

Arabic for Aaron.

Hadeeth, pl. Ahaadeeth [حَدِيْث جـ أَحَادِيْث]

Literally means, "sayings" and could refer to the recorded quotes of anyone. Usually, it is the title given to the collection of recorded words, actions and tacit approvals of the Prophet Muhammad (sal-Allaahu 'alayhi wa sallam), which serve as an explanation of the meaning of the Noble Qur.aan.

Hajj [حَجّ]

The "major pilgrimage". The once in a lifetime obligation (only if one possesses the means) of pilgrimage to Makkah; made up of specified rites performed between the 8th to the 13th day of Dhul-Hijjah (the twelfth month of the Islaamic Hijrah year). It is one of the five pillars of Islaam.

Hajjatul-Wadaa' [حَجَّةُ الْوَدَاع]

The farewell pilgrimage of the Prophet (sal-Allaau 'alayhi wa sallam) before he died.

al-Hakeem [الْـحَكِيم]

From the Beautiful Names of Allaah, meaning The All-Wise.

Hanafee, pl. Ahnaaf [حَنَفِيّ جـ أَحْنَاف]

An adherent to, or a student of the School of Islaamic Jurisprudence which is based upon the teachings of Abu Haneefah Nu'maan ibn Thaabit ibn Zootaa ibn Marzubaan (died in Baghdad 148 AH / 767 AD).

Hanbalee, pl. Hanaabilah [حَنْبَلِي جـ حَنَابِلَة]

An adherent to, or a student of the School of Islaamic Jurisprudence which is based upon the teachings of Abu 'Abdullaah Ahmad ibn Muhammad ibn Hanbal ash-Shaybaanee (died in Baghdad 241 AH / 855 AD).

Hijaab [حِجَاب]

Veil, head covering and cloak covering worn by Muslim women to protec themselves from the gaze of men.

Hikmah, pl. Hikam [حِكْمَة]

Wisdom, sapience, sageness, sagacity, judiciousness, prudence, foresight, insight, reason, reasonableness.

Hizbiyyah [حِزْبِيَّة]

Partisanship, factionalism, party life (spirit, activities), partiality, bias.

Hizbut-Tahreer [حِزْب التَّحْرِير]

Islaamic political organisation founded in Jerusalem, by Taqi-uddeen an-Nabahaanee in 1953.

'Iddah [عِدَّة]

A woman's prescribed waiting period after her divorce or the death of her husband.

Ijtihaad [إِجْتِهَاد]

The effort a jurist makes in order to deduce the law, which is not self-evident, from it sources.

al-Ikhwaan al-Muslimoon [الإِخْوَان الْـمُسْلِمُوْن]

The Muslim Brotherhood. Founded in Egypt, by Hasan al-Banna in 1928.

'Ilmaanee [عِلْمَانِيّ]

A secularist.

Imaam, pl. A.immah [إِمَام جـ أَئِمَّة]

A distinguished and recognised scholar; Generally recognised to be at a level above the 'Allaamah, and often referred to as a Mujaddid (reformer and reviver of the religion). Also used to refer to the one who leads the prayer.

Injeel [إنْـجيْل]

Arabic for the Bible, popularly referred to as The New Testament.

Inshaa.-Allaah [إنْ شَاءَ الله]

Literally means, "if Allaah wills."

Islaam [إسْلام]

Submission, surrender, obedience to the Will of Allaah.

Jamaa'ah, pl. Jamaa'aat [جَمَاعَة جـ جَمَاعَات]

Group, faction, party, community.

al-Jawaad [الـجَوَاد]

Allaah, The All-Generous and Bountiful.

Jihaad [جهَاد]

To strive hard, or to fight to defend one's life, property, freedom, and religion. It can also refer to an attempt to free other people from oppression and tyranny. Importantly, Islaam strongly opposes the kidnapping, terrorising, or hijacking of civilians, even during war.

Jinn [جنّ]

Living beings created from fire. They can observe humans and all that is around them; however the humans cannot see them. It is both the Jinn and the mankind to whom Muhammad (sal-Allaahu 'alayhi wa sallam) was sent as the final Messenger.

GAT

Jumu'ah [جُمُعَة]

The Friday prayer performed in jamaa'ah after the khutbah. This is in place of the Salaat az-Zhuhr.

al-Kareem [الْكَرِيْم]
From the Beautiful Names of Allaah, meaning The Most Noble.

Khalafee [خَلَفِيّ]
One who disagrees with and opposes the approach of the Salafee.

Khawaarij [خَوَارِج]
Insurgent, renegade, dissenter and rebel.

Khaybar [خَيْبَر]
An oasis 93 miles north of Madeenah. It is where the Battle of Khaybar took place in 629AD.

Khurooj [خُرُوْج]
To transgress and rebel against the established leader of the land.

Khutbah, pl. Khutab [خُطْبَة جـ خُطَب]
A public sermon, address, speech.

Khutbatul-Haajah [خُطْبَة الـحَاجَة]
Popularly referred to as the "sermon of need".

Maalikee, pl. Maalikiyyah [مَالكِيّ جـ مَالكِيّة]
An adherent to, or a student of the School of Islaamic Jurisprudence which is based upon the teachings of Abu 'Abdullaah Maalik ibn Anas ibn Maalik ibn 'Amr al-Asbahi (died in Madeenah 179 AH / 795 AD).

Madhhab, pl. Madhaahib [مَذْهَب جـ مَذَاهِب]
School, school of religious law, doctrine, persuasion, sect, way, manner.

Maatureediyyah [مَاتُرِيْدِيّة]
The followers of the 'aqeedah of Abu Mansoor al-Maatureedee, which is a close variant of the Ash'aree 'aqeedah.

Madhhab, pl. Madhaahib [مَذْهَب جـ مَذَاهِب]
School, school of religious law, doctrine, persuasion, sect, way, manner.

Manhaj, pl. Manaahij [مَنْهَج جـ مَنَاهِج]
Methodology, manner, approach, procedure.

Masjid, pl. Masaajid [مَسْجِد جـ مَسَاجِد]

The Muslim's place of worship.

al-Masjid al-Haraam [الـمَسْجِد الـحَرَام]

"The Grand Masjid" in Makkah; which is the holiest masjid in Islaam.

Minbar, pl. Manaabir [مِنْبَر جـ مَنَابِر]

Pulpit, platform, stand, rostrum.

Moosaa [مُوْسَى]

Arabic for Moses.

Mubtil [مُبْطِل]

Abolishing, nullifying, invalidating.

Mufti [مُفْتِي]

Interpreter or expounder of the Sharee'ah; deliverer of legal religious verdicts.

Muslim, pl. Muslimoon [مُسْلِم جـ مُسْلِمُوْن]

An adherent of the Islaamic faith. One who submits himself to the sole worship of Allaah.

Musnad [مُسْنَد]

A collection of traditions listing the names of the Companions in alphabetical order. The most important and exhaustive of all the musnad works available is that of Imaam Ahmad ibn Hanbal.

Nameemah [نَـمِيْمَة]

Defamation, slander, talebearing.

Nooh [نُوْح]

Arabic for Noah.

Qaadiyaaniyyah al-Ahmadiyyah [قَادِيَانِيّة الأَحْمَدِيّة]

Islaamic group founded in India, by Mirza Ghulaam Ahmad al-Qaadiyaanee in 1900.

al-Qadeer [الْقَدِير]

Allaah, The All-Powerful.

Qiblah [قِبْلَة]

Direction of prayer. The direction towards the Ka'bah in al-Masjid al-Haraam in Makkah.

Qur.aan [قُرْآن]

Compiled divine revelations from Allaah to Prophet Muhammad; The Holy Book of the Muslims.

Raafidhah, pl. Rawaafidh [رَافِضَة جـ رَوَافِض]

The correct term applied to the *Shee'ah*, who, amongst other beliefs, rejected [رَفَضُوا] the *khilaafah* of Abu Bakr, 'Umar and 'Uthmaan.

Radhi-yAllaahu 'anhu / 'anhumaa / 'anhum

[رَضِيَ الله عَنْهُ / عَنْهُمَا / عَنْهُمْ]

Literally means, "May Allaah be pleased with him / with the two of them / with them."

ar-Raheem [الرَّحِيْم]

From the Beautiful Names of Allaah, meaning The Ever-Merciful.

ar-Rahmaan [الرَّحْمَن]

From the Beautiful Names of Allaah, meaning The All-Merciful.

Saheeh, pl. Sihaah [صَحِيْح جـ صِحَاح]

Authentic, correct.

Salaf, pl. Aslaaf [سَلَف جـ أَسْلاَف]

The first three generations of Muslims. Popularly referred to as "as-Salaf as-Saalih" - the pious predecessors.

Salafee, pl. Salafiyoon [سَلَفِي جـ سَلَفِيُوْن]

An adherent to the Qur.aan and the authentic Sunnah as understood by the first three generations of Muslims.

sal-Allaahu 'alayhi wa sallam [صَلَّى الله عَلَيْهِ وَ سَلَّم]

Literally means, "May Allaah send prayers and salutations upon him." This is to be said every time reference is made to the final Messenger of Allaah, Muhammad.

as-Samee' [السَّمِيع]

From the Beautiful Names of Allaah, meaning The All-Hearing.

Seerah, pl. Siyar [سِيْرَة جـ سِيَر]

Biography, life history.

Shaafi'ee, pl. Shaafi'iyyah [شَافِعِي جـ شَافِعِيَّة]

An adherent to, or a student of the School of Islaamic Jurisprudence which is based upon the teachings of Abu 'Abdullaah Muhammad ibn Idrees ash-Shaafi'ee (died in Fustat, Egypt 204 AH / 820 AD).

Shahaadah [شَهَادَة]

Martyrdom. Also refers to the testification of one's submission solely to Allaah.

Shaykh, pl. Shuyookh, Mashaa.ikh, Mashaayikh
[شَيْخ جـ شُيُوخ / مَشَائِخ / مَشَايِخ]

Correctly referred to as a religious scholar; however, it is also referred to one who is elderly.

Shaytaan, pl. Shayaateen [شَيْطَان جـ شَيَاطِين]

Satan. The evil one, evil spirit, devil, demon.

Shirk [شِرْك]

Associating partners in worship with Allaah.

Shee'ee [شِيْعِي]

An adherent to the doctrine of the *Shee'ah Raafidhah*.

Soorah, pl. Suwar [سُوْرَة جـ سُوَر]

Chapter; one of the 114 chapters of the Noble Qur.aan.

GAT

Subhaanahu wa Ta'aala [سُبْحَانَهُ وَ تَعَالَى]

Literally means, "How perfect He is, the Almighty"; Complete meaning: "I exalt Him and elevate Him above having any defects or deficiencies.".

Sunnah, pl. Sunan [سُنَّة جــ سُنَن]

Way, mode, manner; correctly referred to as the words, actions and tacit approvals of the Prophet Muhammad (sal-Allaahu 'alayhi wa sallam), which serve as an explanation of the meaning of the Noble Qur.aan.

Ta'teel [تَعْطِيل]

To deny some or all of the Names and Attributes of Allaah.

Taabi'ee, pl. Taabi'oon [تَابِعِي جــ تَابِعُوْن]

Third generation of Muslims. Those who met the Companions of Muhammad (sal-Allaahu 'alayhi wa sallam) as Muslims and died as Muslims.

Tabdee' [تَبْدِيع]

To declare a Muslim an innovator.

Tafseeq [تَفْسِيق]

To accuse a Muslim of open disobedience and transgression against Islaam.

Tahiyyatul-Masjid [تَـحِيَّةُ الْـمَسْجِد]

The two rak'ah prayer offered promptly upon entering the masjid, before sitting down.

Tahreef [تَـحْرِيف]

The distortion, alteration or misrepresentation of the meaning of Allaah's Names and Attributes.

Takfeer [تَكْفِير]

To accuse a Muslim of disbelief and apostasy.

Takyeef [تَكْيِيف]

To ask about, or specifically describe the Attributes of Allaah, beyond what Allaah and His Messenger have informed us.

Tamtheel [تَـمْثِيل]

To resemble, liken or compare Allaah's Attributes to that of His Creation.

Taqwa [تَقْوَى]

Fear, dread, awe. Piety to Allaah, fear of Allaah, warding off Allaah's wrath, being conscious of Allaah, devotion, devoutness.

Tasbeeh [تَسْبِيح]

The glorification of Allaah, as compounded in the saying of [سُبْحَانَ الله].

Tawheed [تَوْحِيد]

Singling out. To single out Allaah ('Azza wa Jall) alone for worship.

Towfeeq [تَوْفِيق]

Success and good fortune granted by Allaah.

Ummah, pl. Umam [أُمَّة جـ أُمَـم]

Community of Muslims, the Muslim nation.

'Umrah [عُمْرَة]

The "minor pilgrimage." It has fewer rites than the "major pilgrimage" (Hajj). In general, it may be performed at any time of the year.

Waajib [وَاجِب]

Obligatory, mandatory, compulsory.

Wahhaabee, pl. Wahhaabiyyah [وَهَّابِيّ جـ وَهَّابِيَّة]

The derogatory term used to refer to an adherent of the *da'wah* of Imaam Muhammad ibn 'Abdil-Wahhaab.

Zakaah, pl. Zakawaat [زَكَاة جـ زَكَوَات]

The alms tax deducted from the qualifying Muslims wealth at a rate of 2.5%, and distributed to the poor and needy. It is one of the five pillars of Islaam.

GAT

Notes